ENTREPRENEURIAL THINKING

ENTREPRENEURIAL THINKING

Mindset in Action

Suzanne Mawson & Lucrezia Casulli

S Sage

1 Oliver's Yard
55 City Road
London EC1Y 1SP

2455 Teller Road
Thousand Oaks
California 91320

Unit No 323-333, Third Floor, F-Block
International Trade Tower
Nehru Place, New Delhi – 110 019

8 Marina View Suite 43-053
Asia Square Tower 1
Singapore 018960

Editor: Matthew Waters
Assistant editor: Charlotte Hanson
Production editor: Sarah Sewell
Copyeditor: Christine Bitten
Proofreader: Clare Weaver
Indexer: Michael Allerton
Marketing manager: Lucia Sweet
Cover design: Francis Kenney
Typeset by: C&M Digitals (P), Ltd, Chennai, India

Library of Congress Control Number: 2023939894

British Library Cataloguing in Publication data

A catalogue record for this book is available from the British Library

ISBN 978-1-5297-9532-5
ISBN 978-1-5297-9531-8 (pbk)

CONTENTS

SECTION 2   GETTING COMFORTABLE WITH ENTREPRENEURIAL AMBIGUITY AND UNCERTAINTY 93

CHAPTER 4 DEVELOPING YOUR PERSISTENCE AND RESILIENCE 97

CHAPTER 5 TACKLING YOUR CORE BELIEFS AND HARNESSING YOUR FEARS 119

CHAPTER 6 DEVELOPING AND REFINING YOUR ENTREPRENEURIAL JUDGEMENT 147

ONLINE RESOURCES

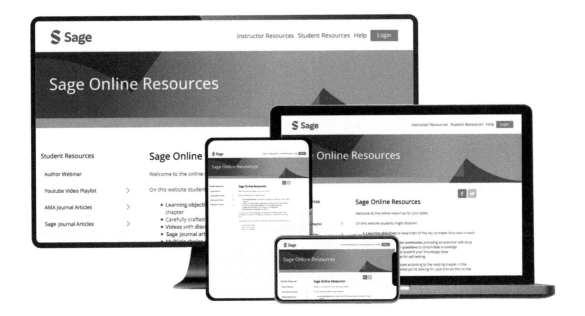

This textbook is accompanied by online resources to aid teaching and support learning. To access these resources, visit: https://study.sagepub.com/mawson-casulli. Please note that lecturers will require a Sage account in order to access the lecturer resources. An account can be created via the above link.

FOR LECTURERS

- **PowerPoints** that can be downloaded and adapted to suit individual teaching needs
- **A Teaching Guide** providing practical guidance and support and additional materials for lecturers using this textbook in their teaching

ACKNOWLEDGEMENTS

We owe a debt of gratitude to so many people for making this book possible.

First, thank you to our students (current and past) at the University of Strathclyde for encouraging us to write this book, providing your own insights and experiences, and helping us to test our ideas and models of competence development. This book is for you.

Thank you to our colleagues who have supported us to develop this book, providing critical feedback, constructive suggestions and wider support. A special thanks to Emilee Simmons, Jillian Macbryde and Carolin Decker-Lange.

We are also grateful to the editorial, production and marketing teams at Sage, particularly Matthew Waters and Charlotte Hanson.

Finally, our heartfelt thanks to those who shared their stories with us to provide cases of entrepreneurial thinking and mindset in practice. Thank you Philip Palios, Becky Pick, Drew Smithsimmons, Marc Reid, Nigel Lockett, Angela Prenter-Smith, Tony O'Neil, Noreen Philips, Lorenzo Conti, Florence Adu, Anna Salvagio on behalf of the Sciacca community, Jérémie Warner and Cecilia Livingston.

PERSONAL ACKNOWLEDGEMENTS

For Arthur, Ross and my family, always. (SM)

Thank you to my family and friends, both near and far, for allowing the space and time to dedicate to this book. Thank you for the understanding when invitations were turned down because the book deadline was looming! Thank you for your patience every time all I could talk about was this book. I promise I will have a larger repertoire of topics for conversation in the future! For Gabriele, Andrew and in loving memory of my dad. (LC)

WELCOME! START HERE!

Hello and welcome! We're delighted that you are joining us as we start on a learning journey about your entrepreneurial thinking and mindset and how this can shape your life!

This book is for anyone looking to develop their own entrepreneurial competences, either informally through independent study or in the context of formal education. We have written this book at the request of our MBA students, who expressed the need for not only a comprehensive source of reference on key entrepreneurial thinking competencies, but also a space for them to work, reflect and put these into practice in their own lives. Whether you are a working professional, a student, or someone looking to think (and act) more entrepreneurially, we hope this book supports you in your own journey of personal discovery.

Suzanne is an Associate Professor of Entrepreneurship at the University of Strathclyde Business School. She is fascinated by how people think and act, and the role that education and training plays in shaping thinking and behaviour. She has applied this interest to various contexts, including within high-growth and scaling ventures, entrepreneurial ecosystems and public policy to support entrepreneurship. She also has a keen interest in pedagogy and andragogy to support the development of competences, linked to a plassion for innovative teaching and learning methodologies and practices.

Lucrezia is an Associate Professor of Entrepreneurship at the University of Strathclyde Business School. She has a life-long passion and interest for understanding how people perceive the world and respond to it. She is particularly fascinated by people that make things happen and do so in unconventional, novel ways. This fascination has found a home in her studies of cognitive processes in the context of entrepreneurial behaviour. Her PhD focused on the role of heuristics and biases in the internationalisation decisions of leaders of smaller firms. Her research interests include how individuals who add value see themselves (entrepreneurial identity), how and why they behave as they do (entrepreneurial action) and what motivates people to add value in different ways.

We have drawn on areas of positive psychology and theories of competence motivation to develop novel approaches to fostering entrepreneurial mindsets in the classroom. We are on a mission to showcase the power of an entrepreneurial mindset to enhance our lives and add value to society.

Our very own attempt to create value is through writing this book and we earnestly hope it will help you to consider how you yourself can create value in your own way.

Suzanne and Lucrezia

WHY IS ENTREPRENEURIAL THINKING AND MINDSET IMPORTANT?

Entrepreneurial thinking used to be the domain of those who started businesses – of our traditional stereotypical 'entrepreneurs'. Recent trends have changed this, however, and brought entrepreneurial thinking to the forefront for all of us.

The rapid pace of innovation and its effect on work means that some jobs will be rendered obsolete in the space of a few years. At the same time, new jobs will emerge that we could not envision as possibilities when we were educated or trained for our profession.[1] Constant global changes and shocks resulting in economic and social disruption are also challenging the nature of work and employment. As a result, most of us should now expect to go through multiple careers over the span of our working lives.

In order to navigate this constantly evolving and complex landscape, it is more important than ever that we develop the competences that allow us to thrive under uncertainty and ambiguity. Throughout history, entrepreneurial individuals have made it their hallmark to embrace the unknown, finding opportunities thrive under conditions of uncertainty and ambiguity. They thus have valuable lessons to offers in terms of how they think and, ultimately, act. Recognising this, politicians, policymakers,[2] educators,[3] economists[4] and psychologists and a host of others have identified ***entrepreneurial competences*** that individuals need if they are to be able to engage in ways of thinking and behaving that will change the status quo and create *value* in the twenty-first century.

These entrepreneurial competences, which comprise knowledge, skills, attitudes, values and behaviours,[5] reflect the best features of entrepreneurial individuals to develop creative solutions and to envision what's possible beyond what is currently being done. At the same

---

[1]Kellerman, G. R. & Seligman, M. E. (2023). *Tomorrowmind: Thriving at Work with Resilience, Creativity, and Connection—Now and in an Uncertain Future*. New York: Simon and Schuster.

[2]Bacigalupo, M., Kampylis, P., Punie, Y. & Van den Brande, G. (2016). *EntreComp: The Entrepreneurship Competence Framework*. Luxembourg: Publication Office of the European Union.

[3]Quality Assurance Agency for Higher Education (2012). *Enterprise and Entrepreneurship Education: Guidance for UK Higher Education Providers*. Gloucester: QAA.

[4]Stiglitz, J. E. & Greenwald, B. (2014). *Creating a learning society*. In J. E. Stiglitz & B. Greenwald, *Creating a Learning Society*. New York: Columbia University Press; Mazzucato, M. (2011). The entrepreneurial state. *Soundings*, *49*(49), 131–142.

[5]Morris M. H., Webb J. W., Fu J. & Singhal S. (2013). A competency-based perspective on entrepreneurship education: Conceptual and empirical insights. *Journal of Small Business Management*, *51*(3), 352–369.

time, they encompass the competences required to thrive in today's world, some of which are not always reflective of our end-of-the-twentieth century stereotypes of the lone heroic entrepreneurial individual (we'll explore this in depth in Chapter 1). They also relate to the concept of the ***entrepreneurial mindset***, which we'll discuss further in Chapters 1 and 2. Entrepreneurial mindset is the interaction of our *thinking* (cognition) and *emotion* in driving entrepreneurial *behaviour*,[6] and will be defined in this book as:

> *a set of learnable cognitive and emotional competences conducive to developing and enacting behaviours to support value creation activity.*[7]

These competences include the development of an ***action orientation***, where we actively gather information and feedback from the environment, evaluate it and engage in ***judgement*** and decision making that determines our plans and actions.[8] To be able to do this, we need to have ***cognitive flexibility*** and to be open-minded through a growth ***mindset*** in order to support our sense of ***self-efficacy*** and ***creativity.*** Our current understanding of entrepreneurial competences recognises the need for collaborative efforts, particularly for tackling the world's 'wicked problems' and injustices. Additionally, now more than ever after the Covid-19 pandemic, it acknowledges the importance of 'a life well spent', putting our efforts into something that is meaningful for us and that matters too.[9]

Entrepreneurial thinking and mindset may manifest in you creating a business; it may also manifest in a wide range of other activities and entrepreneurial contexts (we'll explore these in Chapter 7). Entrepreneurial thinking and action is no longer confined to just starting a new venture – we have the ability to think and act entrepreneurial to create value within our current organisations, within our communities or wider society, as well as in our own personal lives. We all have the need to develop and 'entrepreneurial identity'[10] that enables us to create *value*.

---

[6]Kuratko, D. F., Fisher, G. & Audretsch, D. B. (2021). Unravelling the entrepreneurial mindset. *Small Business Economics*, *57*, 1681–1691.

[7]Mawson, S., Casulli, L. & Simmons, E. L. (2022). A competence development approach for entrepreneurial mindset in entrepreneurship education. *Entrepreneurship Education and Pedagogy*. https://doi.org/10.1177/2515127422114314

[8]Dimov, D. (2010). Nascent entrepreneurs and venture emergence: Opportunity confidence, human capital, and early planning. *Journal of Management Studies*, *47*(6), 1123–1153.

[9]Kellerman & Seligman, *Tomorrowmind*.

[10]Berglund, K., Hytti, U. & Verduijn, K. (2020). Unsettling entrepreneurship education. *Entrepreneurship Education and Pedagogy*, *3*(3), 208–213.

We'll discuss the notion of value further in Chapter 1 (specifically section 1.7), and throughout the rest of the book. Ultimately, all entrepreneurial thinking and action exists to support the creation of value, what we define in this book as:

> *Something new, improved, or in a novel space, that an individual or group of individuals considers to have worth.*

We often talk about value as a synonym for money, but that is only one form of value (economic value). We can create value for ourselves (see Chapter 10) and others (see Chapter 11) to support society (social value), our natural environment (environmental value), things of beauty (aesthetic value) or even cultural heritage (cultural value). We'll explore what value creation looks like for you personally, as well as the value you can create for those around you.

WHAT CAN YOU EXPECT IN THIS BOOK?

You may find that this book looks and feels a bit different to other 'textbooks' you have used before. At least, we hope it does!

This book is a combined textbook–workbook. It is a point of reference for you, but more importantly a place for you to engage with, reflect on and practise key entrepreneurial competences. It is designed specifically for you to annotate, so don't hesitate to scribble, make notes and complete the exercises and activities!

In Section 1 (Chapters 1 to 3) we'll introduce and discuss what we mean by entrepreneurial thinking and mindset. We'll consider your own beliefs, preferences and frames of reference to help you identify where and how you can contribute to entrepreneurial value creation.

In Section 2 (Chapters 4 to 6) we'll build on our discussions from Section 1, focusing on the uncertainty and ambiguity inherent within value creation activity. We'll explore your own personal responses to uncertain situations in order to determine how you can build your persistence and resilience.

In Section 3 (Chapters 7 to 9) we'll shift our focus somewhat, considering not just your own entrepreneurial thinking but also how you can encourage and support entrepreneurial thinking and action among others. We'll explore value creation as a collaborative activity, where effective communication to build and maintain empathetic communication is critical to empowering others.

Finally, in Section 4 (Chapters 10 to 12) we'll build on ideas and concepts introduced throughout the book to consider what entrepreneurial thinking and action means for your own value creation activity – value for yourself as well as value for others.

Importantly, this book is not just for reading and absorbing concepts. We have structured each chapter to support the development of your own entrepreneurial competences (see above) based on the process of competence development from *unconscious incompetence* to *unconscious competence*.

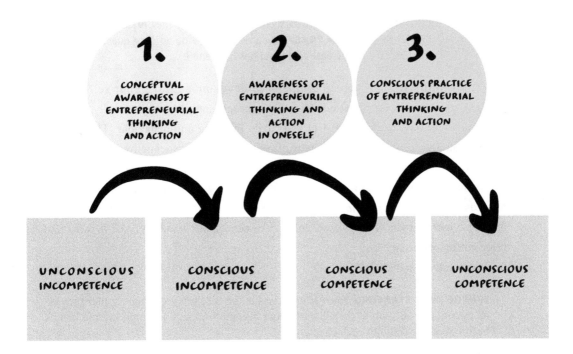

When starting something new, we are usually in a state of *unconscious incompetence* – we aren't yet even aware of our limitations and what we need to foster or improve.

Activities in the first step of competence development are intended for you to learn concepts and to become aware of their relevance. Activities relating to step one will be coloured in BLUE – the colour of focus and learning. This first step will enable you to move towards self-awareness of how the concepts you now know about may apply to you (shifting you from *unconscious incompetence* to *conscious incompetence*).

These activities include:

CHALLENGING ASSUMPTIONS boxes highlight how the concepts and ideas being covered work in practice, providing practical examples as well as highlighting when there are tensions between concepts and their application.

DEEP DIVE activities provide an opportunity for you to learn more about a particular idea or topic through links to videos, readings or other materials.

ENTREPRENEURIAL THINKING AND MINDSET IN PRACTICE cases tell the stories of real individuals who are engaging in entrepreneurial thinking and mindset in practice. They share their insights and experiences linked to the concepts covered in each chapter to give you a sense of what you might yourself see or experience.

CHECK YOUR UNDERSTANDING quizzes at the end of each chapter provide a number of True/False statements (and corresponding answers) to allow you to test your understanding of the ideas and concepts covered.

FURTHER READING resources at the end of each chapter suggest additional popular non-fiction books for you to explore concepts and ideas further.

STOP AND THINK boxes at the end of each chapter look back to the **ENTREPRENEURIAL THINKING AND MINDSET IN PRACTICE** cases and provide guiding questions to help you further make sense of the case and what has happened.

Activities in the second step of competence development take your self-awareness further – from a basic appreciation of how the concepts apply to you personally, to a detailed appreciation of how they manifest in your daily thinking and behaviour. These activities will be coloured in **PURPLE**, the colour of reflection, also associated with so-called 'soft skills'. In this second step, you will engage in guided reflections on your patterns of thinking and behaviour. These activities are intended to shift you from *conscious incompetence* towards *conscious competence*. They do so by inviting you to notice patterns of thought and behaviour that you wish to keep, enhance or change altogether in order to think and act more entrepreneurially.

These activities include:

WHERE AM I STARTING FROM? exercises at the beginning of each chapter provide an opportunity for you to 'benchmark' your current thinking, assumptions and beliefs before working through each chapter.

WHERE AM I NOW? exercises at the end of each chapter think back to where you started from and your responses to the **WHERE AM I STARTING FROM?** exercises. This helps you to reflect on where, how and why personal learning has occurred.

FOOD FOR THOUGHT activities throughout each chapter get you to pause and reflect on how concepts and ideas link to your own life and experiences.

COGNITIVE–BEHAVIOURAL REFLECTION exercises at the end of every chapter provide a structured framework which help you to develop your skill at reflecting on how your thinking and feeling shapes the way you behave entrepreneurially and the actions you take (we'll talk about these elements further in Chapters 1 and 2).

Activities in the third step of competence development are intended to support you as you practise new patterns of entrepreneurial thinking and action. These are coloured in ORANGE, the colour of energy for action. Every new pattern of thinking (and behaving) will require conscious practice over a sustained period of time in order to become so embedded that they are second nature to you (that is, moving from *conscious competence* to *unconscious competence*). To support this, the practice exercises in this section are an essential part of your new habit formation and cognitive 'rewiring'.[11] You can do these as you work through the text, but you can also revisit them time and again as needed to support your learning and development.

---

[11]Doidge, N. (2007). *The Brain That Changes Itself: Stories of Personal Triumph from the Frontiers of Brain Science*. New York: Viking.

These take the form of **PRACTISING ENTREPRENEURIAL THINKING** activities, which can appear both within and at the end of chapters. These provide you with the opportunity to start practising cognitive and behavioural competences introduced in the chapter in order to work towards *mastery*.

In terms of working through this book, we would recommend you follow sections and chapters in order, building from a focus on you and your own entrepreneurial thinking (Section 1) through to how you can communicate and collaborate with others (Section 2) and how this can shape the value you create for yourself and for others (Section 3).

That said, feel free to pick up individual chapters as they meet your needs! Each chapter is self-contained. Where they build upon concepts and ideas from other chapters or sections, you'll be clearly signposted to the relevant material.

WHERE ARE YOU STARTING FROM?

We are so glad to have you with us as you start your journey to develop your entrepreneurial thinking and mindset in support of taking entrepreneurial action to create value for yourself and for others! But, we understand that starting something new can be challenging, particularly when we feel like we're moving outside of our comfort zone. You may find that you're currently feeling a whole range of emotions just now, both positive and negative. This is very normal when we begin a transition to a new activity; we need to reorient ourselves away from what we have just finished (or what is ending) towards a 'new beginning'.[12]

WHERE AM I STARTING FROM?
STARTING YOUR ENTREPRENEURIAL JOURNEY

You've just started on a personal learning journey to develop your entrepreneurial thinking – and ultimately your behaviour and the actions you take! But starting something new can often feel confusing, scary, even overwhelming. Spend a few minutes reflecting on how you are thinking and feeling just now. Record these below.

1. What emotions are you feeling having started this book?

[blank lines for response]

[12]Bridges, W. (2004) *Transitions: Making Sense of Life's Changes*. Cambridge, MA: Da Capo Press.

2. what do you feel worried or concerned about?

3. what do you feel excited or optimistic about?

4. what do you hope to get out of this learning journey?

SECTION 1

CHALLENGING YOUR
ASSUMPTIONS ABOUT
ENTREPRENEURIAL
THINKING AND MINDSET

The first section of this book will introduce and discuss what we mean by entrepreneurial thinking and mindset, looking specifically at this as an outcome of your own sustained effort and practice rather than inherent ability.

CHAPTER 1 will start by considering some of the common perceptions of what entrepreneurship is and, by extension, **who** an entrepreneur is. We will then consider a number of the 'pervasive myths' of entrepreneurship, including that of the 'hero' entrepreneur. Having debunked some of the common myths that shape our views on entrepreneurship (and who can do entrepreneurship), we will then consider entrepreneurial thinking and mindset as a set of skills and competencies that help you to shape your own behaviours as you create value for yourself and for others.

In **CHAPTER 2** we will delve deeper into the concept of mindset – how we become aware of (and make sense of) what we think, how we think and how we leverage that thinking (or not) to pursue our ambitions and goals through our behaviours. We will then consider different ways that we think about situations and how that then shapes our thinking about ourselves and our own abilities. We will then return to the concept of **entrepreneurial mindset**, considering the specific skills, competencies and behaviours that underpin this, and how they support value creation activity.

Finally, in **CHAPTER 3** we will consider the perceptions we hold about ourselves and the world, our so-called frames of reference. We will explore how these frames of reference shape your thinking and action and how we can work to overcome the challenges of mechanised thinking, particularly when looking to create value. We will consider how to shift our frames of reference by building both internal self-awareness and external self-awareness and developing personal reflexivity.

CHAPTER 1

CONTEXTUALISING ENTREPRENEURIAL THINKING AND MINDSET

ENTREPRENEURSHIP COMES IN MANY FORMS —
THE SUPERHERO IS NOT ONE OF THEM.

1.1 INTRODUCTION

Take a moment and consider what comes to your mind when you hear the word *entrepreneurship?* Do you think of a person? A new technology? A start-up? Something else? Why do you think you have this mental image?

WHERE AM I STARTING FROM?
ENTREPRENEURSHIP AND YOU

Spend a few minutes reflecting on your current personal assumptions about entrepreneurship and how these relate to you and your own life. Record these below.

1. What is your own personal understanding of entrepreneurship?

2. What do you think entrepreneurial activity involves?

3. Who do you think engages in entrepreneurship?

4. What is your own experience of entrepreneurial activity?

CONTEXTUALISING ENTREPRENEURIAL THINKING AND MINDSET

The word 'entrepreneurship' is often part of our everyday lives. We may hear it as we read or listen to the news, as we watch television or films, even as we engage in discussions with our friends, families, fellow students at school or university, or with our colleagues at work. It seems that entrepreneurship is, more than ever, visible all around us. Yet how often have you thought about this word and what it actually means, particularly in relation to *you and your life?*

Whether we are aware of it or not, we all have perceptions and make assumptions about entrepreneurship and entrepreneurs. Some of these may be positive, some may be negative, but most importantly these perceptions and assumptions may influence our own behaviour in relation to entrepreneurship. For example, they may lead us to want to either embrace or reject entrepreneurship as a way of thinking and behaving in our own lives, or they may lead us to compare ourselves positively or negatively with public images of famous entrepreneurs. It is for these reasons that tackling these perceptions and assumptions openly is important as you embark on your journey of self-discovery in relation to your own entrepreneurial potential.

This chapter will start by considering some of the common perceptions of what entrepreneurship is and, by extension, *who* an entrepreneur is. We will review and address the two 'pervasive myths' of entrepreneurship before inviting you to reflect on your own views on these common perceptions: the 'hero' entrepreneur and the 'born' entrepreneur. Then, we will consider and explore entrepreneurial thinking and mindset as a set of skills, competencies and linked behaviours that can be developed through sustained effort and practice. These skills and competencies are intended to support you behaving entrepreneurially, as you *create value* for yourself and for others in a range of possible settings and activities.

Once again, we will invite your own reflections on this more recent competences-based view of entrepreneurship. It is important that you do not skip the in-text exercises and activities, however trivial they may seem or uncomfortable they may feel. These are designed to get you thinking about your own attitudes towards entrepreneurship, whether this world is new to you or very familiar.

After working through this chapter, you should be able to:

- query and challenge stereotypical depictions of entrepreneurs and, relatedly, entrepreneurial activity
- articulate the role that thinking (cognition) and emotion play in shaping an entrepreneurial mindset and, in turn, entrepreneurial behaviour

- identify and discuss how entrepreneurial thinking and mindset links to value creation in your own personal and professional lives.

1.2 ENTREPRENEURSHIP IN YOUR CONTEXT

The word 'entrepreneurship' has become commonplace globally. The English term 'entrepreneurship' was originally adapted from the French verb 'entreprendre' or *to undertake*. Yet different cultures (and their languages) have a number of other words or terms to describe 'entrepreneurship' or an 'entrepreneur'. Importantly, these different words or terms often have a different underlying meaning than the English words.

For example, the term 'entrepreneurship' in Arabic is ريادة الأعمال, comprising the words leadership ('riyada') and business ('aamal').

Yet in Mandarin, 'entrepreneurship' can be 创业, 创业精神 or 创业能力, which cover the concepts of 'set up' and 'building from nothing'. An 'entrepreneur' is usually 企业家, which refers to the boss who runs their own business

FOOD FOR THOUGHT
THE LANGUAGE OF 'ENTREPRENEURSHIP'

Take a moment and think about the words used in your own language and culture for 'entrepreneurship' and 'entrepreneur'. Record these below.

1. What word does your language use for 'entrepreneurship'? For 'entrepreneur'?

2. What is the underlying meaning of these words? Is the focus on process (e.g. undertaking, leading) or outcomes? What other assumptions underpin these words (e.g. use of a particular 'gender', active or passive voice etc.)?

3. How do these words and their meanings shape your own thoughts on entrepreneurship and entrepreneurs?

'Entrepreneurship' is also understood differently in different sectors and industries. Some sectors have embraced the notion, while others struggle to identify with it in its current form. Fast pace, fast growth industries such as digital and information technology tend to find themselves at home with the word and the associated business incubators and support infrastructure. Other industries, such as the arts, may struggle to identify themselves with 'entrepreneurship'. Amongst other reasons, this may be because of the perceptions that artists may have of entrepreneurship (i.e. profits-focused, individualistic, etc.).[1] Other sectors have adapted the notion of entrepreneurship based on their specific contextual arrangements. For example, sectors such as engineering and chemistry use the word 'entrepreneurship' as synonymous with the commercialisation of innovations and discoveries.

FOOD FOR THOUGHT
'ENTREPRENEURSHIP' IN YOUR INDUSTRY AND SECTOR

Take a moment and think about the perceptions of 'entrepreneurship' in your industry and sectors. Please record your answers to the questions below.

1. Which industry/sector do you identify with?

---

[1]Coulson, S. (2012). Collaborating in a competitive world: Musicians' working lives and understandings of entrepreneurship. *Work, Employment and Society, 26*(2), 246–261.

2. What would you say is the perception of 'entrepreneurship' in your industry? Is this positive, negative or neutral? Why?

....

....

....

3. To what extent would you say that your employer/self-employment embraces 'entrepreneurship'? In what way?

....

....

....

1.3 THE 'HERO' ENTREPRENEUR?

When we hear 'entrepreneurship', very often the term conjures up mental images of gifted, infallible individuals who single-handedly build hugely successful business empires seemingly overnight and from next to nothing. You may think of, for example, Jeff Bezos, Richard Branson or Elon Musk. This 'hero' entrepreneur is certainly the image celebrated and reinforced by the global media as well as Western popular culture, where an individual is seen to be endowed with special skills and abilities that others do not have.[2] These individuals are also often seen as visionaries and creators; people with drive, ambition and a strong sense of personal direction and purpose who are able to come up with brilliant – seemingly 'world changing' – ideas.

FOOD FOR THOUGHT
PICTURING THE 'ENTREPRENEUR'

Take a moment and think about the first person that comes to mind when the word 'entrepreneur' is mentioned. Find and save an image of this person, before working through the questions below.

---

[2]Warren, L. (2005). Images of entrepreneurship: Still searching for the hero? *The International Journal of Entrepreneurship and Innovation, 6*(4), 221–229.

1. Is this person someone you know personally or know through the media? Are they from your own country or another country?

....
....
....

2. What are the top three characteristics that you would associate with this person?

....
....
....

3. What do you like and dislike about this person? To what extent would you like to be/not be like them?

....
....
....

For some of us, these individuals may be a source of great inspiration. Indeed, it can be motivating to witness people that seem so dedicated and driven every single day, when in fact our own drive can fluctuate and dip at points. However, for others amongst us, these idealised examples may be problematic for a number of reasons. First, it can be hard for us to personally relate in a meaningful way to these individuals, particularly if they do not reflect our own culture, gender, language, or background.[3] Second, when we compare ourselves to the perceptions we have of these 'heroic' individuals, we may end up consciously or unconsciously making a number of unrealistic (or perhaps even unfair) assumptions about ourselves and our own abilities:

---

[3]Swail, J., Down, S. & Kautonen, T. (2014). Examining the effect of 'entre-tainment' as a cultural influence on entrepreneurial intentions. *International Small Business Journal, 32*(8), 859–875.

- we may think that we just need to have a brilliant world-shifting idea as these individuals have (apparently) had and that everything else will fall into place
- we may think that success should come as easily to us as it seemingly does to these individuals
- we may think that if we have to try hard and encounter difficulty we are not entrepreneurial after all
- we may think that we should be able to pursue our goals without ever seeking anyone's input or help and that needing others is a sign of personal weakness or inability
- we may think that, if we have a dip in motivation or energy, we are not the real deal, we are lazy or not that dedicated to our goals.

Would we be justified in thinking the above? We would argue that the answer is NO!

As it turns out, on closer inspection the figure of the 'hero' entrepreneur becomes a lot less heroic and much lonelier. When we start to dig into the lives, decisions and actions of these individuals we often see that their stories are told in a biased and selective way, overemphasising achievement and success, whilst underreporting effort, struggle and even failure. If failures are reported, those are usually told from the vantage point of the success that eventually followed, thus glamorising failure. Yet, the many non-glamourous failed attempts that precede ultimate successes do not always appear in media stories and representations.

Similarly, we usually find that behind the face of the 'heroes' who make it to the cover pages of newspapers and magazines there are armies of co-founders, mentors, investors, skilled and knowledgeable employees, family members and other supporters and contributors who have helped that individual along the way. The latter are often the unsung heroes behind the visible hero.

CHALLENGING ASSUMPTIONS
BEHIND THE HERO ENTREPRENEUR

Many of us know the entrepreneur Elon Musk for his efforts in electric cars, but some will also know him for his passion for space exploration through the SpaceX programme. The success of SpaceX has been showcased all over the world media and rightly so, given its truly ambitious plan: to create reusable rockets that would cut the cost of space exploration. Up until now, it was assumed that rockets would be destroyed after every spaceship launch, at huge cost. Thus, Elon Musk's vision was ambitious and, by his own admission, laughable at first. So, what did it take for this vision to become a reality?

According to publicly available insights into the journey of SpaceX,[4] it took an army of highly skilled, ambitious and dedicated people who shared Musk's vision – to the point of taking risks with their own careers. It also took three failed attempts before a rocket successfully touched down intact on the fourth attempt. Admittedly, Elon Musk was not at all sure that the programme should go for a fourth attempt after the third failure. In **MARS: Inside SpaceX** he tells of the disappointment and doubt that he experienced at that crucial junction in the story.

Looking back from the vantage point of the successful fourth attempt, this story is worthy of celebration, of sharing. But what if we had peeked into SpaceX after the first failed attempt? Or the second? Would we have deemed the story worth telling? What story would this have been? How would it have affected our perception of Elon Musk?

For further information see: **https://money.cnn.com/2015/12/21/news/ companies/spacex-launch-rocket-landing/index.html**

1.4 THE 'BORN' ENTREPRENEUR?

Why then do we hold this 'hero' entrepreneur stereotype? Many of our assumptions about entrepreneurs generally stem from research conducted during the 1960s to the 1980s that assumed that entrepreneurs could be profiled and separated out from 'non-entrepreneurs' through a range of distinguishing *entrepreneurial traits*. Such traits are often considered a central part of each individual's *neuropsychic system*,[5] or the way in which we are 'wired', and are thus stable and cannot be easily changed. Psychological research recognises five universal personality traits in humans – openness, conscientiousness, extraversion, agreeableness and emotional stability (or, conversely, neuroticism) – and entrepreneurs are usually identified as scoring highly on these.[6] Additionally, the 'hero' entrepreneur is also considered to have a number of traits specifically conducive to entrepreneurial action including self-efficacy, achievement motivation, proactive personality, and innovativeness.[7] Does this then mean that entrepreneurs are born with something 'special'?

---

[4]*MARS: Inside SpaceX* [Film]. Directed by: Julia Reagan. USA: Radical Media; 2018.

[5]Allport, G. W. (1966). Traits revisited. *American Psychologist, 21*(1), 1–10.

[6]Antoncic, B., Bratkovic Kregar, T., Singh, G. & Denoble, A. D. (2015). The Big Five personality–entrepreneurship relationship: Evidence from Slovenia. *Journal of Small Business Management, 53*(3), 19–841.

[7]Frese, M. & Gielnik, M. M. (2014). The psychology of entrepreneurship. *Annual Review of Organizational Psychology and Organizational Behavior, 1*(1), 413–438.

Whilst some work continues to explore entrepreneurial genetics,[8] the notion that we can profile who an entrepreneur is based on 'entrepreneurial traits' or genes has largely proved inconclusive. This is not to say that our neurological wiring or biology may not endow some of us with features that are helpful in entrepreneurship, but rather it means that we cannot separate entrepreneurs from non-entrepreneurs purely on the grounds of genetic characteristics.[9] Another issue with the belief in inborn traits is that, in fact, it is difficult to tell if they are inborn at all. Whilst our characteristics may be stable over time, this does not necessarily mean that we are born with them. From a scientific point of view, it is extremely difficult to disentangle whether characteristics are determined by our DNA or through the environment in which we develop our life experiences (the so-called 'nature–nurture' dilemma). The main mechanism scientists currently have to determine whether certain human traits are inborn is to study identical twins who are raised separately. These individuals will have the exact same genetic endowment, but will have been exposed to – and shaped by – different developmental learning experiences as they grow up. Thus, any traits that remain the same in identical twins raised apart can be attributed to genetics. Given the difficulty in identifying subjects for twin studies, research in this area is perhaps unsurprisingly extremely limited.

We also now know that an individual could exhibit all the traits listed above and yet not be involved in entrepreneurial activity. Equally, someone could demonstrate none of these traits and could be highly entrepreneurial.[10] As a result, we now generally recognise that people engaged in entrepreneurial activity are not born with something 'special'. Although there is some limited evidence that being hardwired with specific traits can give individuals an advantage on some entrepreneurial tasks,[11] not having these attributes does not in any way prevent others from taking entrepreneurial action – and succeeding. Despite this understanding, the narrative of the 'hero' entrepreneur persists and, in many instances, may continue to shape your own thinking of what it takes to be entrepreneurial – and whether or not you yourself 'have what it takes'.

---

[8]Nicolau, N. & Shane, S. (2009). Can genetic factors influence the likelihood of engaging in entrepreneurial activity? *Journal of Business Venturing, 24,* 1–22.

[9]Nicolaou, N., Phan, P. H. & Stephan, U. (2021). The biological perspective in entrepreneurship research. *Entrepreneurship Theory and Practice, 45*(1), 3–17.

[10]Gartner, W. B. (1988). 'Who is an entrepreneur?' is the wrong question. *Entrepreneurship Theory and Practice, 12*(4), 11–32; Ramoglou, S., Gartner, W. B. & Tsang, E. W. (2020). 'Who is an entrepreneur?' is (still) the wrong question. *Journal of Business Venturing Insights,* e00168.

[11]Gorgievski, M. J. & Stephan, U. (2016). Advancing the psychology of entrepreneurship: A review of the psychological literature and an introduction. *Applied Psychology, 65*(3), 437–468.

1.5 FROM ENTREPRENEUR TO ENTREPRENEURIAL THINKING

In our increasingly complex world, any entrepreneurial activity relies on a wide range of skills and competencies – beyond what can reside in one individual. It is for this reason that entrepreneurial activity requires multiple people with complementary characteristics that enable them to add value on different tasks, ultimately leading to collective value creation. When considering these more complex, contextualised requirements for entrepreneurial activity, the idea that a single person can be born fully equipped with 'what it takes' becomes even more questionable.

As a result, the notion of 'who an entrepreneur is' has been replaced by a focus on the processes that entrepreneurial activity encompasses. That is, what entrepreneurs and entrepreneurial teams do and the behaviours that they engage in to successfully pursue their ambitions. Because we generally think before engaging in behaviour,[12] a big part of the entrepreneurial process now focuses on how entrepreneurs think[13] and, by extension, how we can all *think entrepreneurially*.

Thinking, or technically **cognition**, is how humans make sense of and process information including perception, memory, learning, judgement and decision making. **Entrepreneurial cognition** considers how our thinking leads to the identification and enactment of opportunities through creative ideas, in doing so learning from setbacks, failures and feedback from the environment in order to create solutions to problems.

A simple way to think about how this works is if we think about your brain as a computer. Within this, you have a number of **cognitive schemas** – your knowledge, beliefs, experiences, etc. – which are the 'files' within your computer's memory. To make use of these, you engage in *thinking processes* (reasoning, judgement, decision making, etc.) which act like computer software programs, opening files, using the data and then saving any new versions of the files. Given the sophistication of our cognitive abilities, and how much 'thinking' we do on a daily basis, we do not always take the time (or put in the effort) to understand how our own 'computers' (brains) work, what 'files' (cognitive schema) our computer is working with, and what 'software' (thinking processes) are working well or in need of updating. Yet, an understanding of both our

---

[12]Ajzen, I. (1991). The theory of planned behavior. *Organizational Behavior and Human Decision Processes, 50*(2), 179–211.

[13]Mitchell, R. K., Busenitz, L., Lant, T., McDougall, P. P., Morse, E. A. & Smith, J. B. (2002). Toward a theory of entrepreneurial cognition: Rethinking the people side of entrepreneurship research. *Entrepreneurship Theory and Practice, 27*(2), 93–104; Mitchell, R. K., Busenitz, L. W., Bird, B., Marie Gaglio, C., McMullen, J. S., Morse, E. A. & Smith, J. B. (2007). The central question in entrepreneurial cognition research 2007. *Entrepreneurship Theory and Practice, 31*(1), 1–27.

thinking processes and the set of information, knowledge and beliefs that our thinking draws on is more important than ever in today's changing world, particularly as we seek to create value for others and for ourselves.

DEEP DIVE
COGNITION

As the entrepreneurship 'guru' Bill Gartner (1988) warned over 30 years ago, 'who is an entrepreneur' is the wrong question.[14] Our thoughts have now shifted from the personality traits or characteristics that entrepreneurial individuals might exhibit, in favour of how they think, feel and ultimately behave. We are now more aware of the importance of **cognition**, how we make sense of and process information, as well as of **metacognition** – how we think about (and make sense of) our own thinking.

If you are new to notions of cognition, thinking and mind, you may find this Ted Talk by John Vervaeke of interest: **www.ted.com/talks/john_ vervaeke_all_the_king_s_disciplines_cognitive_science_rescues_ the_deconstructed_mind**

1.6 ENTREPRENEURIAL THINKING AND MINDSET

When we speak about our thinking, or cognition, we also want to consider the concept of *mindset*. Whilst the terms 'thinking' and 'mindset' are often used interchangeably, they are two different (but interlinked) concepts. Generally, our mindset is how we become aware of (and make sense of) what we think, how we think and how we leverage that thinking (or not) to pursue our ambitions and goals through our behaviours. Our mindset reflects our views and beliefs and how we frame ourselves and the world that we inhabit. It is therefore just as important as our thinking, since our mindset underpins our behaviour – what we chose to do or equally what we choose not to do.[15]

Many people now speak of an *entrepreneurial mindset* and this is increasingly considered to be critical if people want to engage in entrepreneurial activity. However, it is not always clear what exactly this term means and how it is meaningful for us as individuals. We often hear the term entrepreneurial mindset as a soundbite, frequently attached to the narratives of 'hero' or 'born' entrepreneurs that we discussed earlier. This is problematic for a number

---

[14]Gartner, 'Who Is an Entrepreneur?' is the wrong question.

[15]Ajzen, The theory of planned behavior.

of reasons. To start, it implies that there is a single entrepreneurial mindset that we all need to go out and 'get'. Linked to this, when people talk about an entrepreneurial mindset they seldom talk about how we can actively shape and develop our mindset. In reality, mindsets are constructed (and reconstructed) over time through sustained effort and practice. Finally, little attention is paid to differentiating between thinking and mindset. If we want to change our mindset, we need to start by *understanding how we currently think* (our **metacognition**).

So, what do we need to know about entrepreneurial thinking and entrepreneurial mindset? Where can we start?

There is no universally accepted definition of an entrepreneurial mindset and the term may well mean different things to each of us. A useful way to think of an entrepreneurial mindset is to consider it composed of three interlinked elements: cognitions, emotions and behaviours.[16] As we discussed earlier, cognition refers to our thinking – how we process information, acquire knowledge and build understanding. Our cognition is influenced by (and in turn influences) our emotions. Humans are emotional creatures and the emotions we feel shape how we think about the world and ourselves and how we make decisions, even if we think we are acting completely rationally and without emotion.[17] Our emotions can be positive or negative, as well as strong or weak.[18] Combined, our thinking and our emotions influence how we behave in different circumstances or activities. Assuming that our actions are intentional (i.e., not a result of impulsive drives)[19], they are probably planned through thinking (cognition) and moderated (to varying degrees) by emotion. From an entrepreneurial perspective, our thinking and emotions shape how we see opportunities to create value and how we then develop and implement our ideas and solutions. One of the most influential schools of thought on entrepreneurial action is the Theory of Planned Behaviour,[20] which observes that a person's *intentions* shape their behaviour. Intention only exists in our thinking – it is an intangible

[16]Kuratko, D. F., Fisher, G. & Audretsch, D. B. (2021). Unravelling the entrepreneurial mindset. *Small Business Economics, 57*, 1681–1691.

[17]Damasio, A. R. (2000). A second chance for emotion. *Cognitive Neuroscience of Emotion*, 12–23; Adolphs, R. & Damasio, A. R. (2001). The interaction of affect and cognition: A neurobiological perspective. In J. P. Forgas (ed.), *Handbook of Affect and Social Cognition* (pp. 27–49). Mahwah, NJ: Lawrence Erlbaum.

[18]Delgado García, J. B., De Quevedo Puente, E. & Blanco Mazagatos, V. (2015). How affect relates to entrepreneurship: A systematic review of the literature and research agenda. *International Journal of Management Reviews, 17*(2), 191–211.

[19]Lerner, D., Hunt, R. & Dimov, D. (2018). Action! Moving beyond the intendedly-rational logics of entrepreneurship. *Journal of Business Venturing, 33*(1), 52–69.

[20]Krueger, N. F. & Carsrud, A. L. (1993). Entrepreneurial intentions: Applying the theory of planned behaviour. *Entrepreneurship & Regional Development, 5*(4), 315–330.

product of our reasoning. For example, we reason that we'd like to do something (e.g., to run a marathon) and we mentally prepare ourselves for that action (e.g., to train, to eat healthily, etc.), developing the intention to act to achieve our outcome.

Our cognitions, emotions and, ultimately, behaviours are all fluid and can be shaped and developed over time. Critically, we have the power to shape and refine our own entrepreneurial thinking and entrepreneurial mindset. Thus, for the purposes of this book we define entrepreneurial mindset as

> *a set of learnable cognitive and emotional competences conducive to developing and enacting behaviours to support value creation activity.*

We'll delve into this further in Chapter 2, but in essence an entrepreneurial mindset enables us to think in a way that has the potential to create value, shaping our behaviours so we can best engage in purposeful entrepreneurial practice by taking action. Over the remainder of this book, we will introduce a range of entrepreneurial concepts, skills and competencies for you to reflect on in the context of your own personal and professional lives. As we discussed in the Introduction to this book, many of these can be considered *life skills* which will help you regardless of the paths you choose in life.[21] We will encourage you to consider what these concepts, skills and competencies mean for you now and in the future, to identify areas for further development and to consider specific actions you can (and will) take to shape your entrepreneurial thinking and mindset.

STOP AND THINK
BORN NOT MADE

Having worked through the notions of entrepreneurs being 'made' not 'born' and what we mean by 'entrepreneurial mindset', take some time to reflect on what this means for you and any questions that might arise. How might you work towards answering those questions?

1.7 ENTREPRENEURIAL THINKING AND MINDSET FOR VALUE CREATION

Just as we challenged the myth of the 'born' or 'hero' entrepreneur, we also need to consider what entrepreneurial activity looks like. So often we equate entrepreneurship with the

---

[21]Neck, H. M. & Corbett, A. C. (2018). The scholarship of teaching and learning entrepreneurship. *Entrepreneurship Education and Pedagogy, 1*(1), 8–41.

creation of a new business venture. We assume that someone has an idea, they develop a scalable business model, write a plan and then they go and start the business. That is certainly one kind of *entrepreneurial journey*, but not all people who act entrepreneurially will necessarily create – or will even want to create – a new business.

Entrepreneurial activity can and does occur in a range of situations and covers many different types of journey. You may, for example, want to think and act entrepreneurially within an existing company or your current employer. Often called 'corporate entrepreneurship' or 'intrapreneurship', this entrepreneurial activity could involve a range of activities such as developing a new product, refining an existing process (for example, refining how you communicate with your customers), or even changing the culture within your organisation (for example, encouraging and rewarding creative thinking and the development of new ideas).

Perhaps you want to behave entrepreneurially in a non-commercial context or outside of an organisation. Such 'social enterprise' or 'social impact' activity might involve you tackling issues or problems within your community (for example, anti-social behaviour or environmental pollution), working either loosely or formally with other individuals or organisations (e.g., charities) to make a difference.

You may also want to make your own life better, perhaps by turning a hobby into an activity that generates income and thus frees up your time to more of what you love and less of what you don't (often called 'lifestyle entrepreneurship'). Ultimately, no matter where and how we engage in entrepreneurial activity, our entrepreneurial thinking, mindset and behaviour allow us to create *value*, for others or for ourselves.

Value is a bit of a tricky word. We hear discussion of it everywhere yet, like many of the terms we have introduced in this chapter, there is usually a lack of clarity in terms of what it means. When talking about entrepreneurial value creation, many people instantly think of *economic value*.[22] This generally consists of three elements: *perceived value* (i.e., the benefit I think I will have from something), *exchange value* (i.e., what I am willing to give up in order to obtain that something, usually measured in terms of money) and *value in use* (i.e., the benefits I get from using/consuming, which may or not be what I had originally perceived). We are often very comfortable with the concept of economic value as we are used to the idea of quantifying the benefit of something in monetary terms.

However, value can take a much wider range of forms than just economic value[23] and can include, for example:

---

[22]Lackéus, M. (2018). 'What is value?' A framework for analyzing and facilitating entrepreneurial value creation. *Uniped, 41*(1), 10–28.

[23]Hindle, K. & Moroz, P. (2010). Indigenous entrepreneurship as a research field: Developing a definitional framework from the emerging canon. *International Entrepreneurship and Management Journal, 6*, 357–385.

- *social value*, where we seek to help others to reduce their suffering or to make their lives better or happier
- *mental value*, where we derive enjoyment, happiness or a sense of accomplishment from our own entrepreneurial thinking and action
- *environmental/ecological value*, where we address or solve problems occurring within natural ecosystems or spaces
- *aesthetic value*, where we identify or cultivate feelings of pleasure when looking at or experiencing something that we consider to have beauty or attractiveness
- *cultural value*, where we seek to preserve or support cultural heritage.

We can create such value for ourselves, for others, or in tandem – they are arguably 'two sides of the same coin'. As with economic value, these forms of value may also comprise *perceived value*, *exchange value* and *value in use*, although these might look different. For example, if you were creating social value within marginalised communities by providing free access to computers for school children, exchange value might not necessarily be measured in monetary terms but perhaps in less 'tangible' elements such as time or effort.

DEEP DIVE
BALANCING SOCIAL AND ECONOMIC VALUE

As discussed, we are usually very comfortable with the concept of economic value, particularly in the context of profit-oriented organisations. It can be more difficult to think about how such organisations can engage in **social value creation** without this coming at the expense of turnover or profit.

Dan Iversen provides an interesting take on how to balance social and economic value: **www.ted.com/talks/dan_iversen_social_value_creation_an_opportunity_of_a_lifetime/transcript**

Whilst we all have different views on value (and we'll discuss this further in Chapters 10 and 11), for the purpose of this book, we define value as:

The creation of something new, improved, or in a novel space, that an individual or group of individuals considers to have worth.

Ultimately, there is no right or wrong when it comes to thinking about value, so long as your thoughts are meaningful for you and for the people you are looking to create value for.

FOOD FOR THOUGHT

VALUE AND YOU

Value means different things to different people – as it should! When we talk about entrepreneurial thinking and action, it is in the context of creating value for yourself and for others. But what does this mean for you?

Take a moment to consider what value might mean for you, both in terms of your personal life and your professional life. Record these below. We will revisit these later on Chapter 10.

1. What might 'value' mean to you in the context of your personal life?

....

....

....

2. What might 'value' mean to you in the context of your professional life?

....

....

....

1.8 SELF-AWARENESS AS THE FOUNDATION FOR AN ENTREPRENEURIAL MINDSET

We hope that, by now, we are all in agreement that an entrepreneurial mindset is within reach of everyone. You don't need 'special' genetics or traits – just a willingness to engage with your own abilities and to see opportunities for development through sustained effort and practice.

It is a basic principle of this book that fostering an entrepreneurial mindset requires *self-awareness*. The Oxford Dictionary defines self-awareness as knowledge and understanding of one's own character. For the purpose of developing an entrepreneurial mindset, we refer to self-awareness *as one's ability to know and understand one's thinking and feelings and appreciate how they impact – and are impacted by – behaviour.*

Being aware of the mechanisms that regulate our thoughts and behaviours allows us to be in the 'driving seat' as we journey towards fulfilling our entrepreneurial potential. It allows us to become aware of our strengths as well as our areas for improvement so that we can plan what to focus on and how to go about practising for the purpose of improving. Conversely, a lack of self-awareness equates to us trying to drive with our eyes closed – we have no way of knowing where we are and, more importantly, which way we are going.

Many of us believe we are already self-aware because we each hold a sense of who we are – a mental image of ourselves. However, our self-perception can potentially be skewed or inaccurate. Therefore, in order for self-awareness to be truly helpful in guiding our entrepreneurial development, it has to be based on a view that is as objective as possible. One way to accomplish this is to take a balanced perspective of how we see ourselves (our so called 'internal self-awareness') and how others see us ('external self-awareness'),[24] drawing on tools that help us evaluate ourselves impartially. We will use, and build on, these throughout this book and will look at this in further detail in Chapter 3.

1.9 SUMMARY AND NEXT STEPS

This chapter has identified and explored the narratives we often hear and see about entrepreneurs and their activity. We have critiqued a number of the key 'myths' of entrepreneurship – that entrepreneurs are born with special traits or abilities which allow them to behave in superior ways (e.g., the hero entrepreneur). We have also questioned the implicit assumption that entrepreneurial activity is all about creating new businesses and instead discussed *value creation* as the outcome of entrepreneurial activity, whether this is value for yourself or value for others (or both). This entrepreneurial activity (behaviour, action) is shaped by how we think and feel – our mindset. Our mindset is not something we are born with, but rather something that we can shape and develop as we build and refine our skills and competencies over a period of time.

We will build on these concepts over the coming chapters, starting with a deeper discussion of 'mindset' in Chapter 2.

WHERE AM I NOW?
ENTREPRENEURSHIP AND YOU

Having worked through this chapter, spend a few minutes revisiting your assumptions about entrepreneurship and how it relates to you and your own life. Record these below.

---

[24]Eurich, T. (2018). What self-awareness really is (and how to cultivate it)? *Harvard Business Review, 4* January. https://hbr.org/2018/01/what-self-awareness-reallyis-and-how-to-cultivate-it

1. what is your own personal understanding of entrepreneurship?

2. what do you think entrepreneurial activity involves?

3. who do you think engages in entrepreneurship?

4. How does – or how will – entrepreneurial activity relate to you personally?

1.10 CONTINUE YOUR LEARNING

The following activities are designed to support you on your learning journey, building on ideas introduced in this chapter. These can be completed at any time and in any order, although you may find it helpful to begin with the 'Check your understanding' activity before moving on.

CHECK YOUR UNDERSTANDING

1. The translation of 'entrepreneurship' carries the same meaning across all countries globally.

    TRUE

    FALSE (It's false, as different translations have different meanings)

2. The media has a tendency to portray entrepreneurs as heroic and special.

   TRUE (It's true – the media prefers individuals who come across as flamboyant, heroic and of almost unattainable abilities)

   FALSE

3. Researchers have definitely proven that it is possible to profile an entrepreneur based on genetics.

   TRUE

   FALSE (It's false – whilst some genetic factors can play a role in supporting some entrepreneurial behaviour, there is no definitive proof that genetics alone can profile an entrepreneur)

4. Entrepreneurial cognition is about who an entrepreneur is.

   TRUE

   FALSE (It's false – entrepreneurial cognition is about how an entrepreneur *thinks*)

5. In this book, the notion of 'entrepreneurial value creation' is considered broader that the notion of 'venture creation'.

   TRUE (It's true – venture creation is only one potential outcome of entrepreneurial thinking and behaviour; 'value creation' goes beyond just venture creation)

   FALSE

FURTHER READING

1. **The Obstacle is the Way** by Ryan Holiday
2. **Tomorrowmind** by Gabriella Rosen Kellerman and Martin Seligman
3. **Value(s)** by Mark Carney

COGNITIVE–BEHAVIOURAL REFLECTION
BEGINNING THE JOURNEY OF SELF-AWARENESS

As we discussed in Section 1.8, self-awareness is a critical part of developing our entrepreneurial thinking, competences and, ultimately, action. We consider self-awareness to be **one's ability to know and understand one's thinking and feelings and appreciate how they impact — and are impacted by — behaviour.**

Why do this? One way to help us better understand how we think, feel and behave in different situations is to reflect on our experiences using a cognitive-behavioural framework (see image below).

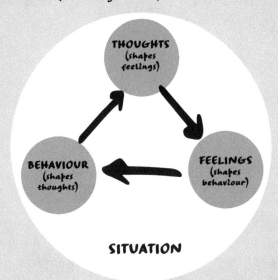

This framework helps to show how changing your thoughts can have an impact on your feelings and behaviours.

As with all things, cognitive-behavioural reflection requires practice, so you'll find these activities throughout this book. To start with, think of (i) a positive situation and (ii) a negative situation that you have been involved in within the past two weeks.

Step 1. Describe these situations in two to three sentences.

Step 2. Describe the thoughts you had in these situations. [This is your *interpretation* of the situation, so make sure you explore it in sufficient detail. We'd recommend about four to eight sentences.]

Step 3. Describe how you felt in these situations. [These are your *emotions*. Be as specific as you can in your language, avoiding general terms like 'happy' or 'sad' in favour of more nuanced terms.]

Step 4. Describe how you behaved (i.e., acted) in these situations. [Focus on how you responded, identifying both positive and negative responses.]

Step 5. Looking back on these situations what sense can you make of them? What do you now better understand about yourself, your feelings and your behaviours?

PRACTISING ENTREPRENEURIAL THINKING
TAKING THE FIRST STEP

When we start something new we can easily feel overwhelmed, intimidated, uncertain or unprepared. Starting something new is hard! Yet it gives us the chance to learn and to improve over time and with effort.

It is so important that we pause every so often to take stock of where we are and how far we've come – to celebrate the victories that we are slowly (but surely) achieving as we build **mastery**. Although it's easy to assume that **mastery** means total (100%) knowledge or skill, this is seldom the case. The more we know, the more we realise we have to learn. For our purposes, mastery is a journey rather than an end state – a continuous drive to improve ourselves, our skills and our competences.

AN EXAMPLE OF MASTERY

There is a very long tradition of London taxicab drivers being some of the most learned individuals in the UK. This is because in order to become an official London cab driver each individual must take a very intensive test called **The Knowledge**. This tests the individual's ability to recall every street in London, without using GPS or a map, and often requires years of study. Originating in 1865, London cab drivers must obtain a result of at least a 60% in order to pass, something **only a minority of individuals who apply achieve.** Even having passed **The Knowledge**, licenced drivers still need to keep up to date as London grows and develops and street patterns evolve.

See: **https://tfl.gov.uk/info-for/taxis-and-private-hire/licensing/ learn-the-knowledge-of-london**

YOUR OWN MASTERY

Take some time to consider what mastery will mean for you.

1. What is it that you are trying to achieve?

2. How will you be able to tell you're making progress?

CHAPTER 2

CONSIDERING YOUR OWN ENTREPRENEURIAL POTENTIAL

"Our life is shaped by our mind; we become what we think"

The Dhammapada (translated by Eknath Easwaran, 2007)

2.1 INTRODUCTION

Now that we have challenged some of the myths and stereotypes of entrepreneurship (see Chapter 1), we can turn our attention away from media representations of big-name entrepreneurs and focus on what is really important – *your own* entrepreneurial potential!

Have you ever thought of yourself as entrepreneurial before? What is appealing about the term or, equally, unappealing? Have you ever spent time considering what skills, competencies, mindset, knowledge and experience you have that will allow you to create value for yourself and for others? As we have touched on, entrepreneurial activity is so much more than the creation of a new business. We can think and act entrepreneurially in many different contexts, some of which might be commercial in nature and others of which might not. But how can we identify our entrepreneurial potential and, more importantly, work to harness it?

This chapter will start by delving deeper into the concept of mindset – how we become aware of (and make sense of) what we think, how we think and how we leverage that thinking (or not) to pursue our ambitions and goals through our behaviours. We will consider different ways that we think about situations and how that then shapes our thinking about ourselves and our own abilities. We will then return to the concept of *entrepreneurial mindset*, considering the specific skills, competencies and behaviours that underpin this, and how they support value creation activity.

After working through this chapter, you should be able to:

- appraise and articulate the concept of mindset
- identify and consider your own mindset, linked to your personal background and context
- articulate the cognitive, emotional and behavioural components of an entrepreneurial mindset.

2.2 THE IMPORTANCE OF MINDSET

As we touched on in Chapter 1, our mindset plays an important role in what we do – or do not do. Our mindsets shift and morph as a result of changing experiences or sustained effort and practice, unlike traits (e.g., introversion, extraversion) which are largely fixed and do not change substantially over time. Critically, our mindsets reflect our thoughts, views and beliefs and ultimately how we think about ourselves.

You may be wondering, why exactly is mindset relevant in any entrepreneurial effort? The reason is to be found in the nature of the entrepreneurial process. Entrepreneurship is not a one-off act. Rather, it is a process that takes place over time, usually starting from an idea for value creation and ending in the realisation of that value. That process may seem straightforward – you know what you want to achieve, you mobilise towards it, put effort in and make it happen. Right?!

This may be the case if the sort of value you want to create is not completely new, that is if there is a charted path that you can follow in order to arrive at the desired result. This is akin to following a recipe and it is what is typically referred to as a 'causation approach'.[1]

Most entrepreneurial processes, however, aim to create value that is different from what has gone before and thus there is no path to be followed – no prescriptive recipe. We may have an idea of what we want to achieve, but are not sure about how to get there. When this is the case, entrepreneurship is more akin to a journey whereby we know where and with what we start but we cannot be sure of how the journey will unfold. We start with an idea and, as we attempt ways to turn it into a reality, we come up against difficulties and setbacks. What we thought would work in a certain way may in reality require finding a different way. This normally requires that we take stock of what has not worked and modify our approach – we pivot, change path altogether or go back to the drawing board.

DEEP DIVE
EFFECTUATION

Research has found that many of the most effective entrepreneurial individuals adopt what is called 'effectual logic', whereby instead of focusing on the 'end' (e.g., what they will create), they instead start with the 'means' available to them (e.g., who they are, what they know, who they know).

Saras Sarasvathy, the researcher behind this concept, explains what this means at https://youtube/tSHtW4Nqt-E

What underpins this entrepreneurial journey, then, are two core attitudes that are now believed to unlock any entrepreneurial path: 1) our perseverance, even when things are not going to plan, and 2) our belief in learning and improving.

A key part of our mindset for acting entrepreneurially, therefore, is how we think about ability to learn versus natural talent. Most of us would agree that human beings are capable

[1]Sarasvathy, S. D. (2001). Causation and effectuation: Toward a theoretical shift from economic inevitability to entrepreneurial contingency. *Academy of Management Review, 26*(2), 243–263.

of learning. We can learn to play the piano, learn to drive, learn how to add and multiply numbers, etc. Yet, despite the fact that learning is a fundamental part of the human experience, we do not always fully recognise or appreciate the ups and downs of the learning process. Learning can be hard. And sometimes it feels like no matter how much effort we are putting into a task, someone else is able to do better or more easily, which can affect how we think about ourselves and our ability.

These kinds of thought patterns have been found to be important in terms of our mindset, influencing whether we demonstrate a *fixed* vs. *growth* mindset, or an *open* vs. *closed* mindset, which we will now look at in more detail.

2.2.1 FIXED VS GROWTH MINDSET

In this section we will discuss the core ideas of a fixed vs growth mindset. However, before you read on, please pause at this point and answer the questions in the box below.

WHERE AM I STARTING FROM?
FIXED VS GROWTH MINDSET

We all perceive ourselves in different ways. There is no 'right' or 'wrong' mindset to have. What is important is that we recognise the way we think about ourselves so that we can consider how our mindset is shaping our behaviour for better — or for worse.

1. Spend a few minutes looking through the key principles of the growth and fixed mindsets below and tick (a) those that you think best apply to you. Try to be honest with yourself — there is no need for impression management here!

GROWTH MINDSET	(a)	FIXED MINDSET	(a)
I believe that...		I believe that...	
My intelligence can grow	☐	My intelligence is fixed	☐
Hard work is the most important	☐	Natural talent is the most important	☐
Hard work makes me smart	☐	If I have to work hard I don't have what it takes	☐
Uncomfortable challenges are opportunities for me to learn	☐	Uncomfortable challenges should be avoided so I don't lose status or reputation	☐

I should try my best regardless of the outcome ▢	Cheating/lying/avoiding are appropriate if I want a positive outcome ▢
Failing means I am not there yet and I must try again ▢	Failing means I am a failure and I must give up ▢

2. What mindset best reflects your own outlook? How do you feel about this result? Why? Record this below.

....

....

....

Researchers have for some time tried to understand what motivates people to make an effort and take action to achieve their potential (so-called *competence motivation*).[2] Interestingly, they have found that inborn ability or talent is not as significant as whether or not people believe that results come from hard work. This has led to the identification of two different outlooks or mindsets, popularised by the work of Carol Dweck – a *growth mindset* and a *fixed mindset*. In essence, individuals with a growth mindset hold a strong belief that they can accomplish anything by working hard at it, whereas those with a fixed mindset hold a strong belief that without being naturally talented or 'gifted' certain accomplishments are out of reach no matter how hard they try.[3]

With the issue of personal learning through effortful practice (and potentially failure) at its heart, a growth mindset often manifests in the following ways:

- Belief that your ability to learn can improve through practice. It can be exercised, much like you would a muscle. Thus, your intelligence can also grow over time.
- Belief that hard work is what's important, not natural talent.

---

[2]Dweck, C. S. & Molden, D. C. (2017). Mindsets: Their impact on competence motivation and acquisition. In A. J. Elliot, C. S. Dweck & D. S. Yeager (eds), *Handbook of Competence and Motivation: Theory and Application* (pp. 135–154). New York: The Guilford Press.

[3]Dweck, C. S. (2006). *Mindset: The New Psychology of Success*. New York: Random House; Dweck, C. S. (2017). From needs to goals and representations: Foundations for a unified theory of motivation, personality, and development. *Psychological Review, 124*(6), 689–719.

- Belief that the experience of hard work makes you smarter. Hard work does not denote a lack of ability.
- Belief in the importance of continuous personal learning and development – the so-called *learning orientation*.
- Belief that uncomfortable challenges are opportunities to learn and should be embraced rather than avoided.
- Belief in taking action, even if it feels hard or scary. Choosing an *action orientation* over procrastination.
- Belief that we all have more to learn and so seek to understand by being curious and asking 'why'.
- Belief that mistakes and failures are opportunities for learning and personal development, rather than the 'end of the road'.
- Belief that mistakes and failures do not define your identity or mean that you are flawed.

As we noted earlier, there is no 'right or wrong' when it comes to our mindset. However, when we are considering entrepreneurial thinking and action, the beliefs aligned to the growth mindset are particularly powerful. When we are creating value, we are operating the space of the 'unknown' – instead of looking for what is, we need to look for *what could be*. Are we willing to see potential, rather than how things are currently? Can we work in spaces where boundaries or requirements are not particularly clear? Can we not only identify opportunities for us to act on, but to also develop the ideas that help us to act? In this way, we need to be curious, action oriented and not afraid to try and – very likely – to fail in our first attempt. As with our views on entrepreneurship,[4] our mindsets are shaped by the culture, people (e.g., family, friends) and institutions (e.g., school, work, religion, government) that we are surrounded by. These can shape our views on effort, learning, failing and personal ability.

DEEP DIVE
GROWTH MINDSET

The concept of growth mindset has been popularised by the work of Professor Carol Dweck, bestselling author of **Mindset** and Stanford University Professor of Competence Psychology. Professor Dweck explains what a growth mindset is and how we can work to develop this outlook for ourselves at **www.youtube.com/watch?v=hiiEeMN7vbQ**

[4]Drakopoulou Dodd, S., Jack, S. & Anderson, A. (2013). From admiration to abhorrence: The contentious appeal of entrepreneurship across Europe. *Entrepreneurship & Regional Development, 25*(1–2), 69–89.

Just as it is important to understand what a growth mindset is, we also need to consider what a growth mindset is not. Since the term is so widely used, a number of 'myths' have developed around the concept just as they have for entrepreneurship.

Having a growth mindset...

- does NOT mean blindly accepting feedback that feels unfair, inaccurate or outright wrong – or assuming that the individuals or sources of feedback know better than you do
- it is NOT about growing *things* (e.g., a business), but rather about *your own growth* in terms of personal abilities[5]
- it is NOT an excuse for not making the effort (i.e., not aiming for your own best possible performance given ability at the specific point in time) – indeed, putting in your full effort regardless of the outcome is a key principle of a growth mindset
- does NOT mean never having self-doubt or having a can-do attitude at all costs and regardless of circumstances.

Whilst a growth mindset allows us to recognise that our abilities can be enhanced over time and through practice,[6] based on our ability to retrain or 'rewire' our thinking thanks to our brain's **neuroplasticity**, a growth mindset in and of itself does not necessarily mean that we will know how to open up to the inputs from which we can learn and adapt our behaviours.

The ability to be open to inputs from others, and from our environments, requires an *open mindset*, as we will explore in the next section of this chapter.

DEEP DIVE
NEUROPLASTICITY

If you have not come across the term 'neuroplasticity' before, have a look at this TED Talk:

www.ted.com/talks/michael_merzenich_growing_evidence_of_brain_plasticity

2.2.2 OPEN VS CLOSED MINDSET
An *open mindset*, also referred to as a deliberative mindset,[7] refers to our tendency to be open to feedback from the external environment and adapt our thinking and behaviour in response to new, relevant information.

[5]Grant, H., Slaughter, M. & Derler, A. (2018). 5 mistakes companies make about growth mindsets. *Harvard Business Review*, 23 July.

[6]Dweck, *Mindset: The New Psychology of Success*.

[7]Reeve, J. (2014). *Understanding Motivation and Emotion*. Hoboken, NJ: John Wiley & Sons.

An open mindset is associated with the concept of *cognitive agility* – our ability to consider multiple alternatives without prejudice before we choose the most promising one.[8] Cognitive agility is best captured by the quote below:

> *It is the mark of an educated mind to be able to entertain a thought without accepting it.* (Attributed to Aristotle[9])

Generally, most of us would claim that we have an open mindset – that we are 'open minded' towards other peoples' different ideas and perspectives. This is, however, only part of what we mean by having an open mindset. In addition to accepting alternative viewpoints, we also need to consider our willingness to adapt and change when these perspectives of observations call into question our '*blind spots*' (we'll come back to this idea in Chapter 6).

WHERE AM I STARTING FROM?
OPEN VS CLOSED MINDSET

1. Spend a few minutes looking through the key principles of the open and closed mindsets in the table below and tick (a) those that you think best apply to you. Try to be honest with yourself – there is no need for impression management here!

OPEN MINDSET	(a)	CLOSED MINDSET	(a)
I...		I ...	
Am willing to have my ideas challenged and to be proven wrong	☐	Dislike being wrong and resist having my ideas challenged	☐
Am focused on pursuing the truth, whatever it may be	☐	Am focused on seeking confirmation for what I think/know	☐
Engage in debates in order to learn	☐	Engage in debates in order to defend my own position	☐

---

[8] Kellerman, G. R. & Seligman, M. E. (2023). *Tomorrowmind: Thriving at Work With Resilience, Creativity, and Connection—Now and in an Uncertain Future*. New York: Simon and Schuster.
[9] From Bennion, L. L. (1959). *Religion and the Pursuit of Truth*. Salt Lake City: Deseret Book Company.

Prefer to ask questions [ ]   Prefer to make statements [ ]

Focus on what is unknown [ ]   Focus on existing knowledge [ ]

Prefer to interact with those who challenge me [ ]   Prefer to interaction with those who agree with me [ ]

2. What mindset best reflects your own outlook? How do you feel about this result? Why? Record this below.

An open mindset recognises – and embraces – the fact that we don't and can't know everything. We always have blind spots, which result from a lack of access to all the relevant information needed to make a full assessment about a situation. We need to recognise, however, that just because we don't have that information does not mean that the information itself does not exist somewhere. This forces us to consider, and ultimately embrace, the *unknown unknowns*. These occur when we do not know what information we may be missing because we are not aware that the information exists or that it is relevant. A useful example of this is when Sir Tim Smit, the Founder and CEO of the environmental conservation EDEN Project in Cornwall, UK [www.edenproject.com/] asked his construction team the following question at the start of their work:

If you were me, what questions should I be asking you so that I can make sure that the project is delivered on time and on budget?

This question wonderfully illustrates Sir Tim's open mindset by highlighting his focus on his blind spots. He recognised that he did not have all the relevant insight to ask meaningful questions, so looked to those with alternative knowledge to identify where to look and what questions to ask. This deliberative thinking and self-awareness are of particular importance when we move beyond mindset generally and start to consider the concept of an *entrepreneurial mindset*.

CHALLENGING ASSUMPTIONS

COMPARING MINDSET IN CORPORATE CULTURE AT APPLE AND AMAZON

Written by Philip Palios

15 January 2023

'Are right, a lot'. The fourth of Amazon's 16 leadership principles, is an interesting marketing spin on the ethos of a closed mindset. Of course, I am sure Amazon would join myself and most newcomers to Gottfredson's definition and evaluation of mindsets in shock upon scoring as close-minded despite being self-described as open-minded. What is Amazon getting at with the principles that shape their corporate culture and how does it relate to Gottfredson's model? Going from theory to practice, what is it like to work within a company whose leadership values close-mindedness and how does it manifest in product development? In this essay, I will compare and contrast my own experiences as a software engineer working at Amazon and Apple from 2012 through 2020 with particular attention to the role of corporate culture in promoting growth vs fixed and open vs closed mindsets.

When I first joined Amazon in 2012, I was assigned to lead software quality for the first Prime Video iOS app. I was good at what I did and through the strenuous efforts of myself and the handful of engineers I worked with, we had a very successful app launch. Myself and the other engineers had little to no input in how the product would function, we followed a very traditional software engineering approach of being given designs and specifications from management which we were tasked with building. My role as a quality engineer was not to say whether or not the product was of high quality in my opinion, but to measure whether it met the provided designs and specifications. The product's business success, measured in user uptake and increased minutes of video streaming, was the result of the decisions that management had made and our ability to execute them. Celebrations ensued and I was soon placed on a special, secret project. Within software engineering, this is coveted. Everyone in the field knows the 'good' engineers go to special projects and the 'bad' ones go to sustained engineering (fixing bugs and general upkeep of existing software).

While my job was to evaluate software against its specifications, I couldn't help but speak up when I believed those specifications were faulty. In the case of the iOS app, I didn't have significant objections to the design or specifications. Once placed on the special project, that changed. Thanks to the passing of time and expiration of non-disclosure agreements, I am now free to share details of the project and my experience. What it ultimately boils down to is that when a team of product managers and designers who were hired because of their close-minded belief that they 'are right, a lot' produce a specification and receive strong objections from engineers, also hired because of their belief that they 'are right, a lot', what ensues is deadlock and friction, rather than collaborative innovation.

The project, known to the outside world as the infamous Fire Phone, was a wildly ambitious new venture dreamed up by Amazon's top brass. After successful launches of the Kindle Fire tablet and Fire TV, the company was riding high, seeing itself joining Apple, Google and Microsoft as a platform developer and device manufacturer. While built on top of Google's Android operating system (which the Kindle Fire and Fire TV also ran on), the Fire Phone was intended to be worlds apart. Most significantly, and likely driving the wild idea, was the desire to own the digital marketplace of smartphone users — ensuring that apps, music, videos, books and other digital media were purchased and consumed through Amazon (rather than Google with all existing Android phones or Apple with iPhones). What management underestimated was how hard it would be to build and launch a smartphone. Myself and the hundred or so engineers assigned to the project were extremely concerned and vocal about the product's mismatch between vision and reality.

So why did the project launch and suffer such great failure? What sets this apart from Apple is not that Apple doesn't have similar flops — it's that Apple's open-minded culture prevents most flops from making it to market. One of the first things that people working in software engineering learn is that the earlier in the product development lifecycle problems are identified and resolved, the lower the cost. Fixing issues in design and planning before they go to engineering is ideal, fixing them in engineering before release eats up additional engineering time and money, fixing them post-launch is the most risky and expensive. I got into software quality engineering because I wanted my role to be that of a gatekeeper helping prevent problems from making it to launch and being more costly to fix. But according to Amazon, my job was merely to ensure the product matched the design, not to critique the design itself. The same went for the engineers. So if there were problems with the design, they would only be revealed upon launch, no matter how much noise was made by the engineers building the project.

'Think different'. The classic slogan embossed on endless Apple adverts. What does it mean? Does it suggest an open or closed mindset? Most importantly, is it merely marketing or does it reflect the corporate culture? My opinion, based on working within the engineering teams on Apple TV, Apple Music and Apple Maps, is that there is indeed a unique corporate culture created and supported from the top down which encourages an open mindset. In a way, it is practically the opposite of Amazon's 'be right' attitude; instead I would say Apple has a 'be foolish' attitude. While being offered a job at Apple is extremely competitive and an opportunity only available to those with top skills and experience, there are additional essential ingredients that Apple evaluates for when hiring and encourages once hired, including mindset.

I was originally hired at Apple to work on a secret project, it was really exciting and I felt a similar sense of exclusivity to when I was first assigned to the Fire Phone project at Amazon. What I was working on had already been years in the making and was a real innovation, unlike the hastily-executed, gimmick-ridden Fire Phone. I'm not going into details here because the project I was originally hired at Apple for was never released. As my time at Apple continued, I learned that it was quite common for projects to be put on hold or set aside entirely. The idea being that only projects that meet a very high bar are released to market. There is no need to 'be right' to start a project, and it is only through time and testing that a decision is made, usually based on the input of many people and with supporting data. So while Apple (mostly) appears to release polished, highly successful projects, this is not due to a 'be right, a lot' attitude, but actually the opposite. Everyone at Apple is invited to innovate and share ideas for new features or entirely new projects, these ideas don't go into a void either, every time I ventured out to test the waters I was surprised by the response of the teams I got in contact with, they were genuinely interested in employee input and some of my suggestions even made it into products that I was not directly involved with as part of my 'job.'

Encouraging employees to experiment, knowing most of what will be produced is not something that is viable, is an amazing freedom and creates a very unique culture. Rather than merely grow in my skillset, I grew in my thinking while working at Apple. It was serene to be working alongside people, however accomplished, who had humility and a sense of foolishness, a willingness to be wrong and be challenged in the search for great products.

While both Amazon and Apple are massive corporations, they can be better understood as entrepreneurial labs. Unlike older, non-tech businesses, working for these companies, especially in engineering, means exploring new ideas with the resources and support of a massive business behind you (and owning rights to everything you produce). When they are thought of as entrepreneurial labs, the influence of mindset can be studied in a similar way to how it might be studied at 'real' start-ups, which are primarily just teams of engineers and business people with fewer resources and support.

Recruiting employees with and/or encouraging/developing an open mindset is not an 'easy win' because it breaks down the efficiency and structure of a traditional top-down business, where everyone below the executives are hired to do as they are told and not ask questions. The difference is whether a business sees its success as being first or being best; it is rare that anyone achieves both. Apple is almost never first, but almost always best. Amazon has been first in many instances (save the Fire Phone) but rarely the best. These different strategies have different reliance on mindset. To be first, there is no time to be questioned. To be best, questioning is essential.

From a financial standpoint, one could compare Apple and Amazon, with their starkly different cultures of mindset, and say that either an open or closed mindset can lead to profitability, at least in the short-term. However, when considering long-term resiliency of the business as well as the amount of technological innovation and social impact, it becomes easier to see the difference produced by the differing mindsets.

SOURCES

Amazon's leadership principles: **www.aboutamazon.com/about-us/leadership-principles**

Apple's careers site: **www.apple.com/careers/us/index.html**

Gottfredson: **https://ryangottfredson.com/blog/2020/08/10/mindsets-the-circuit-board-of-our-mind/**

Fire phone perspectives on failure:

https://en.wikipedia.org/wiki/Fire_Phone

www.forbes.com/sites/jeanbaptiste/2014/06/19/4-reasons-the-amazon-fire-phone-will-fail/?sh=546734f7fd48

www.businessinsider.com/jeff-bezos-on-big-bets-risks-fire-phone-2014-12

www.zdnet.com/article/hands-on-with-amazons-fire-phone-gimmicks-over-purpose/

www.theguardian.com/technology/2014/aug/26/amazon-fire-phone-sales-data

www.cnet.com/tech/mobile/fire-phone-one-year-later-why-amazons-smartphone-flamed-out/

2.3 DEVELOPING AN ENTREPRENEURIAL MINDSET

We introduced the basic concept of entrepreneurial mindset in Chapter 1 as the interaction of *thinking* (cognition) and *emotion* in driving entrepreneurial *behaviour*,[10] defining it as:

> *a set of learnable cognitive and emotional competences conducive to developing and enacting behaviours to support value creation activity.*[11]

So what then are these competences? And, more importantly, why do they matter for our behaviour?

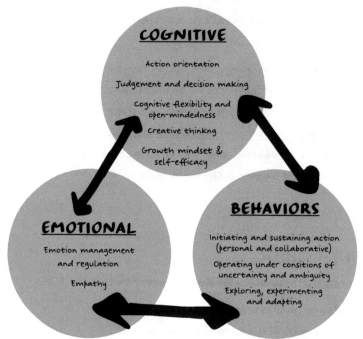

2.3.1 COGNITIVE ASPECTS OF ENTREPRENEURIAL MINDSET

Thinking is a critical part of what we do as humans. Our cognition allows us to take in and process information, leading to decisions of what we do (or don't do).

This concept of action is at the heart of entrepreneurship – we *do* something in order to create value. This involves starting an action, as well as sustaining and coordinating this over a longer period of time – the so-called 'entrepreneurial journey'.[12] To achieve this, a critical entrepreneurial

---

[10]Kuratko, D. F., Fisher, G. & Audretsch, D. B. (2021). Unravelling the entrepreneurial mindset. *Small Business Economics, 57*, 1681–1691.

[11]Mawson, S., Casulli, L. & Simmons, E. L. (2022). A competence development approach for entrepreneurial mindset in entrepreneurship education. *Entrepreneurship Education and Pedagogy,* https://doi.org/10.1177/25151274221143 14

[12]McMullen, J.S. & Dimov, D. (2013). Time and the entrepreneurial journey: The problems and promise of studying entrepreneurship as a process. *Journal of Management Studies, 50*(8), 1481–1512.

competence is the development of an ***action orientation***, where we actively gather information and feedback from the environment, evaluate it and then determine our plans and actions.[13]

This evaluation process itself is important. We need to engage in *judgement and decision making* that is fast and responsive, but that is also appropriate for the situation in which we find ourselves (we'll go into this further in Chapter 6).

To be able to do this, we need to have ***cognitive flexibility*** and to be *open-minded* which we just considered in Section 2.2 (and which we'll explore further in Chapter 3).

This ability to take on board feedback and to adapt is fundamental to our ability to look beyond what we see and to think about what is possible, engaging in *creative thinking*. Creative thinking can be difficult as we explore problems, experiment and challenge our frames of references whilst facing limitations in our knowledge and experiences.

To thrive, we benefit from the *growth mindset* we discussed earlier, where we prioritise effort and practice and embrace learning from both successes and setbacks, developing and supporting our own sense of ***self-efficacy*** as a creator of value.

PRACTISING ENTREPRENEURIAL THINKING
CHANGING ROUTINES

Cognitive flexibility can refer to our ability to separate from one task and respond to another, or think about multiple concepts at the same time.

A simple way to work on your own cognitive flexibility is to think about – and alter – your daily routines. For example, do you take the same route to school/work each day? If so, try taking a different route (or form of transport). Even a small change like this can result in you being more aware of your surroundings and yourself.

1. What routine can you change today? (You could consider changing the time you get up, the order in which you get ready for the day, how you get to/from work or school and so on.)

....

....

---

[13]Dimov, D. (2010). Nascent entrepreneurs and venture emergence: Opportunity confidence, human capital, and early planning. *Journal of Management Studies, 47*(6), 1123–1153.

2.3.2 EMOTIONAL ASPECTS OF ENTREPRENEURIAL MINDSET

As we've talked about, our thinking does not occur in isolation. Our cognition is instead influenced by (and in turn influences) our emotion. We don't often spend a lot of time thinking about our emotions; many of us may have even been encouraged to not think about our feelings, particularly in educational or workplace situations. Not only is it largely impossible to suppress our feelings (particularly those strong ones), it is actually counterintuitive when it comes to our thinking and action. It is only when we understand how we feel about something that we can start to consider why we think and behave in a particular way with regard to it.

Our emotion and our cognition continually interact, no more so than we are trying to create value. Entrepreneurial activity can have significant ups and downs, full of excitement one minute and then worry or fear the next. As we discussed in Chapter 1, we can think about our emotions being positive or negative, as well as either strong or weak. Yet our emotions are not in themselves positive or negative. These labels only become relevant when we *interpret* our emotions (though our thinking) and apply the label we think is most appropriate.

We thus need to make sure that the way we are interpreting our emotions is not clouding our rational thinking, judgement or decision making[14] and can do so by engaging in *emotional management and regulation* where we harness our emotions and actively shape our responses. Just as an overly negative interpretation of emotions may prevent us from acting, overly positive interpretations may have the potential to cloud our decisions and ultimately actions.

---

[14]Delgado García, J. B., De Quevedo Puente, E. & Blanco Mazagatos, V. (2015). How affect relates to entrepreneurship: A systematic review of the literature and research agenda. *International Journal of Management Reviews, 17*(2), 191–211.

Linked to emotional management and regulation of our own emotions is the ability to appreciate those of others. **Empathy** involves understanding and appreciating the thoughts, feelings and experiences of others.[15] This not only helps us to understand what problems people may face and what they might want or need (i.e., the value we can create for them), empathy is also a powerful skillset when collaborating with other people. As we talked about in Chapter 1, entrepreneurial activity isn't the domain of 'heroic' individuals, but rather people working together in pursuit of a common interest or goal. Empathy is critical within these collaborations (which we'll cover further in Chapter 7) as it allows us to develop trust with individuals and a safe environment where people feel free to experiment and learn.

2.3.3 BEHAVIOURAL ASPECTS OF ENTREPRENEURIAL MINDSET

Ultimately, our cognitive and emotional skills and competences allow us to shape our behaviours, taking action to create value (think back to Chapter 1) through entrepreneurial behaviours.[16]

Whilst the context of our entrepreneurial action may differ (e.g., inside an existing organisation, amongst our family, in a start-up), as may the value we are creating, entrepreneurial action requires a number of behaviours which are positively influenced by the cognitive and emotional skills and competencies just discussed.

First, it is not just enough to take action – we need to also be able to sustain that action and *persist* even when things become difficult. This isn't to say we should keep going at all cost (we'll discuss this more in Chapter 4), but we need to be able to continue despite setbacks or challenges.

Second, when taking action we will in all likelihood be facing many unknowns (or even unknown unknowns). Entrepreneurial action involves thinking about what is possible. This usually means we need to work with limited information, data or past precedent in an environment or set of circumstances that we don't yet understand or feel wholly comfortable with. We thus need to become comfortable operating under conditions of **uncertainty** and *ambiguity*, where situations could change rapidly and we need to be able to embrace feedback, to try, to fail and to learn.

Finally, in trying we need to practise *exploring, experimenting* and, depending on how things go, *adapting*. New and challenging endeavours seldom go smoothly,[17] so we need to be able to be flexible and to change course when appropriate.

---

[15]Korte, R., Smith, K. A. & Li, C. Q. (2018). The role of empathy in entrepreneurship: A core competency of the entrepreneurial mindset. *Advances in Engineering Education, 7*(1), n1.

[16]McMullen, J. S. & Shepherd, D. A. (2006). Entrepreneurial action and the role of uncertainty in the theory of the entrepreneur. *Academy of Management Review, 31*(1), 132–152.

[17]McMullen & Dimov, Time and the entrepreneurial journey.

These behaviours may come easily to some of us. For others, they may seem daunting. However, we can develop our comfort and ability through effort and practice, particularly through engaging in self-reflection.

ENTREPRENEURIAL THINKING AND MINDSET IN PRACTICE
BECKY PICK AND THE JOURNEY TO PICK PROTECTION

The case study is intended to illustrate the following:

- the evolving nature of the entrepreneurial journey
- the growth mindset and the open mindset needed to navigate it.

This is the case study of Becky Pick, a university student who was looking for a solution to keep students like herself safe from attacks and ended up founding lone workers solutions company Pick Protection. The case is narrated in Becky's own voice.

PICK PROTECTION TODAY

Pick Protection provides lone worker and employee protection solutions. Our target market is companies that have got employees that work by themselves and that could perhaps be a social worker going into somebody's house, it could just be somebody that works in a bank and they carry their laptop with them, which puts them at risk. So there's a whole range of risk profiles. We work with organisations to make sure they keep their employees as protected and safe as possible.

A lot of our clients are public sector, such as local authorities, social workers, housing officers, but we also are trying to move much more into this large corporate market, with banking and finance being a target market for us. And then looking at other sectors such as manufacturing logistics security could be quite interesting.

The lone worker solutions themselves can be something that an employee can have on them, such as a wearable device to activate if they need help. They press a button, it would then connect to an alarm receiving centre which is a 24/7 centre with highly trained operators who will receive an alert come through from the person, they'll receive the GPS location of the person and it will open up to the audio call so they can hear everything that's happening. They can record everything that's happening so that they could later use it as evidence in potential court cases. A verified emergency send the police as a level one response, putting them ahead of the 999 queue. It could send an ambulance and they'll follow the escalation procedure.

There are three parts to any lone worker solution. The first part is the mechanism that the employee uses to raise the alarm and that could be either an app or a dedicated device or it could be a satellite device or Bluetooth button. There's a whole range of mechanisms that we employ. Those will all link into the second part, which is an online management platform where the managers of the lone workers can see in real time what's happening, who's doing what, because we know you know where they are. They can set a timed risk period as well. There's lots more than just the SOS alarm, so they can see all that in the portal. And then the third part and probably most important part is the response side of it, so that when somebody presses that button, someone's there to facilitate the response.

The online platform is the middle part of our software. We've built that in house and we've also built the smartphone applications in house there and protection. We've bought in the dedicated device I talked about, our satellite device, because there are companies that specialise in that and they can make them really cheaply. So it's not worth us doing that when we can buy them on the shelves and then just configure them to integrate into our portal.

The third part is the alarm receiving centre. To create one of those, you need so much capital to start. I mean, they need to be bombproof bulletproof glass. It really is a huge investment so we outsource it. We've got a partnership with a company and they already have that in place – they are a supplier to us of that service for our customers.

PICK PROTECTION: THE JOURNEY

It sounds like the business model is well figured out now, but that was not always the case.

It all started when I was in my third year of a university degree in Entrepreneurship and Marketing. I just had an idea. My neighbour was attacked and nobody came to help her. So that was when I thought that we should all have something on us all the time that we know if we activate, we will get a response. I started doing a bit of research into what was on the market in terms of personal protection and I found that there were personal attack alarms but none of them would guarantee a response if activated. The business evolved from there. I had no idea at the time that I was going to go on to start a business. It was just an idea that I had. I worked with the entrepreneurship support network of my university to see how I could take the idea a bit further. They advised me on grants and competitions to apply for to get funding. I did that, got a bit of money, developed a little 3D printed alarm that would click on a bra strap and absolutely loved it. Then, through my networks at the university's entrepreneurship support, I met a lady who's involved in an angel investment syndicate. She encouraged me to pitch for investment, which came as shock to me. I did not think I was anywhere near ready at that point. I was still to complete my dissertation! Nevertheless, I did the pitch, the investors liked it and at that point the offering was very much a personal attack alarm that could be sold to end users such as students.

The first round of investment was a key milestone. It triggered a mental switch so that I realised that I had a real opportunity to create a business, whereas up to that point I was playing with the ideas just to see how far it would go. But the investment made me take the business seriously and I decided to do my best.

I started working with the investment director, who was a lovely guy with a great background in technology. He's worked with start-ups from pre-revenue to global sales before so he was really experienced. we worked on the business and we figured out that there's a whole other market that was underserved. There were over 6 million lone workers in the UK and every nine minutes one of them gets attacked.

And then at that point, we thought we would serve both markets: lone workers and students. At that point I was trying to develop a solution that would work for both and everybody else I spoke to knew it was a bad idea, but I just could not let go of one market.

Also at that point, I met some investors from the next round, who were experienced and successful. Through conversations with them, it became apparent that we needed to choose one thing to focus on, one focal market, in order to serve it well.

with the investors we figured out that the Business-to-Consumer route would have needed millions of pounds of investment in order to yield a suitable return on investment, whereas the corporate, Business-to-Business market would have required less investment. So we choose the latter.

Having chosen the B-to-B market, all the product development and all the research that we had done was no longer relevant, so we had to start all over again.

We started going out to customers that use lone worker solutions and asked them what they did not like about existing solutions. We received great feedback that supported the decision that this was the right market to go for because we could make a big difference in it. From there onwards, three years from the original start, we started to develop this solution, which at the time was just the smartphone applications, going to the online portal.

By chance, I met the chief executive chairman of a company that does logistics security and told him about what I was doing. He responded that they had a security division with an alarm receiving centre and proposed that we work together. Furthermore, he offered to invest as well. At that point, not only did we had a bit more money but, crucially, we had their support and buy-in to be able to use their alarm receiving centre and start to develop our offering.

Sales were pretty slow to start with, to be honest, it was really hard to build a reputation for something that people have to take so seriously when you are a start-up with very little experience. But we kept on chipping away at it and doing what we could and all the while sales were not coming in and cash was running out and it was getting a bit scary. However, the investors could see that we were on the right track and it was just a case of a little bit more time. So, we did get a little bit more money in. And at that point, our biggest competitor, for some reason, got rid of their entire regional sales team. And at that point, what we needed was really good sales people that had a good network of people. We managed to get three of the salespeople we've now got that used to work for our competitor.

That completed the picture. We built our product a range further, we've got a really easy to use product and we started to get some really good customers on board.

BECKY'S MINDSET

I have asked my mentor why he wants to work with me. I was curious because he came on as my mentor without getting paid and he was spending way more time in the business than we could have asked for.

He said a couple things. One is that I am super, super eager to learn, so people know that if they do work with me, I will really appreciate it and secondly, I will absolutely take on board what people say. I think sometimes entrepreneurs get criticised for having a vision that they want to pursue and they won't deviate or listen to advice. Whereas I'm happy that I know a lot of people who know a lot more than I do, so I can draw on their knowledge. In fact, I'd not be that sensible if I didn't take their advice on board. So I guess they know that I do appreciate it and I will listen and I think that's why they would work with me.

I mean, they always say 'it takes seven years to create an overnight success' or something like that. You just see people create these businesses and it all looks great and I absolutely thought that was how it would work. Yet, six years down the line and we've still got so much to do as a business, we are still just at the beginning of the journey. There have been so many ups and downs, ups and downs. I would not have expected it to be this hard. The only way to navigate it is to learn as you go. Being really open to feedback and listening to customers. I think everybody starts a business because they've got an idea or something that they want to fix or address and it's just unbelievable how much more you can learn that you thought you already knew just by talking to people and listening to other perspectives.

2.4 SUMMARY AND NEXT STEPS

This chapter has delved deeper into the concept of mindset. We have considered why mindset is important, particularly in the context of the entrepreneurial journey where we face uncertainties, changing conditions, difficulties and setbacks. We have explored a number of different elements of mindset, including fixed vs growth mindset and open vs closed mindset. Whilst there is no right or wrong mindset to have, we have considered the impact that our mindset can have on our ability to positively engage (and ultimately thrive) during the entrepreneurial journey. Building on this idea of mindset, we have outlined the specific concept of entrepreneurial mindset as a set of cognitive and emotional competences linked to behaviours that support our value creation efforts.

WHERE AM I NOW?

MINDSET

Having worked through this chapter, what are your reflections now on your mindset?

1. What kind of mindset(s) would you say you have?

2. How does this make you feel?

3. Do you feel these are reflective of your skills/competences/ capabilities?

4. What does this understanding of your mindset mean for you going forward?

For further insight into your mindset, you may want to take the Gottfredson Mindset test (available at **https://ryangottfredson.lpages. co/personal-mindset-assessment-1/**) and then repeat the reflective questions above.

2.5 CONTINUE YOUR LEARNING

The following activities are designed to support you on your learning journey, building on ideas introduced in this chapter. These can be completed at any time and in any order, although you may find it helpful to begin with the 'Check your understanding' activity before moving on.

CHECK YOUR UNDERSTANDING

1. Having a 'growth mindset' means having a desire to grow one's business.

   ☐ **TRUE**

   ☐ **FALSE** (It's false – having a growth mindset means believing that one's intelligence can grow)

2. Having an 'open mindset' is synonymous with being tolerant of different view and beliefs.

   ☐ **TRUE**

   ☐ **FALSE** (It's false – whilst having an open mindset also includes considering the view of others, it is broader than this aspect alone)

3. An entrepreneurial mindset has interconnected cognitive, emotional and behavioural components.

   ☐ **TRUE** (It's true, as per definition of entrepreneurial mindset in the chapter)

   ☐ **FALSE**

4. Whether we are aware of it or not, our emotions continuously shape and are shaped by our thoughts.

   ☐ **TRUE** (It's true – emotions are a form of feedback that helps us think and make choices)

   ☐ **FALSE**

5. Behaving entrepreneurially under uncertainty means waiting to have the perfect idea before putting the idea in practice.

   ☐ **TRUE**

   ☐ **FALSE** (It's false – behaving entrepreneurially under uncertainty means that the perfect solution cannot be identified 'a priori' and that one requires to start from somewhere and experiment)

FURTHER READING

1. **Mindset: The New Psychology of Success** by Carol Dweck

2. **How Not To Be Wrong: The Art of Changing Your Mind** by James O'Brien

3. **Bounce** by Matthew Syed

STOP AND THINK

BECKY'S JOURNEY

Having read through Becky's journey to Pick Protection, consider how her story aligns to the cognitive, emotional and behavioural aspects of an entrepreneurial mindset.

1. What cognitive aspects of entrepreneurial mindset did Becky exhibit in starting her business? How were these portrayed in the case study?

2. What emotional aspects did Becky exhibit? And how do you think these link to her success?

3. What behaviours did Becky exhibit?

4. How did Becky utilise her network in her entrepreneurial journey? How did this help and/or hinder her experience?

COGNITIVE-BEHAVIOURAL REFLECTION
RESPONDING TO MISTAKES

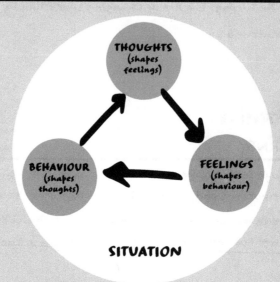

Drawing on the cognitive-behavioural framework introduced in Chapter 1, consider a situation in the last one to two weeks where you made a mistake, and your mistake was noticed by others. Example of situations could be:

- gave the wrong answer during a presentation or assessment

- made an error in a document you prepared, etc.

Why do this? Tracking your response to making a mistake shortly after the mistake happens will give you a more accurate picture of how your emotions affect your thinking about it.

Step 1. Describe this situation in two to three sentences.

Step 2. Describe the thoughts you had in this situation. [This is your interpretation of the situation, so make sure you explore it in sufficient detail. We'd recommend about four to eight sentences.]

Step 3. Describe how you felt in this situation. [These are your emotions. Be as specific as you can in your language, avoiding general terms like 'happy' or 'sad' in favour of more nuanced terms.]

Step 4. Describe how you behaved (i.e., acted) in this situation. [Focus on how you responded, identifying both positive and negative responses.]

Step 5. Looking back on this situation, what sense can you make of it? What do you now better understand about yourself, your feelings and your behaviours?

The purpose of this exercise is to explore your fixed/growth mindset and your responses to mistakes.

PRACTISING ENTREPRENEURIAL THINKING
SHIFTING FROM 'SHOULD' TO 'COULD'

As we've discussed in this chapter, it is important to be aware of your behaviours and how you react in different situations – particularly in those that we find difficult!

Many of us are nervous about public speaking, particularly to larger groups. Have you ever had to give a presentation and felt like you were going to 'freeze' or forget what to say? Have you worried about people asking you questions that you do not know how to answer?

Being able to approach a situation differently can help. One way to shift how you approach challenging situations is instead of thinking of what you **'should'** do, you should focus on what you **'could'** do.

For example, you might be thinking:

If I know enough, I **should** be able to impress the audience.

Instead of focusing on what you 'should' do, try focusing on what you **could** do.

To show I know enough, I **could** outline the information I have collected and explain how I am using that information.

The next time you find yourself in a situation where you question yourself on what you 'should' be doing, then take a moment to think and reflect on how you could refocus your energy on what you 'could' do instead.

1. What was the situation?

....

....

....

....

2. How did you shift from should to could?

....

....

....

....

Acknowledgement: Emilee Simmons, 2023

CHAPTER 3

CHALLENGING YOUR FRAMES OF REFERENCE

As the parable tells, the blind men were all touching the same animal, but each thought they were touching something different.

3.1 INTRODUCTION

In the preceding chapters we have discussed the foundations of entrepreneurial thinking and mindset and explored them as the preconditions for entrepreneurial behaviour, or *action*. We have talked about how we can shape our thinking and our mindset over time and the importance of self-awareness in this process.

A large part of developing this self-awareness requires us to understand how and why we view the world – and of course ourselves – in the way that we do. Like the ancient blind men, we each have different perceptions of the world depending on the angle from which we experience it. Have you even given thought to how you view the world? To the assumptions you hold about how the world works and your role in it? Have you considered how these perceptions have been influenced by your family? Your friends? Your culture? Your education or workplace experience?

The perceptions that we have are shaped by our upbringings, our formal education and other life experiences and as such they can shift and morph over time. Despite the fact that we all hold perceptions about ourselves and the world, we don't usually spend nearly enough time thinking about these. More specifically, we seldom think about how our perceptions have been shaped and are currently being reinforced (or reconfigured) and how our perceptions may differ from how others view us and the world. We also seldom consider how our perceptions, preferences and *frames of reference* are shaping our current decisions and behaviours.

This chapter will begin by looking more deeply into some of the perceptions you hold about yourself and the world, your so-called frames of reference, in order to consider where and how they have the potential to shape your entrepreneurial thinking and action. Building further on the principles of self-awareness and personal reflexivity, we will consider how our experiences and prior knowledge also shape how we can engage in value creation – *something new, improved, or in a novel space that an individual or group of individuals considers to have worth.*

After working through this chapter, you should be able to:

- identify, at a high level, your current frames of reference linked to your personal and professional background
- articulate the link between your worldview and your strengths in relation to value creation
- articulate the link between frames of reference and mechanised thinking
- consider how to engage in reframing to support your own value creation activity.

3.2 IDENTIFYING OUR FRAMES OF REFERENCE AND WORLDVIEW

As we mentioned in Chapter 1, we all hold different views and beliefs about ourselves, our world and the place in that world that we inhabit yet we often fail to explore what these are and how they have come to be. The notion of 'frames' or 'framing' is widely used to help in unpacking these views and beliefs, from how we construct our sense of self to how we see ourselves in relation to others, even in terms of the language that we use to articulate and reinforce these understandings and identities.[1]

In essence, frames of reference can be thought of as *the mental structures that allow us to understand our own reality and to create a sense of (personal) meaning.*[2] As with so many things, our frames of reference are influenced by a range of factors including our upbringing, our education, our culture and our lived experiences which shape the assumptions, attitudes and beliefs underpinning our frames.

A related notion to frames of reference is that of **worldview**:

> *Worldview provides a nonrational foundation for thought, emotion, and behaviour. Worldview provides a person with presuppositions about what the world is really like and what constitutes valid and important knowledge about the world.*[3]

Our worldview provides us with the information through which we understand the world (i.e. our frames of reference). The information forming our worldview is not all necessarily factual or accurate. Rather, it is a mixture of objective facts, personal interpretation of facts and presuppositions about how things work. For this reason, it is not necessarily rational but rather subjective. Put differently, two people who have been through the same experience and know the same facts are likely to have different interpretations of those facts and experiences and, therefore, different worldviews. Despite this, we may not be aware that our personal worldview is just one of many and may conclude that it is 'the' worldview! This is especially the case if we surround ourselves with individuals who are so similar to us that they share the same information, social networks and views.[4]

---

[1]Bendford, R. D. & Snow, D. A. (2000). Framing processes and social movements: An overview and assessment. *Annual Review of Sociology, 26,* 611–639; Goffman, E. (1974). *Frame Analysis: An Essay on the Organization of Experience.* Cambridge, MA: Harvard University Press.

[2]Entman, R. (1993). Framing: Toward a clarification of a fractured paradigm. *Journal of Communication, 43,* 51–58.

[3]Cobern, W. W. (1996). Worldview theory and conceptual change in science education. *Science Education, 80*(5), 579–610, p. 584.

[4]Granovetter, M. S. (1973). The strength of weak ties. *American Journal of Sociology, 78*(6), 1360–1380.

Over time many of our assumptions, attitudes and beliefs become 'hard wired' so that we no longer actively think about them. However, just because we don't actively think about our frames of reference does not mean they are not important. If our mindset considers how we become aware of (and make sense of) what we think (see Chapter 2), our frames provide the structures in which we develop our mindset. Ultimately, our frames of reference influence our thinking and action – sometimes for the better and sometimes to our detriment.

3.3 THE LINK BETWEEN WORLDVIEW AND VALUE

The way we view the world is inextricably linked to what we perceive to be of *value* – that is, what is worth investing our time and effort in. In Chapter 1, we mentioned a few different examples of value creation (social value, environmental value, aesthetic value, etc.). Here, we wish to offer some examples on how different worldviews may make us keener on certain forms of value rather than others. It is important to note that the examples offered below are just that – examples. They are not intended to cover the rather extensive and elusive landscape of worldviews out there.

One way in which worldview varies in entrepreneurial behaviour is the extent to which we perceive the world as *competitive versus collaborative (*more on this in Chapter 7). For example, some research from Scotland suggests that those engaged in entrepreneurial activity in the creative industries value collaboration, co-creation and sharing over individual success and achievement.[5] The worldview that underpins such behavioural preferences for these individuals is therefore diametrically opposite to the more Darwinian (e.g. 'survival of the fittest') and transactional one from other entrepreneurs involved in non-creative industries. The latter are likely to see the world in terms of win–lose, whereas the former consider togetherness and sharing the ultimate win, the end in itself.

Another variation in worldview stems from our formal training. For example, those who have been formally trained in science, technology, engineering and mathematics (STEM) subjects may view the world in terms of *structured problems with knowable solutions,* or with right or wrong answers. Conversely, those trained in social sciences and humanities are more likely to view *issues as less structured and with no right or wrong answers,* compared to their STEM counterparts. STEM-trained individuals often conceive of value creation as solving lab-based problems through technical innovations. Social scientists and business-trained people are likely to look for value in how such innovations solve problems in the imperfect world of human beings![6]

---

[5]Knox, S., Casulli, L. & MacLaren, A. (2021). Identity work in different entrepreneurial settings: Dominant interpretive repertoires and divergent striving agendas. *Entrepreneurship & Regional Development, 33*(9–10), 717–740.

[6]Bosman, L. S. & Fernhaber, S. (2018). Defining the entrepreneurial mindset. In L. Bosman & S. Fernhaber (eds), *Teaching the Entrepreneurial Mindset to Engineers* (pp. 7–14). Cham: Springer International Publishing.

Our *identities* also shape our worldview. For example, journalists who conceive of themselves as reporters of the truth about events in the world may value freedom of speech over remuneration of service and other commercial interests.[7] The same has been reported to be the case for artists, who value their freedom of expression and aesthetic value creation over creation of revenues.[8]

FOOD FOR THOUGHT
IDENTIFYING YOUR FRAMES OF REFERENCE

Spend a few minutes reflecting on some of the assumptions, attitudes and beliefs you hold linked to your upbringing and current life.

1. What was your family upbringing (e.g., family structure, family values and expectations)?

2. What was your cultural upbringing (e.g., place of origin, place of residence, religious tradition, racial identity, languages, cultural diversity)?

---

[7]Caplan, J., Kanigel, R. & Tsakarestou, B. (2020). Entrepreneurial journalism: Teaching innovation and nurturing an entrepreneurial mindset. *Journalism & Mass Communication Educator, 75*(1), 27–32.

[8]Knox et al., Identity work in different entrepreneurial settings.

3. What is your formal training and profession (e.g., engineer, accountant, artist)?

4. How would you describe yourself to others? (e.g., thoughtful, studious, shy, lively, awkward, nervous, athletic, etc.)

5. How would your colleagues describe you? (e.g., thoughtful, studious, shy, lively, awkward, nervous, athletic, etc.)

6. What are your current socio-demographic characteristics? (e.g., age, gender identity, ethnicity, education level, income level)

CHALLENGING YOUR FRAMES OF REFERENCE 71

In terms of our entrepreneurial thinking and mindset, it is particularly important to be aware of our frames of reference. As these become firmly entrenched into our subconscious, we may find ourselves viewing the world in a way that no longer aligns with what we are trying to accomplish. This is particularly relevant when we consider the issue of **value creation.**

A key principle of value creation is novelty – we are doing something new, something in a new way, or something in a new space. This forces us to look beyond what there is, or what has been, to consider possibilities, or what *could be.* In this space, *creativity* is essential. We'll come back to this further in section 3.4, but creativity entails both thinking ('creative thought') and action (the act of creation) and is *the ability that human beings have to think beyond 'what is' in order to develop novel objects, ideas, processes or behaviours.* Thinking back to our myths from Chapter 1, many of us often assume that creativity is also something that some 'special' people have, some sort of innate gift or ability. Yet creativity is a critical human capability – something we all have the potential to foster and develop – in order to operate within our complex, dynamic and uncertain world.

3.4 HOW FRAMES OF REFERENCE SHAPE OUR THINKING AND ACTION

Working in this space of creation, we are often challenged to let go of the prior assumptions, approaches, beliefs and framings that limit our cognitive flexibility and our ability to adapt to changing circumstances and requirements. We may be inherently sceptical about our own creative abilities as well. A study conducted by Adobe[9] investigated how important people considered creativity to be to their lives and to society. They sampled 5,000 people across the US, UK, Germany, France and Japan and found that the vast majority of respondents (c. 80%) considered creativity to be critical to daily life. Less than half of the respondents, however, considered themselves to be creative and only one quarter felt they were living up to their own creative potential.

WHERE AM I STARTING FROM?
BELIEFS SURROUNDING CREATIVITY

Our views on our own creative abilities are shaped by our frames of reference and our worldview. What beliefs do you hold? Is creativity something innate in 'special' individuals, or do you believe it is something that can be developed?

---

[9]Adobe (2012). *State of Create Study: Global Benchmark Study on Attitudes and Beliefs about Creativity at Work, School and Home.* Available at: www.dexigner.com/images/article/22456/Adobe_State_of_Create.pdf

Spend a few minutes looking through the key principles below. For each row, tick the box (a) that best reflects your thoughts. Try to be honest with yourself – there is no need for impression management here!

I BELIEVE THAT...	(a)	I BELIEVE THAT...	(a)
Creativity is rare	☐	Creativity is everywhere	☐
Creativity is a talent that some people have	☐	Creativity is something that is available to everyone	☐
Creativity cannot be taught	☐	Creativity can be developed through training and effort	☐
Creativity is an individual process	☐	Creativity can exist within individuals, pairs and teams	☐
Creativity manifests in 'breakthrough' or 'lightbulb' moments	☐	Creativity manifests in bits and pieces over time	☐
Creative outputs are works of art or scientific discoveries	☐	Creative outputs are possible in all contexts, organisations and jobs	☐
Creative outputs are the result of personal talent	☐	Creative outputs are the result of sustained effort and hard work	☐

If you ticked more principles on the left-hand side, you probably subscribe to the 'elite' view of creativity, that creativity is both something special that cannot be taught, and that also manifests in ground-breaking works.

If you ticked more principles on the right-hand side, you probably subscribe to the 'developmental' view of creativity, that creativity is something that can be learned and developed by all, where creativity is a process rather than a singular event.

1. What view best reflects your own outlook? How do you feel about this result? Why? Record this below.

....

....

2. How does this view relate to your own frames of reference and worldview? Record this below.

Adapted from Feldman (1979)[10]

Our views on creativity, linked to our frames of reference and worldview have an important influence on our ability to think and act entrepreneurially. Our frames of references are closely linked to the ***einstellung effect***,[11] sometimes called the 'setting effect'. The einstellung effect describes the tendency for people to behave or respond in a way that they have done before – even if it is no longer the most appropriate (or effective) way given the current circumstances. It draws on the principle of heuristics (which we'll consider in more detail in Chapter 6), whereby we try to find cognitive 'short cuts' to either make our lives easier, or to help us make sense of a situation or problem that is new to us. We thus end up drawing on existing cognitive structures (patterns of thought).

We are all influenced in some way by the einstellung effect, although this effect is recognised to be even more pronounced (a) amongst 'experts' (i.e., individuals with technical or experiential knowledge, who tend to display more 'cognitive rigidity' over time)[12] and (b) when people are operating in particularly stressful and uncertain conditions[13] – a defining characteristic of most entrepreneurial activity (which we'll consider further in Section 2). Whilst drawing on established patterns of thinking and acting may seem like a good idea, it can in fact do us more harm than good. First, our approach is unlikely to be the most efficient or productive way of tackling the issue in front of us. Second, we can easily become disheartened when our 'tried and true' methods or approaches fail to work – in all likelihood because they are no longer the most appropriate! This frustration may cause us to mentally

---

[10]Feldman, D. H. (1979). Toward a nonelitist conception of giftedness. *Phi Delta Kappan, 60,* 660–663.

[11]Luchins, A. S. & Luchins, E. H. (1959). *Rigidity of Behaviour: A Variational Approach to the Effects of Einstellung.* Eugene, OR: University of Oregon Books.

[12]Bilalić, M., McLeod, P. & Gobet, F. (2008). Inflexibility of experts – reality or myth? Quantifying the Einstellung effect in chess masters. *Cognitive Psychology, 56*(2), 73–102.

[13]Sahai, R. & Frese, M. (2019). If you have a hammer, you only look for nails: The relationship between the einstellung effect and business opportunity identification. *Journal of Small Business Management, 57*(3), 927–942.

disengage, making us more likely to give up rather than persist (we'll talk about persistence in more detail in Chapter 4).

The einstellung effect is closely related to the concept of functional fixedness, another cognitive bias driven by our frames of reference where we think in a 'mechanised way' and fixate on the typical use of something.[14] A good way to think of this is what you would do if you were given a hammer – you would likely go look for some nails! If you were given some screws, you would seek out a screwdriver.

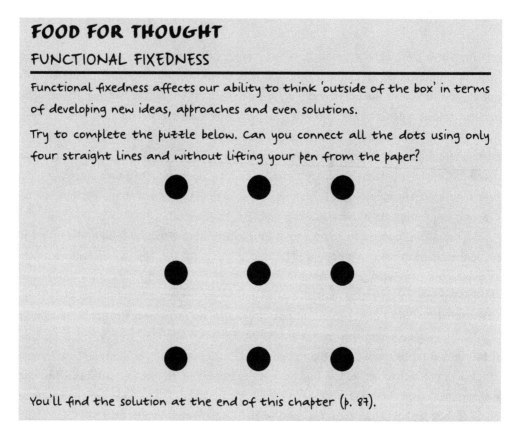

FOOD FOR THOUGHT

FUNCTIONAL FIXEDNESS

Functional fixedness affects our ability to think 'outside of the box' in terms of developing new ideas, approaches and even solutions.

Try to complete the puzzle below. Can you connect all the dots using only four straight lines and without lifting your pen from the paper?

You'll find the solution at the end of this chapter (p. 87).

Functional fixedness applies to both tangible objects (e.g. a hammer) as well as intangible concepts. We become so caught up in the properties of what we're working with that we struggle to think about alternative applications, uses or approaches – we see only *what is,* rather than *what could be.* This is a particular challenge when we are working to think and behave entrepreneurially to address problems or needs, particularly in uncertain situations.

---

[14]Duncker, K. (1945). On problem-solving. *Psychological Monographs, 58*(5, Whole No. 270), 1–113.

CHALLENGING ASSUMPTIONS
DO SCHOOLS KILL CREATIVITY?

As we've discussed, our worldview and frames of reference are shaped and (re)enforced by our own experiences. A large part of this includes our upbringing and education. Given how central creative thinking and action is in our dynamic and ever changing world, there has been a lot of interest in the role that schools play in shaping our own creative skills and efforts.

The late Sir Ken Robinson was a vocal advocate for fostering creativity from the very earliest years in school, something he noted was paradoxical with the educational system itself. He argued that it was in fact that school system – the very place that ought to be building creative thinking skills – discouraging creative thinking and action.

How does this relate to your own educational experiences? Did your own school encourage creative thinking or alternative approaches? How did this align with wider societal values and belief systems? What impact do you think this has had on you now?

See: **www.ted.com/talks/sir_ken_robinson_do_schools_kill_creativity?utm_campaign=tedspread&utm_medium=referral&utm_source=tedcomshare**

So how can we shift our frames of reference to look beyond what is and what we have done before to think about what we can do, be and *create?*

3.5 SHIFTING OUR FRAMES OF REFERENCE

Although our frames of reference become increasingly 'hard wired' over time, that is not to say we cannot work to become aware of them and to actively work to shift them through building our self-awareness and personal reflexivity. As we discussed in Chapter 1, self-awareness refers to our ability to know and understand our thinking and feelings and appreciate how they impact – and are impacted by – behaviour. Building our self-awareness can be hard. It may force us to confront observations about ourselves that are uncomfortable, unsettling and perhaps even upsetting. Yet if we don't consider who we are, it becomes nearly impossible to consider who we can become.

Therefore, in order for self-awareness to be truly helpful in guiding our entrepreneurial development, we need to build a balanced perspective of how we see ourselves. We need to consider not only how we see ourselves, or *internal self-awareness,* but also how others see us, or *external self-awareness.* [15]

3.5.1 INTERNAL SELF-AWARENESS THROUGH REFLECTION

We can often recount what we do – the actions we take. But how often do we stop to understand why we behave (or do not behave) in certain ways? When it comes to behaving entrepreneurially or not, how often do we take the time to reflect on the thought processes that made us decide to play it safe rather than being bolder? Or to approach a task in the way we always have rather than experimenting with something new? Our thought processes may be impacted by deeper layers of feelings such as fears or other uncomfortable emotions. Uncovering these layers through self-reflection is to hold up a mirror to ourselves – that is indeed why it is called 'reflection'!

True reflection is effortful. It requires that we deliberately think about our own thinking – a process known as ***metacognition***. Entrepreneurship scholars have found that individuals who use metacognitive processes are well placed to take on board feedback and behave more adaptively.[16] This is important because adapting and pivoting are key behaviours required during entrepreneurial activity.

In our experience, we find that it is much easier for people to report and reflect on what's going on in their external world than what is going on in their inner world. This is because the external world is visible, thus what happens in it just has to be observed. On the other hand, what's going on in our thoughts is not clearly visible. Here we need metacognition in order to become able to 'look inside our own thoughts' (i.e., in order to develop self-insight). Metacognition may be new to you as a term, though you may have some familiarity with it in practice.

For example, you may have engaged in metacognition if you have ever kept a journal or diary to record your experiences and thoughts. Journaling can be particularly helpful in building internal self-awareness and personal reflexivity as you identify (perhaps hidden) thoughts, emotions and areas for further development. Journaling requires time and effort over a sustained period of time and often works best done as a 'stream of consciousness' – you should not force yourself to put thoughts on paper in any particular form as doing this may shift your focus to form rather than on content. If you are used to formal writing, this may take some getting used to. What to write in a journal depends on the area you want

[15]Eurich, T. (2018). What self-awareness really is (and how to cultivate it)? *Harvard Business Review, 4 January.* Available at: https://hbr.org/2018/01/what-self-awareness-reallyis-and-how-to-cultivate-it

[16]Haynie, J. M., Shepherd, D. A. & Patzelt, H. (2012). Cognitive adaptability and an entrepreneurial task: The role of metacognitive ability and feedback. *Entrepreneurship Theory and Practice, 36*(2), 237–265.

to improve on. For example, if you currently tend to overthink situations and feel like you never 'take the plunge' (i.e., take action) on something you want to do, then you may want to reflect on and write about the inner conversations that you have with yourself that stop you from taking action.

An example of the power of journaling for self-awareness comes from one of our former students, who we will call Chris. Chris reported to us that he'd wake up every morning with a different entrepreneurial idea. He could not go one day without spotting a new opportunity for adding value. However, when it came to putting any of these ideas into practice, Chris would freeze. Frustrated with this realisation, Chris decided to work on his action orientation and started journaling to figure out what was stopping him. At first, in his journal he reported being afraid that the ideas might not actually work and observed that he couldn't choose between his ideas as he wasn't confident about which one was the 'best'. Over time, Chris started to realise that the common theme in his journal entries was 'wanting to get it right straight away' and that the reason he would not take action was that there was no certainty about what was 'right'. A deeper investigation into his own need to get it right (beyond the financial resources at risk) was that Chris grew up in a culture where getting it wrong was associated with social stigma. This realisation took Chris a long time to arrive at, but he now has greater awareness of both himself as well as his areas for further development.

3.5.2 EXTERNAL SELF-AWARENESS THROUGH FEEDBACK

Whilst personal reflection can give us important insight into our (sometimes hidden) thoughts and feelings, they don't fully how capture how we are perceived by others – particularly in terms of the skills, abilities and strengths that we have. It is easy to downplay (or overplay) our abilities to ourselves, so it is useful to get external feedback to balance our own self-perceptions and self-image. External feedback is also critical in challenging our assumptions about ourselves and our place in the world,[17] linked to our frames of reference.

As with internal self-awareness, developing external self-awareness can be difficult. It requires us to have an open mindset and a growth mindset (think back to what we covered in Chapter 2) – we need to be prepared to take on board feedback, as well as to consider opportunities for personal development and learning rather than considered points of feedback to be indications of failure. If we don't think that we can improve, negative criticism from others can feel damning.

We can approach gathering external feedback in a number of ways, either through formalised approaches (e.g., the 360-degree feedback process[18]) or more informal means.

---

[17]Brookfield, S. D. (2017). *Becoming a Critically Reflective Teacher,* 2nd edn. San Francisco, CA: Jossey-Bass

[18]Zenger, J. & Folkman, F. (2020). What makes a 360-degree review successful? *Harvard Business Review, 23 December.* Available at: https://hbr.org/2020/12/what-makes-a-360-degree-review-successful

Generally, it can be useful to collate information from different individuals, whether this is in a professional or personal setting, in order to capture a range of views and observations. It is important to remember that external feedback alone is not enough – it needs to be combined with our own internal self-awareness and insights to ensure we are not vulnerable to other peoples' biases, assumptions and frames of reference.

Critically, it is not about the feedback we receive but what we do with that external feedback – how does this help us to better understand ourselves and our potential.

DEEP DIVE
FEEDBACK VS FEEDFORWARD

Many people worry about receiving feedback from others, particularly if there is a sense of judgement. Not all feedback is created equal! A related concept that may help is *feedforward* – a focus not on what has happened, but on the future (and what could be done to make that future better).

Joe Hirsch talks about the power of feedforward and how, as both receivers and givers of feedback, we can shift our approach to getting and giving feedback: **www.ted.com/talks/joe_hirsch_the_joy_of_getting_feedback**

3.6 REFRAMING FOR VALUE CREATION

Once we have developed internal and external self-awareness, and are open to feedback and development, we are in a better position to both understand our current frames of reference and to challenge where they are helping us and where they are hindering us. As we have discussed, when thinking about creating value – whether for ourselves or for others – we need to consider how we can look beyond what is and think about *what is possible.* This may require us not only to challenge our own frames of reference with relation to ourselves as individuals, but also the frames of reference we hold with regard to situations, experiences and problems that we and others face as we seek to develop creative ideas and novel solutions.

To do so, we can actively engage in the process of reframing. This allows us to see beyond what we've thought or done before and gives us the opportunity to change the number and range of possible responses and solutions we can offer.[19] By engaging in reframing, we can also influence and shape how others respond (we'll consider the importance of interpersonal collaboration for value creation in

---

[19]Seelig, T. (2013). How reframing a problem unlocks innovation. *Fast Company*. Available at: www. fastcompany.com/1672354/how-reframing-a-problem-unlocks-innovation

Section 3). A key approach to reframing is considering our use of language – how we structure and articulate our thinking about a situation. Framing can be thought of in terms of three key elements:[20]

Language – The words, phrases and language structures we use to describe something, including jargon, metaphors and stories. Our use of language also includes the way we communicate objectivity, legitimacy and, conversely, bias.

Thought – The mental models that shape what we chose to frame and how we choose to frame it, linked to our assumptions and beliefs about our own reality and our place in the world (i.e., our personal frames of reference).

Forethought – How we exert control over our communication of frames based on our awareness and consciousness (i.e., how we can think and act in a purposeful manner, rather than reacting spontaneously and without thinking).

The act of (re)framing gives us the opportunity to actively craft the 'space' in which we are living and working, rather than simply discovering a space that we then need to respond to or work within. This is very important from an entrepreneurial value creation perspective, as studies have highlighted that the time and effort spent at the earlier part of the creative process (e.g., exploring, ideation and framing a problem or solution) is directly linked to the ultimate quality of the output.[21]

But what does (re)framing look like in practice? Drew Smithsimmons, co-founder of Braided Communications explains his experience of reframing below.

ENTREPRENEURIAL THINKING AND MINDSET IN PRACTICE
DREW SMITHSIMMONS, BRAIDED COMMUNICATIONS

This case study is intended to illustrate the process of looking at problems from different perspectives, drawing on the concept of reframing. It is the case study of Drew Smithsimmons, a trained Cognitive Behavioural Psychotherapist who co-founded **Braided Communications**, a firm that aims to support the health and performance of astronauts on deep space missions.

The case is narrated in Drew's own voice.

---

[20]Fairhurst, G. T. (2005). Reframing *The Art of Framing*: Problems and prospects for leadership. *Leadership*, *1*(2), 165–185.

[21]Getzels, J. & Czikszentmihalyi, M. (1976). *The Creative Vision: A Longitudinal Study of Problem Finding in Art*. New York: Wiley.

EARLY EXPERIENCES AND WORLDVIEW

I have a strong sense of fairness, and that society is organised for the comfort of a privileged few and to the detriment of everybody else, and that sense of fairness and kindness will have come out of my own childhood and experiences. I was always motivated to stand up for people who are having a hard time or are being treated unfairly.

From about eight to fifteen I was in a school where there were only two people of colour in the whole school of maybe over a thousand and one of them was my best friend. So every single day for years we had running battles getting beaten up because Peter wasn't white, and they used to shout horrible things at him. We would never win, but we stood up. We stood up together. My experiences were of exclusion and bullying and isolation and fear.

That's how I and my fellow students were trained — to be agents of change, using a social model of disability to remove obstacles for full participation for everybody.

I'm quite psychologically minded.

When I went to university, in my classes we'd be ridiculed for having done the reading and being interested in the topic and also I did not sound like someone from the area, so I was treated as though I did not belong there. There continued this sense that there is a hierarchical structure in our society, and I was not part of these groups.

EDUCATIONAL EXPERIENCES

I went to Edinburgh University to do a masters in social anthropology and development. I started that in the late nineties. I was there over the millennium, and I took a year and a half break in the middle, because my father died in the middle and I was out of money. So I went to work as a TEFL teacher in Taiwan to earn enough money to come back. The university held my place for me. I came out with a first-class masters in social anthropology with development. I wanted to do international development work. Before my grades were out, I was already in Mongolia to set up a research project there. I wanted to study the transmission of HIV across the Chinese border into the Gobi Desert, which totally made sense at the time. I didn't really think through that neither the Chinese nor the Mongolian governments might not want that to be studied.

But I got quite far: I got a permit, I had a translator, and we were going to interview and track drivers and migratory sex workers along that. When it became really clear what our intentions were, the questions we were going to ask, and that we wanted to write up and publish this data, the project got shut down. I left Mongolia and went back to Taiwan to do some more teaching work to try and save some money.

A lot of the people I was working with in Mongolia were really impressive, and it wasn't the international NGOs. I saw some pretty detestable behaviour from expats in Mongolia, but there were local people doing amazing projects, particularly in Ulaanbaatar, the main city, where there were thousands and thousands of children living in the sewers. Then that gets down to like minus forty degrees in the winter, and they're living in the sewers down there because it's warm. These local folks would help them get food, get into shelters where they could have a room, get them back into school. I just found that so impressive, and it was so clear to me that to do some of the best work, it's often best if it's your community. If you're from within that community, you understand the needs, you're more efficient with your resources. You can see where to spend those resources.

In coming back to Scotland, I wondered what I could do within my own community. I retrained as a social worker and I went off to work in the north of Glasgow. I specialised in mental health services, and I got particularly involved in doing family work for psychosis. On my first day as a social worker I was allocated 40 cases and every one of those cases was for somebody experiencing a psychotic illness of one kind or another, and they were often in the most vulnerable, complex contexts. We would team up with a therapist or a psychologist so I basically ended up doing more and more structured psychological type of work. So I went to back to university for a third time and trained as a cognitive behavioural psychotherapist.

EMPLOYMENT EXPERIENCES

When I became a CBT therapist, I went out to work for the National Health Service in the north and islands of Scotland. These are areas with quite extreme weather and quite often the ferries were cancelled and I wouldn't be seeing patients. I couldn't deliver a cadence and frequency of therapy that is designed to deliver results. I began using technology through video suites in the local hospital so that, even when the weather was bad, I could still deliver therapy by video, which was really controversial at the time. I was disciplined by the hospital managers for delivering therapy by video.

That was the beginning of what went on to be a career around using technology to increase access to psychological therapists. I got involved in a number of services, companies, technologies, in the UK as well as in Scandinavia, Denmark and the United States, using technology to increase access to psychological therapies.

FRAMING PROBLEMS DIFFERENTLY

Within all of that, as a therapist I was always picking models and approaches that were grounded in attachment theory. Attachment and emotion regulation are my specialisms, and that made me well placed to work on NASA's problem around what's going to happen for really isolated people on a deep space mission when they're so far away from their closest friends and family. I could draw on all of that clinical knowledge to think about a problem in a very different sector.

I invented a technology to help keep astronauts healthy in deep space missions, using technology so that their nervous systems are able to co-regulate with the nervous systems of their loved ones even when there's a really big time delay. That's what Braiding was designed for, and that will keep those astronauts healthy and more able to cope with a lot of the other challenges and it will support their performance. I probably spent two years just thinking about the invention while having lots of other jobs in mental health and technology.

THE BIRTH OF BRAIDED COMMUNICATIONS

In 2019, I co-founded the company with an ex colleague who's got lots of experience in telecoms and an astrophysics degree. I haven't really stopped being a therapist because I still look at the world through that lens. I don't think I've stopped being a social worker either, because I'm still trying to remove barriers to participation in society for the terrestrial side of the work we do and I am trying to remove barriers to psychological support for the space side of what we do. I am still working on the same problems.

In 2017 NASA announced the Artemis program. Along with that came a lot of information about details of the mission itself and particularly around the human health part and the problems that they were having that needed to be solved in order for these missions to progress, and I was spending a couple of hours a day reading this, researching it. Space exploration is a special interest of mine. So in the evenings, to relax I spent hours reading these documents and trying to understand the problem of astronaut isolation. I got very interested in that as a problem. The way it was framed by the space agencies was that the distance involved between the ship and the ground is so large that there will be a time delay, therefore, very reasonable to assume no synchronous communication can happen. Therefore, the crew will be isolated, and not have synchronous contact with their family and friends on the ground. That's the way it was framed. It's impossible, because of the physical limitation. I just remember reading that and thinking, of course. Yeah, of course you can't get around physics. But what about the humans here? Because my specialism is the wonderfully complex workings of human minds. The human impulse to communicate is so strong that even in this context of difficult physical limitations there would be a way for people to structure dialogue to have meaningful communication. I didn't know what the answer was. I just thought it was possible. How might it work? What might the dialogue look like?

What I was pretty sure of is that latency was being conflated with the concept of synchrony. So if there's any latency there can't be synchrony. I thought that that was a misunderstanding of synchrony, because in music you have syncopated rhythms where people are following different rhythms, but it's still synchronous.

There are different kinds of rhythm, and I thought you could have a dialogue where people are in it at the same time, they're just in slightly different places. My framing of it was that it is synchrony under latency. I thought about what may be the structure of a dialogue that you could wrap around the latency. I kept seeing patterns of interweaving braids. I would see that in my mind's eye as a sort of rotating weave of a rope.

That's not a hallucination – just daydreaming! I began to see that pattern in nature. I saw it in designs. I saw it in people's clothes. I saw it in a carpet in a hotel, which represented it so beautifully. I took a picture of it, and that really helped me focus. If each of those strands is a sub-strand of a dialogue, if each strand was a sub-topic, you could wrap those sub-topics in a certain pattern.

Source: Pixabay

So if you were looking at it from side on, you would have these interweaving braids going between the ship and the ground.

What would that experience be like as the data's coming in? If the software controls the rhythm of the data transfer, for a user at either end that could be experienced as having constant dialogue coming in to interact with. If you're having constant dialogue to interact with, and the other person is doing exactly the same with you at that same moment, if your attention and behaviour is synchronised to the same central clock to the same metronome, that's synchrony. The whole idea stemmed from framing the problem differently than the way it has been framed before.

3.7 SUMMARY AND NEXT STEPS

This chapter has further considered some of the assumptions you hold about yourself and your place in the world – your frames of reference – and how these have been influenced by your upbringing and wider professional experience(s). We have considered how our frames of reference can shape our thinking, specifically how they can cause us to engage in mechanised thinking based on previous experiences. Whilst experience is a wonderful thing, we need to be able to look beyond what has worked in the past (i.e., overcoming the einstellung effect and functional fixedness) in order to consider what will be the most appropriate course of action based on current circumstances. To do so, we need to challenge our frames of reference, developing our internal self-awareness as well as external self-awareness and utilising feedback to help us develop our skills and competences. We can also engage in the process of reframing in relation to value creation activity, tackling not only our personal frames of reference but also the frames we create around an opportunity, problem or solution.

WHERE AM I NOW?
IDENTIFYING YOUR FRAMES OF REFERENCE

Having worked through this chapter, spend a few minutes revisiting your assumptions, attitudes and beliefs you hold linked to your upbringing and current life.

Now consider the following:

1. How do your assumptions/attitudes/beliefs influence how you frame yourself?

2. How do your assumptions/attitudes/beliefs influence how you frame yourself in relation to others?

3.8 CONTINUE YOUR LEARNING

The following activities are designed to support you on your learning journey, building on ideas introduced in this chapter. These can be completed at any time and in any order, although you may find it helpful to begin with the 'Check your understanding' activity before moving on.

CHECK YOUR UNDERSTANDING

1. A 'worldview' means having an opinion on world affairs.

   ☐ **TRUE**

   ☐ **FALSE** (It's false – a worldview provides a person with presuppositions about what the world is really like and what constitutes valid and important knowledge about the world)

2. We are usually unaware of our worldview.

   ☐ **TRUE** (It's true – our worldview is usually not part of our deliberate thoughts)

   ☐ **FALSE**

3. Our worldview is shaped by our formal training.

   ☐ **TRUE** (It's true – our understanding of the world may be very different if we are trained in science compared if we are trained in arts)

   ☐ **FALSE**

4. What we consider of 'value' is unrelated to our worldview.

   ☐ **TRUE**

   ☐ **FALSE** (It's false – our worldview informs and is informed by what we consider of value)

5. We tend to disregard our worldview when we approach new problems.

   ☐ **TRUE**

   ☐ **FALSE** (It's false – we tend to fall into patterns of mechanised response that are informed by our previous experiences and our worldview)

FURTHER READING

1. *Frames of Mind* by Howard Gardner

2. *Originals* by Adam Grant

3. *Out of Our Minds: Learning to be Creative* by Ken Robinson

FOOD FOR THOUGHT
FUNCTIONAL FIXEDNESS

Functional fixedness affects our ability to think 'outside of the box' in terms of developing new ideas, approaches and even solutions. In the case of this task, we need to look beyond the 'box' that we assume exists around the dots.

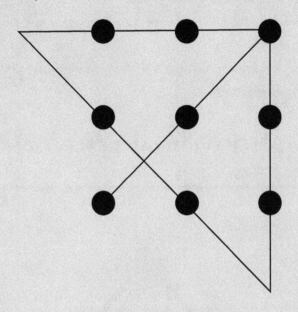

1. **How do you feel after having tried this task?**

2. **Do you find boundaries to be helpful to your thinking, or do you have trouble looking beyond the constraints?**

STOP AND THINK
DREW'S WORLDVIEW

Looking back to Drew's story, consider the impact that his worldview and frames of reference had on the formation of Braided Communications and the value that this organisation creates.

1. How did Drew's early experiences shape his views on the world and on others?

2. How has his worldview influenced the decisions he has taken in creating Braided Communication?

COGNITIVE–BEHAVIOURAL REFLECTION
SOLVING PROBLEMS

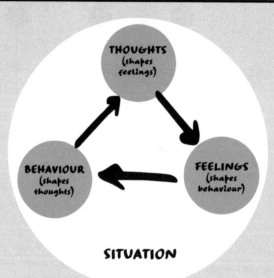

Drawing on the cognitive-behavioural framework introduced in Chapter 1, consider a situation the last one to two weeks where you were faced with a problem where you struggled to think of a new solution.

Why do this? Through the '**WHERE AM I NOW**?' box above, you have already reflected on your frames of reference at a high level. Doing this cognitive–

behavioural reflection will give you a more detailed understanding of how you use your frames of reference to solve problems.

Step 1. Describe this situation in two to three sentences.

Step 2. Describe the thoughts you had in this situation. [This is your **interpretation** of the situation, so make sure you explore it in sufficient detail. we'd recommend about four to eight sentences.]

Step 3. Describe how you felt in this situation. [These are your **emotions**. Be as specific as you can in your language, avoiding general terms like 'happy' or 'sad' in favour of more nuanced terms.]

Step 4. Describe how you behaved (i.e., acted) in this situation. [Focus on how you responded, identifying both positive and negative responses.]

....
....
....
....
....
....

Step 5. Looking back on this situation, what sense can you make of it? What do you now better understand about yourself, your feelings and your behaviours? How do these relate to your own frames of reference and worldview?

....
....
....
....
....
....

PRACTISING ENTREPRENEURIAL THINKING
REFRAMING

As we discussed in this chapter, our frames of reference and worldview shape the way we see ourselves, the world, and our place in this. At times, these frames can help us to see new possibilities, but at times they can prevent us from seeing beyond what we have already experienced.

To create value, we often need to challenge our frames of reference to think about the world differently – we need to think *creatively*. One way in which we can develop our reframing and creative thinking skills is through puzzles.

Take, for example, the puzzle below. You can see that the shapes on the left-hand side can be divided into four equal parts/shapes.

The shape on the right-hand side has yet to be divided. Can you divide this into four equal parts/shapes? (we suggest tracing onto a separate piece of paper so you can try and try again as needed!)

Solution:

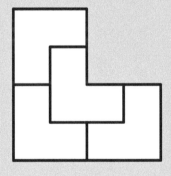

Acknowledgement: Emilee Simmons, 2023

PRACTISING ENTREPRENEURIAL THINKING
FOUR STRATEGIES FOR CREATIVITY

In the Harvard Business Review Articles below, Gabriella Rosen kellerman and Martin Seligman outline four strategies that we can use to think more creatively: https://hbr.org/2023/01/cultivating-the-four-kinds-of-creativity

Now consider how you could apply each of the four strategies to create something of value in your organisation:

1. **Integration.** What features, functions or other could you bring together in the same service, process, product? What extra value could this integration create?

2. **Splitting.** What could you split into its constituent parts so that each can be put to a different use?

3. **Figure-ground reversal.** Are there problems you are trying to solve by focusing on what is clearly visible to you rather than what's hidden? What perspective can you get if you focus on what's hidden?

4. **Distal thinking.** What would you (product, service, process) look like if you skipped two or three steps ahead in its evolution?

SECTION 2

GETTING COMFORTABLE WITH ENTREPRENEURIAL AMBIGUITY AND UNCERTAINTY

The second section of this book will consider the fundamental link between entrepreneurial activity and uncertainty. It will explore how people respond to uncertainty generally and will guide you to consider your own personal responses to ambiguous, uncertain and psychologically challenging situations. It will then consider how you can develop comfort with uncertainty, specifically how you can build personal persistence and resilience, develop new forms of thinking and harness your fears as catalysts to action rather than viewing them as barriers.

CHAPTER 4 will start by considering the link between entrepreneurial activity – the creation of value – and uncertainty. We will think about how creating value requires us to follow uncharted paths, where we are subject to uncertainty, ambiguity and risk. We will consider how our responses to these conditions are shaped and reflect on our own personal preferences and perceptions, before considering the importance of persistence and resilience to thrive in uncertainty, rather than just survive.

In **CHAPTER 5** we will build on the concepts of persistence and resilience from Chapter 4, considering how deeply embedded fears affect our thinking, feelings and actions under uncertainty and our ability to act resiliently. We will start by exploring the concept of *core beliefs*, the deep-seated assumptions we hold about ourselves and the world, and how they link to our fears. Building on this, we will consider how our core beliefs and related fears shape our entrepreneurial thinking and action (or inaction), identifying a number of common fears linked to self-worth and 'imposter' syndrome/phenomenon in order to challenge the assumptions we hold about our own entrepreneurial abilities and potential.

Finally, in **CHAPTER 6** we will consider the concept of entrepreneurial judgement – how we make decisions to act (or not). We will start by exploring two main styles of judgement, the fast and intuitive 'System 1' and the slower and more deliberate 'System 2'. We will consider how these styles relate to your own preferences and dominant forms of decision making, linked to concepts from Chapters 4 and 5. We will then identify the trade-offs and implications of these two different styles particularly under situations of uncertainty where we have limited information.

CHAPTER 4

DEVELOPING YOUR PERSISTENCE AND RESILIENCE

"**JUST BEGIN...** THE GREATEST JOURNEYS ALL START WITH A SINGLE STEP. WHEN YOU STAND AT THE BOTTOM OF A MOUNTAIN, YOU CAN RARELY SEE A CLEAR ROUTE TO THE TOP. IT IS TOO FAR AWAY AND THE PATH TOO TWISTY AND HIDDEN BEHIND OBSTACLES. THE ONLY WAY TO CLIMB THE SUCKER IS TO START – AND THEN KEEP PUTTING ONE FOOT IN FRONT OF THE OTHER, ONE STEP AT A TIME."

– BEAR GRYLLS,
TODAY.COM (2013)

4.1 INTRODUCTION

In Section 1 we looked in detail at you, your thinking, emotions, behaviours and overall mindset. As we discussed, and as you yourself have practised at the end of each chapter through cognitive–behavioural reflection, we think, feel and act in response to different *situations*. Different situations elicit different responses from us, some for the better and some perhaps for the worse.

When considering entrepreneurial thinking and action for value creation, we are often working within situations with limited information, few answers and significant dynamism and change. Have you ever considered how you personally respond to such environments? Does uncertainty and ambiguity fill you with excitement or with dread? What can we do to better cope in such circumstances and what skills and competences do we need to develop?

This chapter will start by introducing the link between entrepreneurial activity (i.e. the creation of value – *something new, improved, or in a novel space, that an individual or group of individuals considers to have worth*) and uncertainty, grounded in the principles of economic dynamism and *information asymmetry*. We will then delve further into the concepts of uncertainty, risk and ambiguity, including how these are shaped by our upbringing, background, culture and context (linked back to our discussions from Section 1). Finally, we consider how you can learn to not only survive but to thrive in uncertain situations, drawing on the concepts of persistence and resilience.

After working through this chapter, you should be able to:

● articulate the link between entrepreneurial activity for value creation and uncertainty
● differentiate between uncertainty, ambiguity and risk, reflecting on your own preferences and responses to these conditions
● consider the link between uncertainty and persistence.

4.2 THE LINK BETWEEN VALUE CREATION AND UNCERTAINTY

As we discussed in Chapter 1, value creation may mean different things in different contexts – and to different individuals (e.g., economic value creation, social value creation, environmental value creation, etc.). Also, the nature of the activities that lead to the creation of value vary widely. These may involve the development of new products or services, new market development or entry, new organisational processes or even new forms of partnership. These can be developed within new ('start-up') ventures or established organisations ('corporate venturing') or even amongst groups from community to pan-national level.

Regardless of the context, creating value is synonymous with novelty – value creation is, after all, the development of something *new, improved, or in a novel space*. Importantly, this novelty is likely to be as relevant to the 'creators' themselves as it is to the potential customers, users, or beneficiaries. Put simply, when we look to create value we can't simply replicate what we have already seen or done. We need to look beyond what we have and think about what is possible rather than what is (think back to our discussions from Chapter 3). As a result, value creation seldom allows us to follow a path we have followed before, or something that has already been mapped out. Rather it requires us to follow an uncharted path – one where we cannot be sure at the outset what we will encounter or what sequence of actions will lead us to the (successful) realisation of value. This is what we refer to as *uncertainty*.

WHERE AM I STARTING FROM?
WORKING IN UNCHARTED TERRITORY

Spend a few minutes reflecting on a situation where you embarked on a project that was completely new to you and for which there was no 'how to' guidance and no person to whom you go to for help or specific direction.

1. What was the nature of the situation?

2. How did you feel during this situation?

3. How did you respond to a lack of direction or plan which you could draw on?

4. Did your experience shape your thinking about – and approach
to – achieving your desired outcome?

....

....

4.3 ENTREPRENEURIAL UNCERTAINTY, RISK AND AMBIGUITY

Since the earliest days of research on entrepreneurship, **_uncertainty_** has been considered a cornerstone of the entrepreneurial journey.[1] This is because entrepreneurial activity nearly always involves:

- working in dynamic environments where change can be difficult to plan for or to predict (e.g., personal consumption preferences, technological developments, etc.)
- being subjected to sudden external 'crises' or 'shocks' that are difficult to plan for or to predict (e.g., natural disasters or pandemics)
- working in environments where there may be limited knowledge or _information asymmetries_ (where one side knows more than the other, and thus there are unfair power dynamics)
- working in environments where there may be ill-defined problems or few 'boundaries' to the nature of the work
- working in environments where resources (e.g., funding, human capital) may be scarce or hard to access

As a result of these '**V**olatile **U**ncertain **C**omplex **A**mbiguous' conditions (which we'll discuss further in Chapter 11), uncertainty and entrepreneurial action go hand in hand. This is important when considering your own entrepreneurial thinking and action, as a key capability of entrepreneurial individuals is considered to be their ability to operate – and ultimately thrive – under uncertainty.[2]

But what is uncertainty, exactly? We can think of it in terms of three interlinked elements: state, effect and response.[3]

---

[1]McMullen, J. S. & Shepherd, D. A. (2006). Entrepreneurial action and the role of uncertainty in the theory of the entrepreneur. _The Academy of Management Review, 31_(1), 132–152.

[2]Casson, M. (1982). _The Entrepreneur: An Economic Theory_. Washington, DC: Rowman & Littlefield.

[3]Milliken, F. J. (1987). Three types of perceived uncertainty about the environment: State, effect, and response uncertainty. _Academy of Management Review, 12_, 133–143.

State uncertainty exists when we observe or perceive an environment to be unpredictable. *Effect uncertainty* exists when we cannot predict what impact a future (or potential future) change will have on us. Combined, state and effect uncertainty comprise *environmental uncertainty*, where we have a limited set of courses of action but a wide range of possible outcomes from that action.

Response uncertainty exists when we don't know what we can do/how we can respond, linked to the inability to predict the consequents of our responses/actions. More simply, we can think about these in terms of three questions we can ask ourselves:[4]

1. What's happening out there? (state uncertainty)
2. How will it impact me? (effect uncertainty)
3. What am I going to do about it? (response uncertainty).

Given this interplay, we can think of uncertainty as something complex, multifaceted and ever changing.

DEEP DIVE
DEALING WITH UNCERTAINTY

Recent years have seen significant political, environmental and social change which has resulted in significant **environmental uncertainty**. We are often tempted to make predictions to try to overcome our own **response uncertainty**, but as we'll discuss further in Chapter 6 our judgement can be subject to bias.

So how do we cope within situations of uncertainty? Former professional poker player Caspar Berry explores how we respond to – and make decisions in – volatile and uncertain conditions: **www.ted.com/talks/caspar_ berry_dealing_with_uncertainty?utm_campaign=tedspread&utm_ medium=referral&utm_source=tedcomshare**

Very often, we hear of 'uncertainty and risk'. These two concepts are often grouped together, but it is important to differentiate between the two. While they are related, uncertainty is not the same as risk. The key difference lies in what is knowable and what is unknowable.

Simply, uncertainty cannot be mapped out in advance. We never know what will happen. Yet we are able to identify and consider the probable risks of undertaking an activity before we actually start. For example, before starting a new initiative we will be aware

---

[4]McMullen & Shepherd, Entrepreneurial action and the role of uncertainty in the theory of the entrepreneur.

that we could potentially lose the time that we spend on this or any money that we invest in it. The precise likelihood or chance of these risks actually occurring, however, is less clear largely because of the uncertainty surrounding what could go wrong once we start!

We all have our own preferences when it comes to working under uncertain conditions, as we do when it comes to risk. The part of our thinking that determines how we behave in relation to risk is referred to as 'regulatory focus'[5] – whether we prefer to seek safety ('prevention focus') or to seek advancement ('promotion focus')[6] through the taking of (calculated) risks.

WHERE AM I STARTING FROM?
PREVENTION OR PROMOTION FOCUS

We all perceive ourselves in different ways. There is no 'right' or 'wrong' mindset to have. What is important is that we recognise the way we think about ourselves so that we can consider how our mindset is shaping our behaviour for better – or for worse.

1. Spend a few minutes looking through the key principles of prevention and promotion focus below and tick (a) those that you think best apply to you. Try to be honest with yourself – there is no need for impression management here!

PREVENTION FOCUS	(a)	PROMOTION FOCUS	(a)
I am...		I am...	
Focused on maintaining my safety		Focused on achieving advancement	
Motivated to do the best I can with what I have to offer		Motivated to reach a better version of myself	
Focused on my current duties and responsibilities		Focused on my dreams and aspirations	

[5]Higgins, E. T. (1998). Promotion and prevention: Regulatory focus as a motivational principle. *Advances in Experimental Social Psychology, 30*, 1–46.

[6]Brockner, J., Higgins, E. T. & Lowe, M. B. (2004). Regulatory focus theory and the entrepreneurial process. *Journal of Business Venturing, 19*(2), 203–220.

Trying to avoid negative outcomes		Trying to create positive outcomes	
Cautious in my actions		Bold in my actions	
More comfortable when 'playing it safe'		More comfortable when trying new things	
Focused on tasks that are urgent		Focused on tasks that are important	

2. What focus best reflects your own outlook? How do you feel about this result? Why? Record this below.

....

....

In entrepreneurial endeavours, there is a longstanding prevailing view that entrepreneurs are 'risk takers' and that it is this inclination to take risks that they are rewarded for when the gamble pays off.[7] More recent views of risk-taking give us a nuanced view of when and how being prone to risk is appropriate in different tasks involved in creating value.

The more risk-prone *promotion focus* serves us well when producing ideas, so that our creative thinking is not hampered by our inner voice asking 'but what if this doesn't work?!'. Equally, this overly positive attitude that disregards potential risks is helpful when persuading others (e.g., collaborators, investors, employees) of the power of our ideas to address problems or enact change.[8]

However, a more risk-averse attitude, manifesting in a *prevention focus*, is helpful when we are working through or screening our ideas for potential, foreseeable flaws. Equally, it is helpful when those we need to persuade are themselves risk averse and not easily convinced by good ideas alone. In such cases, people with a prevention focus will be better at producing robust research and data to underpin or substantiate an idea. Also, because those with a prevention

---

[7]Casson, *The Entrepreneur: An Economic Theory*.

[8]Brockner et al., Regulatory focus theory and the entrepreneurial process.

focus are better at anticipating problems, they are also less likely to give up on the problems they foresaw manifest because they were prepared for them.[9]

As with so many of our preferences (and as we explored throughout Section 1), our tolerance for uncertainty and our risk preferences are shaped by our own personal contexts, including our early schooling/education, upbringing and family life and current working or educational environment. These preferences also manifest at the level of our national culture, adding another dimension of influence to our own preferences.

A pioneer on studies of national culture, Geert Hofstede, identified the concept of *uncertainty avoidance*, or the degree to which the members of a society feel uncomfortable with uncertainty and ambiguity. Research has found that strong uncertainty avoidance manifests in strong national codes of belief and behaviour which discourage new ideas and atypical behaviours. Weak uncertainty avoidance, on the other hand, manifests in more relaxed societal attitudes towards new ideas and practices.

DEEP DIVE
UNCERTAINTY AVOIDANCE

Studies of national culture have yielded some fascinating insights into cultural preferences, perceptions and behaviours. If you've not come across the work of Professor Geert Hofstede before, spend some time having a look through his model of national culture: **www.hofstede-insights.com/models/national-culture/**

As we discussed above, a key dimension of national culture is uncertainty avoidance. In the following video Professor Hofstede summarised this dimension and what it means: **https://youtu.be/fZFGLyGne7Q**

CHALLENGING ASSUMPTIONS
UNCERTAINTY AND RISK IN THE DIGITAL ERA

While some argue we are living in times of unprecedented uncertainty, are we really feeling the full impact of that?

---

[9]Ibid.

The rise of Artificial Intelligence (AI), machine learning and algorithms for behavioural prediction have been not only automating routine tasks, they have also in many ways been helping to reduce uncertainty for organisations. Amazon, for example, has been using AI across its range of operations and services for many years.

How might AI help us to make sense of situations when we face state, effect or response uncertainty? How could the use of data and predictive analytics help us shape our responses and decisions? Does AI have the potential to make predictions with such accuracy that imagined furthers come to pass? See: **https://youtu.be/2DtyjCOUxTw**

4.4 THRIVING IN UNCERTAINTY AND AMBIGUITY

While we all have different preferences when it comes to uncertainty (some of us love it and some of us hate it), the reality is that we will all have experienced circumstances of uncertainty before and will do so again. Particularly as we seek the 'novel' in pursuit of creating value! With this in mind, we want to think about how we can better operate within uncertainty so that we not only survive but *thrive*.

4.4.1 DEVELOPING YOUR PERSISTENCE

Working under uncertainty and ambiguity can be hard. We may not be able to see what is coming and, even when something happens, we may not ever get answers as to why events unfolded as they did. We may also need to try different courses of action to see what leads to our desired outcome with no guarantee that we are going to get where we are hoping to (or achieve what we are hoping to achieve). To be able to keep going within these challenging circumstances we need to develop **persistence**.

Persistence (or 'willpower') is the *combination of our own internal motivation and the skill to mobilise our energies and keep going, regardless of setbacks*. Related to the concept of 'grit',[10] persistence explains our tendency to sustain interest in – and effort towards – very long-term goals. It is something that takes time and effort to develop and is not something we can easily switch on or off. You may want to think of persistence as you would a muscle[11] – it might be weak at first but can be strengthened through continuous training.

It is important to note that persistence is inherently context specific – we all have our own preferences, identities and values which shape our actions. We thus are likely to find it harder (or easier) to persist in some contexts or situations than others. For example, if you are physically fit

[10]Lee, T. H. & Duckworth, A. L. (2018). Organizational grit. *Harvard Business Review, 96*(5), 98–105.

[11]Baumeister, R. F. & Tierney, J. (2011). *Willpower: Rediscovering the Greatest Human Strength*. New York: Penguin.

and enjoy pushing your own athletic boundaries, you may find it easier to keep going in the face of extreme physical challenges such as climbing a mountain than others. Equally, if you have been learning how to paint still-life scenes using watercolour paints, you may find persistence comes more easily if you are engaging in an artistic challenge. Linked to the diversity of situations we also want to consider the issue of personal *meaning*.[12] When we are doing the things that align to our own interests, values or visions of the future, we are more likely to be able to persevere than if we are doing something we consider irrelevant to us. This sense of meaning helps us to forge the *resolve* to keep going, even if we encounter anxiety or even boredom along the way.[13]

Most critically, persistence under uncertainty requires us to accept that things will not always go as planned – and that we are likely to experience setbacks, delays or 'failures'. As we face the possibility (or manifestation) of these outcomes our outlook often changes – we become worried, cautious and more pessimistic. These feelings change how we think about our abilities and the possibilities available to us, often impacting our ability to embrace change and stick with our goals, aspirations and activities. When things go wrong, we also need to 'fill in the blanks' to make sense of what has happened, without necessarily having all the information or insight we need. We can think of this as attribution – a way of explaining what we *attribute* the outcome to.

WHERE AM I STARTING FROM?
ATTRIBUTION STYLE

We all have our own attribution style. This may even differ between contexts (e.g., work vs home).

Take a few minutes to complete the 'Optimism Test' based on the principles of attribution style. This should take you about 10 minutes. Access and complete the test at: **www.authentichappiness.sas.upenn.edu/questionnaires/optimism-test**

Note: You will need to first 'Register' to create a new profile before you can complete the test.

1. Consider your results and how you feel about these. Record your thoughts below.

[12]Csikszentmihalyi, M. (2002). *Flow: The Classic Work on How to Achieve Happiness*. London: Rider.
[13]Ibid.

There is now significant scientific evidence that links our style of *attribution* and our ability to keep going – to *persist* – even in uncertain and challenging circumstances. In his work, esteemed psychologist Martin Seligman has identified that the way we attribute the causes and impact of events has a direct impact on both our ability to persist as well as on our overall wellbeing and ability to thrive. He has identified two 'explanatory styles', based on three foundational elements, each of which can be explained from a *pessimistic* or *optimistic* perspective:

- *Personalisation* – the degree to which you attribute events to be a result of your own flaws or other external circumstances

  'I failed the math test because I'm stupid and don't understand math' (*pessimistic*)

  vs

  'I failed the math test because the room was noisy and I couldn't concentrate fully' (*optimistic*)

- *Pervasiveness* – the degree to which you attribute events to be global (e.g., covering every area of your life) or local (e.g., a specific event or context)

  'I should choose a different career path since I can't do math' (*pessimistic*)

  vs

  'I may have failed this time, but this is just one test of many' (*optimistic*)

- *Permanence* – the degree to which you attribute events to be permanent or temporary.

  'I will never be able to do math' (*pessimistic*)

  vs

  'I failed this test, but I can do better next time' (*optimistic*)

These influence how we think about the world, and how we mentally start making judgements about situations (particularly under uncertainty), which in turn influence our actions. From this, Seligman[14] identified what he called *learned optimism*, a strategy for framing events whereby we cultivate a positive outlook and way of thinking and communicating. As he explains:

> *The basis of optimism does not lie in positive phrases or images of victory, but in the way you think about causes.*[15]

---

[14]Seligman, M. E. (2018). *Learned Optimism: How to Change your Mind and Your Life*. New York: Vintage Books.

[15]Seligman, M. E. P. (2007). *The Optimistic Child: A Proven Program to Safeguard Children Against Depression and Build Lifelong Resilience*. New York: Houghton Mifflin.

To do so, we need to first become aware of current explanatory style and then look to shape our thinking towards 'optimistic' explanation to minimise unnecessary self-blame while recognising and taking responsibility for our actions and failures in order to learn from them (think back to our discussions on growth mindset from Chapter 2!).

	OPTIMISTIC EXPLANATORY STYLE	PESSIMISTIC EXPLANATORY STYLE
WHEN A GOOD EVENT HAPPENS...	Personal (internal) Pervasive Permanent	External (people, circumstances) Local Temporary
WHEN A BAD EVENT HAPPENS...	External (people, circumstances) Local Temporary	Personal (internal) Pervasive Permanent

FOOD FOR THOUGHT
YOUR EXPLANATORY STYLE

Take a moment and think about how you would normally frame events. Record your thoughts below.

1. What kind of explanatory style would you normally adopt?

> ....
> ....
> ....

2. Does this differ across different aspects of your life (e.g., home, education, work)?

> ....
> ....
> ....

4.4.2 WHAT PERSISTENCE IS NOT

Despite the need to develop our ability to keep going when things get difficult, it is important that we differentiate persistence from 'stubbornness'. The two are not the same thing!

In many circumstances, particularly when we are trying to create something new or in a new way, persistence may mean actively choosing not to listen to critical voices – others may be unable to fully grasp our vision, let alone appreciate or share it.[16] We may need to keep going despite encountering resistance or critical feedback. However, persistence that verges into an inability to be open to feedback and new information is just as unhelpful as giving up 'at the first hurdle'.[17] Overconfidence – and a stubborn belief in the original plan of action despite new information – prevents us from correcting course and can actually take us further away from where we want to be (or where we should be).[18]

Persistence also doesn't mean that we never give up. Society often values our ability to keep going to the extreme, with those who stop an activity labelled (perhaps unfairly) a 'quitter'. This may lead us to believe that once we start an endeavour we have to see it through to completion no matter the consequences, particularly if the endeavour has become public knowledge and 'quitting' would be equally public. So is it OK to give up? Absolutely! The question of when to stop an activity will be very personal and change from context to context, but evidence suggests that we should stop *when the efforts in one area of our lives are at the expense of other areas of our life*.

For example, perhaps you've been working to increase your income by starting a new 'side-hustle' alongside your job. If this side-hustle starts to impact your ability to do your job well, or it eats into your time and space to exercise, sleep or maintain your physical and emotional health then the decision to stop persevering is a sign of strength rather than weakness.[19]

4.4.3 PERSISTENCE VS RESILIENCE

Whilst persistence is critical when engaging in entrepreneurial thinking and action, we need to separate persistence from resilience.

As we've discussed, persistence is a choice to keep going – to continue pursuing a course of action in the face of opposing forces (e.g., positive vs negative feedback). ***Resilience***,

[16]Holland, D. V. & Shepherd, D. A. (2013). Deciding to persist: Adversity, values, and entrepreneurs' decision policies. *Entrepreneurship Theory and Practice*, *37*(2), 331–358.

[17]Green, S. & Palmer, S. (eds) (2019). *Positive Psychology Coaching in Practice*. Abingdon, Oxon: Routledge.

[18]Trevelyan, R. (2008). Optimism, overconfidence and entrepreneurial activity. *Management Decision*, *46*(7), 986–1001.

[19]Green & Palmer, *Positive Psychology Coaching in Practice*.

on the other hand, refers to our ability to grow in the face of adversity.[20] Resilience, like persistence, is a dynamic process rather than a characteristic or inherent property.[21] It is something we can cultivate and build through purposeful action and practice, as we learn to adapt to feedback (positive and negative) in order to bend rather than break when the going gets tough.[22]

In terms of entrepreneurial thinking and action, resilience plays a special role as the 'shield that protects [our] intentions from the negative impact of fear of failure'.[23] We'll talk more about fear of failure linked to resilience shortly in Chapter 5.

4.5 SUMMARY AND NEXT STEPS

This chapter has explored the fundamental link between entrepreneurial activity and uncertainty. When we seek to create value – *something new, improved, or in a novel space, that an individual or group of individuals considers to have worth* – we are nearly always working in a space of uncertainty where there is no charted path for us to follow. We thus need to consider our own personal responses to uncertainty, or risk more broadly, including how these have been shaped by our background, culture and context. Whilst we may have particular preferences, we can alter how we cope within situations of uncertainty and ambiguity. We have discussed the role of persistence (and, relatedly, resilience) in building our capacity to not only survive under conditions of uncertainty but also develop and grow.

WHERE AM I NOW?

PERSISTENCE

Having worked through this chapter, spend a few minutes considering your own thoughts and preferences with regard to your ability to persist. Now consider the following:

---

[20]Masten, A. S., Best, K. M. & Garmezy, N. (1990). Resilience and development: Contributions from the study of children who overcome adversity. *Development and Psychopathology, 2*(4), 425–444.

[21]Martin, R. (2012). Regional economic resilience, hysteresis and recessionary shocks. *Journal of Economic Geography, 12*(1), 1–32.

[22]Seligman, M. (2011). *Flourish*. London: Nicholas Brealey Publishing.

[23]Monllor, J. & Murphy, P. J. (2017). Natural disasters, entrepreneurship, and creation after destruction: A conceptual approach. *International Journal of Entrepreneurial Behavior & Research, 23*(4), 618–637, p. 628.

1. How do you respond to situations where you face ambiguity and uncertainty? In your own life, do these kinds of situations happen frequently or infrequently?

....

....

2. Are there particular situations in which you are more likely to be able to keep going, despite facing uncertainty? Why?

....

....

3. Are there particular situations in which you may struggle to keep persevering? Why?

....

....

4.6 CONTINUE YOUR LEARNING

The following activities are designed to support you on your learning journey, building on ideas introduced in this chapter. These can be completed at any time and in any order, although you may find it helpful to begin with the 'Check your understanding' activity before moving on.

CHECK YOUR UNDERSTANDING

1. We can create new value (something new, improved or in a novel space) without having to grapple with uncertainty.

☐ **TRUE**

☐ **FALSE** (It's false – the creation of new value means not having a chartered path, which implies that there is going to be a degree of uncertainty)

2. State uncertainty is one of four elements of uncertainty.

    ☐ **TRUE**

    ☐ **FALSE** (It's false – Milliken lists three elements of uncertainty: state, effect and response)

3. When we ask ourselves the question 'what is happening out there?' we are effectively grappling with a question of state uncertainty.

    ☐ **TRUE** (It's true – state uncertainty is about uncertainty surrounding the current situation)

    ☐ **FALSE**

4. If you are a 'prevention focus' you are more focused on the pursuit of your dreams than you are on fulfilling your duties and obligations.

    ☐ **TRUE**

    ☐ **FALSE** (It's false – a prevention focus means you are more focused on your obligations and duties than on your aspirations and dreams)

5. People who consider the causes of bad situations to be temporary and situation specific are less likely to give up.

    ☐ **TRUE** (It's true – an explanatory style where bad things are temporary and specific is more conducive to optimism and persistence)

    ☐ **FALSE**

FURTHER READING

1. **Learned Optimism: How to Change Your Mind and Your Live** by Martin Seligman

2. **Grit: Why Passion and Resilience are the Secrets to Success** by Angela Duckworth

3. **Mind Fuel: Simple Ways to Build Mental Resilience Every Day** by Bear Grylls

COGNITIVE–BEHAVIOURAL REFLECTION
TRYING AND TRYING AGAIN

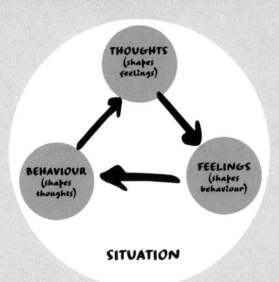

Drawing on the cognitive-behavioural framework introduced in Chapter 1, consider a situation in the last one to two weeks where despite trying more than once, you did not get the result you were aiming for. Example situations could include, but should not be limited to:

- getting a promotion/pay rise

- securing a new client/contract

- fitting exercise into your working day

- sticking to your (new year's) resolutions, etc.

Why do this? Focusing on a specific instance of a setback will give you a more accurate understanding of how you deploy your explanatory style in your daily experiences.

Step 1. Describe this situation in two to three sentences.

Step 2. Describe the thoughts you had in this situation. [This is your **interpretation** of the situation, so make sure you explore it in sufficient detail. We'd recommend about four to eight sentences.]

....

....

....

Step 3. Describe how you felt in this situation. [These are your **emotions**. Be as specific as you can in your language, avoiding general terms like 'happy' or 'sad' in favour of more nuanced terms.]

....

....

....

Step 4. Describe how you behaved (i.e., acted) in this situation. [Focus on how you responded, identifying both positive and negative responses.]

....

....

....

Step 5. Looking back on this situation, what sense can you make of it? What do you now better understand about yourself, your feelings and your behaviours?

....

....

....

The purpose of this exercise is to explore your ability to persevere and persist in action when things are not going in your favour.

PRACTISING ENTREPRENEURIAL THINKING
PERSISTENCE IN NEW, UNCOMFORTABLE TASKS

As we discussed in this chapter, persistence is context-specific. We feel more or less able to persevere in different situations depending on our knowledge, skills, background and interests which shape our familiarity and comfort in these situations.

We can learn a lot about our own drive and motivation when we do something that feels different or uncomfortable – something just outside our so-called 'comfort zone'. As Mihalyi Csikzentmihalyi observes, 'One cannot enjoy doing the same thing at the same level for long. We grow either bored or frustrated'. In pushing beyond our comfort zone, we can 'stretch our skills or discover new opportunities for using them'.[24]

So, here goes! Grab a pen/pencil and a piece of blank paper.

1. Hold your pen/pencil in your non-dominant hand – this is the hand that you do not normally use!

   - If you normally write with your right hand, hold your pen/pencil in your <u>left hand.</u>

   - If you normally write with your left hand, hold your pen/pencil in your <u>right hand.</u>

   - If you are ambidextrous and can write equally well with both hands, hold your pen/pencil in between your toes!

2. Set a timer for 60 seconds and draw a picture of an elephant.

3. Repeat, either until you draw it to your satisfaction or until you wish to stop.

4. Now, reflect on the following:

   - What was/were the source/s of uncertainty for you in this task?

   - Did you stick with it even as it became easier? If not, why not?

   - Did you stick with it even as it became harder? If not, why not?

---

[24]Csikszentmihalyi, *Flow: The Classic Work on How to Achieve Happiness*, p. 75.

You may have found that the source of uncertainty stems both from ambiguity about what an elephant looks like (creative uncertainty – we are having to think of the limited, fuzzy images we hold in our mind about where its legs are, how big its ears are in relation to its body, etc.) and the lack of clear instruction on why we are doing this particular task (environmental uncertainty – uncertainty about the purpose of this specific challenge in the bigger picture of what we are trying to achieve – in this case, develop persistence). Both the latter are over and above the discomfort of doing something new without knowing whether we have the drawing skills necessary to succeed.

5. Next, let's remove one element of creative uncertainty from the task. Below, you have an image of an elephant that you can attempt to replicate. Now, you have one less source of ambiguity as you don't have to think of where the lines are to be drawn, but you are still faced with the creative uncertainty of drawing with your non-dominant hand.

6. Set a timer for 60 seconds and draw a picture of the elephant.

7. Repeat, either until you draw it to your satisfaction or until you wish to stop.

8. Now, reflect on the following:

- How did you find drawing the elephant this time?
- Did you stick with it even as it became easier? If not, why not?*
- Did you stick with it even as it became harder? If not, why not?

* Both anxiety about our skills or boredom with repetition can be a source of lack of perseverance, particularly if we don't manage to get to a point where we are enjoying an activity.[25]

---

[25]Csikszentmihalyi, M. (2000). *Beyond Boredom and Anxiety*. San Francisco, CA: Jossey-Bass.

CHAPTER 5

TACKLING YOUR CORE BELIEFS AND HARNESSING YOUR FEARS

"PAIN IS TEMPORARY
QUITTING LASTS
FOREVER."

— Lance Armstrong,
Every Second Counts
(with Sally Jenkins)
(2003)

5.1 INTRODUCTION

By now we have considered and reflected on how our thinking and action are shaped by our own contexts and experiences; these also have an important influence on our preferences about – and responses to – conditions of entrepreneurial uncertainty and ambiguity. As we just discussed in Chapter 4, we not only need to develop our persistence within these conditions, but also our resilience. Very often our ability to persist (or not) is shaped by our *fears* about what we can or cannot do.

Have you ever considered what the 'little voice' in your head is saying to you when you are doing something beyond your comfort zone or skill set? Does it empower you, or make you feel incapable? What kind of words does it use and where does this come from?

This chapter will build on the concepts of persistence and resilience from Chapter 4, considering how deeply embedded fears affect our thinking, feelings and actions under uncertainty and our ability to act resiliently. We will start by exploring the concept of *core beliefs*, the deep-seated assumptions we hold about ourselves and the world, and how they link to our fears. Building on this, we will consider how our core beliefs and related fears shape our entrepreneurial thinking and action (or inaction), identifying a number of common fears linked to self-worth and 'imposter' syndrome/phenomenon in order to challenge the assumptions we hold about our own entrepreneurial abilities and potential.

After working through this chapter, you should be able to:

- explain the concept of core beliefs and understand the relationship between your beliefs and your fears
- identify and articulate a number of common fears linked to entrepreneurial thinking and action
- consider your own fears and the beliefs that underpin them.

5.2 A BRIEF INTRODUCTION TO CORE BELIEFS

The term 'core beliefs' may be new to you. They are hardly ever part of classroom or workplace conversations. In fact, they are often considered such a private matter that you may never have even discussed them with your family or closest friends – or even paused to consider them yourself! Despite this, it is increasingly recognised that our beliefs play a critical role in shaping our thinking and our behaviour, particularly our ability to think about possibilities beyond our past experiences and frames of reference (think back to Chapter 3).

So what exactly is a core belief? *Core beliefs* are, simply, the deep-seated beliefs we hold about ourselves, the world and our future. As with most of our preferences, core beliefs are built from our own lived experiences and how we have interpreted these experiences;[1] they in turn inform the way we look at and interpret the world.[2]

---

[1]Kelly, G. (1955). *Personal Construct Psychology.* New York: Norton.
[2]Kelly, G. A. (1963). *A Theory of Personality: The Psychology of Personal Constructs.* New York: WW Norton & Company.

Our understanding of the impact of core beliefs on thinking, feeling and behaviour stems from clinical settings,[3] where core belief inventories have been developed and adopted to help individuals make sense of themselves and the world. In recent years, however, these inventories have been updated and adapted for wider public use[4] with important implications for both personal and professional development.

WHERE AM I STARTING FROM?
IDENTIFYING YOUR CORE BELIEFS

For each of the 100 statements below, circle either True(T) or False (F) according to whether you think the statement is mostly true or mostly false. When you're not sure which to choose, go with your first impulse.

1.   T F   I am worthy of love and respect

2.   T F   My world is a pretty safe place

3.   T F   I perform many tasks well

4.   T F   I am in control of my life

5.   T F   I feel loved and cared for

6.   T F   I can rely upon myself

7.   T F   The world is neither fair nor unfair

8.   T F   I feel a strong sense of belonging in my family and community

9.   T F   Most people can be trusted

10. T F   I set reasonable standards for myself

11. T F   I often feel flawed or defective

12. T F   Life is dangerous – a medical, natural, or financial disaster could strike at any time

13. T F   I am basically incompetent

---

[3]Young, J. E. (1999). *Cognitive Therapy for Personality Disorders: A Schema-Focused Approach.* Sarasota, FL: Professional Resource Press/Professional Resource Exchange.

[4]McKay, M. & Fanning, P. (1991). *Prisoners of Belief.* Oakland, CA: New Harbinger Publications Inc.

14.   T F   I have very little control over my life

15.   T F   I've never felt really cared for by my family

16.   T F   Others can care for me better than I can care for myself

17.   T F   I get upset when I don't get what I want – I hate to take no for an answer

18.   T F   I frequently feel left out of groups

19.   T F   Many people would like to hurt me or take advantage of me

20.   T F   Very little of what I do satisfies me – I usually think I could do better

21.   T F   I feel Ok about myself

22.   T F   I can protect myself from most dangers

23.   T F   Doing some things comes easy for me

24.   T F   I have the power I need to solve most of my problems

25.   T F   I have at least one satisfying intimate relationship

26.   T F   It's Ok to disagree with others

27.   T F   I accept it when I don't get what I want

28.   T F   I fit in well with my circle of friends

29.   T F   I rarely need to protect or guard myself with other people

30.   T F   I can forgive myself for failure

31.   T F   Nobody I desire would desire me if they really got to know me

32.   T F   I worry about getting sick or hurt

33.   T F   When I trust my own judgement, I make wrong decisions

34.   T F   Events just bowl me over sometimes

35.   T F   My relationships are shallow – if I disappeared tomorrow, no one would notice

36.   T   F   I find myself going along with others' plans

37.   T   F   There are certain things I simply must have to be happy

38.   T   F   I feel like an outsider

39.   T   F   Most people think only of themselves

40.   T   F   I'm a perfectionist; I must be the best at whatever I do

41.   T   F   I have legitimate needs I deserve to fill

42.   T   F   I am willing to take risks

43.   T   F   I am a competent person, as capable as most people

44.   T   F   My impulses don't control me

45.   T   F   I feel nurtured in my family

46.   T   F   I don't need the approval of others for everything I do

47.   T   F   Things tend to work out, even in the end

48.   T   F   People usually accept me as I am

49.   T   F   I seldom feel taken advantage of

50.   T   F   I set achievable goals for myself

51.   T   F   I'm dull and boring and can't make interesting conversation

52.   T   F   If I'm not careful with my money, I might end up with nothing

53.   T   F   I tend to avoid new challenges

54.   T   F   I fear I'll give in to overwhelming crying, anger, or sexual impulses

55.   T   F   I'm afraid of being abandoned – that a loved one will die or reject me

56.   T   F   I don't function well on my own

57.   T   F   I feel I shouldn't have to accept some of the limitations placed on ordinary people

58. T F People don't usually include me in what they're doing

59. T F Most people can't be trusted

60. T F Failure is very upsetting to me

61. T F I count for something in the world

62. T F I can take care of myself and my loved ones

63. T F I can learn new skills if I try

64. T F I can usually control my feelings

65. T F I can get the care and attention I need

66. T F I like to spend time by myself

67. T F Most of the time I feel fairly treated

68. T F My hopes and dreams are much like everyone else's

69. T F I give people the benefit of the doubt

70. T F I'm not perfect and that's OK

71. T F I'm unattractive

72. T F I choose my old, familiar ways of doing things over risking the unexpected

73. T F I don't perform well under stress

74. T F I'm powerless to change many of the situations I'm in

75. T F There's no one I can count on for support and advice

76. T F I try hard to please others and I put their needs before my own

77. T F I tend to expect the worst

78. T F Sometimes I feel like an alien, very different from everybody else

79. T F I must be on my guard against others' lies and hostile remarks

80. T F   I push myself so hard that I harm my relationships, my health, or my happiness

81. T F   People I like and respect often like and respect me

82. T F   I don't worry much about health or money

83. T F   Most of my decisions are sound

84. T F   I can take charge when I need to

85. T F   I can depend on my friends for advice and emotional support

86. T F   I think for myself, I can stand up for my ideas

87. T F   I am treated fairly most of the time

88. T F   I could change jobs or join a club and soon fit in

89. T F   I'd rather be too gullible than too suspicious

90. T F   It's Ok to make mistakes

91. T F   I don't deserve much attention or respect

92. T F   I feel uneasy when I go very far from home alone

93. T F   I mess up everything I attempt

94. T F   I'm often a victim of circumstances

95. T F   I have no one who hugs me, shares secrets with me, or really cares what happens to me

96. T F   I have trouble making my own wants and needs known

97. T F   Although my life is objectively Ok, I have a lot of trouble accepting some parts that aren't the way I'd like them to be

98. T F   I don't feel I belong where I am

99. T F   Most people will break their promises and lie

100. T F   I have very clear, black-and-white rules for myself

Now score YOUR ANSWERS:

1. Value _____ points

Look at your answers for items 1, 21, 41, 61, 81. For each T circled, give yourself one point. Now look at your answers for items 11, 31, 51, 71, 91. For each F circled, give yourself one point. Record your total points in the space above. On a scale of 1–10 this indicates how much you agree with the statement 'I am worthy'. The higher your score, the more valuable you believe you are as a person.

2. Security _____ points

Look at your answers for items 2, 22, 42, 62, 82. For each T circled, give yourself one point. Now look at your answers for items 12, 32, 52, 72, 92. For each F circled, give yourself one point. Record your total points in the space above. On a scale of 1–10 this indicates how much you agree with the statement 'I am safe'. The higher your score, the more safe you feel.

3. Performance _____ points

Look at your answers for items 3, 23, 43, 63, 83. For each T circled, give yourself one point. Now look at your answers for items 13, 33, 53, 73, 93. For each F circled, give yourself one point. Record your total points in the space above. On a scale of 1–10 this indicates how much you agree with the statement 'I am competent'. The higher your score, the more competent you feel.

4. Control _____ points

Look at your answers for items 4, 24, 44, 64, 84. For each T circled, give yourself one point. Now look at your answers for items 14, 34, 54, 74, 94. For each F circled, give yourself one point. Record your total points in the space above. On a scale of 1–10 this indicates how much you agree with the statement 'I am powerful'. The higher your score, the more you feel in control of your life.

5. Love _____ points

Look at your answers for items 5, 25, 45, 65, 85. For each T circled, give yourself one point. Now look at your answers for items 15, 35, 55, 75, 95. For each F circled, give yourself one point. Record your total points in the space above. On a scale of 1–10 this indicates how much you agree with the statement 'I am loved'. The higher your score, the more you feel nurtured.

6. Autonomy _____ points

Look at your answers for items 6, 26, 46, 66, 86. For each T circled, give yourself one point. Now look at your answers for items 16, 36, 56, 76, 96.

For each F circled, give yourself one point. Record your total points in the space above. On a scale of 1–10 this indicates how much you agree with the statement 'I am autonomous'. The higher your score, the more independent you feel.

7. Justice _____ points

Look at your answers for items 7, 27, 47, 67, 87. For each T circled, give yourself one point. Now look at your answers for items 17, 37, 57, 77, 97. For each F circled, give yourself one point. Record your total points in the space above. On a scale of 1–10 this indicates how much you agree with the statement 'I am treated justly'. The higher your score, the more likely you are to accept what you get in life as fair or reasonable.

8. Belonging _____ points

Look at your answers for items 8, 28, 48, 68, 88. For each T circled, give yourself one point. Now look at your answers for items 18, 38, 58, 78, 98. For each F circled, give yourself one point. Record your total points in the space above. On a scale of 1–10 this indicates how much you agree with the statement 'I belong'. The higher your score, the more you feel secure and connected to family, friends, acquaintances and humanity in general.

9. Others _____ points

Look at your answers for items 9, 29, 49, 69, 89. For each T circled, give yourself one point. Now look at your answers for items 19, 39, 59, 79, 99. For each F circled, give yourself one point. Record your total points in the space above. On a scale of 1–10 this indicates how much you agree with the statement 'People are good'. The higher your score, the more likely you are to trust others and to expect them to behave positively towards you.

10. Standards _____ points

Look at your answers for items 10, 30, 50, 70, 90. For each T circled, give yourself one point. Now look at your answers for items 20, 40, 60, 80, 100. For each F circled, give yourself one point. Record your total points in the space above. On a scale of 1–10 this indicates how much you agree with the statement 'My standards are reasonable and flexible'. The higher your score, the more likely you are to judge your own and others' actions compassionately.

Source: McKay, M. & Fanning, P. (1991). *Prisoners of Belief*. Oakland, CA: New Harbinger Publications Inc.

5.3 THE LINK BETWEEN CORE BELIEFS AND FEARS

Our core beliefs are inherently linked to our *fears*. Just as with our core beliefs, we may avoid thinking about our fears beyond simply acknowledging them.

Fear has been defined in a number of ways, but for our purposes can be thought of as a temporary emotional state stemming from our perception of threats.[5] The word perception is important here – we may hold fears that we consider critical threats but that are actually unlikely to come to pass.

Some of you may be sceptical about discussing your core beliefs and fears. We find that this is often very uncomfortable for people – and people usually avoid doing things that feel uncomfortable! We are also often asked whether discussing our fears might in turn cause us more problems:

> *Is acknowledging our fears going to make us feel even more afraid?*
>
> *Are other people going to perceive us as weak if we disclose our fears to them?*

These are very relevant concerns, yet the evidence base would suggest that the answers to these questions is a resounding 'NO!'. Given that our core beliefs and fears are mostly hidden from our conscious mind (i.e., we are usually not actively thinking about them), we often fail to see resulting patterns in our behaviour. Yet becoming more aware of them does not further strengthen our fears or worries. In fact, research shows the opposite – that actively acknowledging and addressing our fears and beliefs causes them to lose their hold over us. This isn't to say that we will no longer be afraid. Our fears may continue, but they are less likely to control how we feel, think and behave, giving us a greater sense of empowerment.

There are also benefits to discussing our inner beliefs and fears with others, despite our worries of being judged, provided this is done in a receptive and safe environment (see Chapter 8 for a discussion of psychologically safe environments). First, by sharing our own fears, we allow others to do the same. What we are likely to find is that all of us have fears, despite the fact that we tend to assume that we are alone in having them. Establishing that fears are common can be a powerful way of normalising fear and often highlights that many of us have fears in common. Take, for instance, the fear of failure. We'll discuss this in further detail in a moment, but this is a largely universal fear – we all (at one time or another) have a fear that we will fail, whether in a specific activity/endeavour or in our lives more widely.

---

[5]Cacciotti, G. & Hayton, J. C. (2015). Fear and entrepreneurship: A review and research agenda. *International Journal of Management Reviews, 17*(2), 165–190.

FOOD FOR THOUGHT
PERSONAL FEARS

Take a moment to consider what fears you might hold. To do so:

1. Complete the following sentence:

In my life, I am most afraid that

....
....

2. Consider where this fear may stem from. How does it link to your own
   core beliefs?

....
....
....

We often find that people's fears centre around a number of common themes,
which we'll explore further in Section 4. We'll also share with you some 'fear
statements' that we've collected from our own work, which you may find
helpful as you reflect on your own personal fear(s).

5.4 THE INFLUENCE OF CORE BELIEFS AND FEAR ON ENTREPRENEURIAL THINKING AND ACTION

But why do we need to consider our core beliefs and fears in relation to entrepreneurial thinking and action?

Ultimately, when we seek to create value we are going to find ourselves in situations of uncertainty (think back to Chapter 4) where we need to explore possibilities that are in all likelihood beyond our expertise, skill or knowledge (see Section 4). In doing so, most of us will need to confront a number of fears, linked to our own core beliefs about our capabilities. It is increasingly recognised that these play an important role in our thinking and in our behaviour, including our ability to think and act entrepreneurially. The views a person holds about themselves and the world – linked to their fears – directly influences the choices that they make and whether or not they actually engage in entrepreneurial action.[6]

---

[6]Laguna, M. (2013). Self-efficacy, self-esteem, and entrepreneurship among the unemployed. *Journal of Applied Social Psychology, 43*(2), 253–262.

5.4.1 THE ROLE OF CORE BELIEFS

It is now widely acknowledged that individuals who think entrepreneurially and subsequently take entrepreneurial action are more likely to hold a number of core beliefs relating to their ability to cope, specifically within challenging and uncertain situations. These fall under the labels of 'self-efficacy' and 'self-esteem'.

The concept of **self-efficacy** has long been linked to entrepreneurial thinking and behaviour. Simply, self-efficacy refers to how we judge our personal capabilities. It is the belief we hold in our own ability to cope with specific tasks or situations.[7] Individuals who exhibit what is called 'global self-efficacy' – a generalised confidence in their own ability to act in complex and challenging situations[8] – have been found to be more able and willing to engage in entrepreneurial thinking and action, particularly under uncertainty.[9] Thus self-efficacy (i.e. belief in oneself) is often considered to be an indicator of a person's readiness to engage in entrepreneurial activity.[10]

Often conflated with self-efficacy is the core belief of **self-esteem**. It is important to emphasise that self-efficacy and self-esteem, while interlinked, are not the same thing. Self-esteem is how we judge our own worth. Our capabilities may feed into this, but we make judgements on our self-worth independently of the skills and capabilities that we may (or may not) have. These judgements mean we generally hold either a positive or negative attitude about ourselves and our own worth.[11]

Our core beliefs play a central role when we think about taking entrepreneurial action. There may be instances where we *believe that we have the ability* to take action, but we *do not believe that we are worthy* of the accomplishments that may stem from that action (self-efficacy without self-worth). On the flipside, we may *not feel competent or capable* to take action but hold the *belief that we are worthy* of the accomplishments that taking action would lead to (self-worth without self-efficacy). Research shows that it is those with *high self-worth* that are more likely to take action and be resilient in the face of mistakes, failures and setbacks. They are also more likely to pursue their goals and to take risks to do so.[12]

---

[7]Bandura, A. (1997). *Self-Efficacy: The Exercise of Control*. New York: Freeman.

[8]Stajkovic, A. D. & Luthans, F. (1998). Self-efficacy and work-related performance: A meta-analysis. *Psychological Bulletin, 124*, 240–261.

[9]Markman, G. D., Baron, R. A. & Balkin, D. B. (2005). Are perseverance and self-efficacy costless? Assessing entrepreneurs' regretful thinking. *Journal of Organization Behavior, 26*, 1–19.

[10]Bosma, N., Hill, S., Ionescu-Somers, A., Kelley, D., Levie, J. & Tarnawa, A. (2020). *Global Entrepreneurship Monitor 2019/2020*. Available at www.gemconsortium.org/report/gem-2019-2020-global-report

[11]Rosenberg, M. (1989). *Society and Adolescent Self-Image,* revised edn. Middletown: Wesleyan University Press.

[12]Laguna, Self-efficacy, self-esteem, and entrepreneurship among the unemployed.

DEEP DIVE

THE UNSPOKEN IMPORTANCE OF SELF-WORTH

As discussed above, self-worth (our sense that we are worthy regardless of our achievements) paradoxically leads us to the resilient behaviour that creates achievement. Whilst we often speak about self-esteem, we speak less about **self-worth.**

University of Chicago Psychologist, Adia Gooden, provides an informative and compelling case for the importance of the often-unspoken notion of self-worth at **www.youtube.com/watch?v=EirlZ7fy3bE**

5.4.2 THE ROLE OF FEAR

Our fears are deeply rooted in our own core beliefs, both formed and reinforced by our lived experiences and the assumptions we now make about ourselves and the world around us. Unfortunately, entrepreneurial thinking and action usually go hand in hand with fear, a result of the uncontrollable and unknowable circumstances in which value-creating activity takes place. Whilst we all have a range of fears, in terms of entrepreneurial thinking and action we want to specifically consider four key fears: fear of failure; fear of success; fear of social esteem loss; and fear of not realising our potential.

FEAR OF FAILURE

Perhaps the fear most commonly considered in relation to entrepreneurship, a fear of failure is widely recognised to be the critical point influencing whether individuals take entrepreneurial action or not. Whilst we may have the intention to take action to create value, we may never actually act on that intention because of the fear that we will fail.[13]

> *I am most afraid that I will lose my professional career and reputation by not fulfilling my full inherent promise and not have the funds to support my family.*

Yet, despite this seeming simplicity, the fear of failure is a bit more complex than we often assume. First of all, we often assume that fear of failure is a fixed 'trait' that some people have. However, current research demonstrates that fear of failure is in fact a *mental state*[14] that can be both enabling and constraining depending on our preference/perspectives/frames of reference and how the fear is experienced, interpreted and managed.

---

[13]Bosma et al., *Global Entrepreneurship Monitor 2019/2020.*

[14]Cacciotti, G., Hayton, J. C., Mitchell, J. R. & Giazitzoglu, A. (2016). A reconceptualization of fear of failure in entrepreneurship. *Journal of Business Venturing, 31*(3), 302–325.

For some of us, fear of failure can be a barrier to taking action. It can make us feel panicked, anxious, depressed and unable to focus. These feelings often stem from a number of underlying core beliefs, including the worry that we will: (i) experience shame and embarrassment; (ii) devalue our own self-esteem; (iii) have an uncertain future; (iv) upset important others; and (v) have those important others lose interest.

For others of us, fear of failure can actually act as a source of motivation to take action, or continue taking action. It can make us feel excited, motivated to keep trying, a desire to conquer our fear and a sense of satisfaction in conquering the fear. These feelings often stem from the core beliefs that: (i) hard work can conquer anything; (ii) failure does not define a person; (iii) failure is a learning opportunity; and (iv) failure is not shameful.

FEAR OF SUCCESS

Whilst we often hear about fear of failure, we don't often talk about the flip side of this – a fear of success. Just as we can worry about things going wrong for us, equally we can worry about what will happen if things work out. We can be anxious that achieving our goals or being successful in an endeavour will cause others to look at us differently, perhaps causing us to face disapproval or even rejection.[15] Research has found fear of success to be more important within some groups, including women, those from cultural backgrounds that emphasise the collective rather than individual achievement and those individuals working in occupations that are not traditional for their gender.[16]

CHALLENGING ASSUMPTIONS
THE FEAR OF SUCCESS

We often believe that fear of failure is the main enemy of resilient behaviour. But what if, for some of us, succeeding was scarier than failing? What if, for some of us, having something to lose is scarier than having nothing at all?

Jemele Hill talks us through the reasons why success can be scarier than failure at **https://youtu.be/bjzlTnc7PCE**

FEAR OF SOCIAL ESTEEM LOSS

Linked to fear of failure and fear of success is the fear of losing social esteem. This is particularly the case when we think about entrepreneurial activity, when we are trying something new or different that people around us may not (yet) understand or support. We

---

[15]Colman, A. M. (2015). *A Dictionary of Psychology*. Oxford: Oxford University Press.

[16]Horner, M. S. (1972). Toward an understanding of achievement-related conflicts in women. *Journal of Social Sciences, 28*(2), 157–175.

may fear disappointing our families, losing the trust and respect of those around us such as close colleagues or friends, or losing our reputation within our wider professional networks.[17]

> *I am most afraid that I will not be able to meet the expectations that other people have for me.*

> *I am most afraid that I will make a mistake and let people down.*

Fear of loss of social esteem relates to the notion of *social identity* – we need to feel connected to, and accepted by, our social group of reference. If we fall short of their approval, the sense of self that we derived from our social identity may be jeopardised.[18]

FEAR OF NOT REALISING OUR POTENTIAL

Finally, we may also hold the fear that we are underachieving, stagnating, or just generally not realising our potential. We may not be achieving what we're defining as success, or equally we may feel like we're losing the creativity, motivation or even joy in our lives.[19]

> *I am most afraid that I won't find meaningful, fulfilling work that I am passionate about, where I can share my experience, knowledge and skills.*

> *I am most afraid that I settle and don't push myself to try different things.*

Interestingly, fear of not progressing in our self-development is often considered a key motivation to undertake entrepreneurial action and create value, be it in the context of a new or established organisation or in our own lives more widely.

5.4.3 THE IMPOSTER PHENOMENON

Having considered both core beliefs and fears, we can see that the two are closely interlinked and have a huge impact on what we think and feel and in turn what we do (or do not do). Some negative core beliefs, aligned to fears such as the fear of failure, can manifest in what is commonly termed 'imposter syndrome' or, more accurately, ***imposter phenomenon*** as this is not a medical condition as the term syndrome implies!

Imposter phenomenon, something that is often experienced during times of transition or uncertainty,[20] is an experience of being a 'phoney'. In other words, we believe that we

---

[17]Cacciotti et al., A reconceptualization of fear of failure in entrepreneurship.

[18]Brewer, M. B. & Hewstone, M. (eds) (2004). *Self and Social Identity*. Oxford: Blackwell Publishing.

[19]Amabile, T. & Kramer, S. (2011). *The Progress Principle: Using Small Wins to Ignite Joy, Engagement, and Creativity at Work.* Boston, MA: Harvard Business Press.

[20]LaDonna, K. A., Ginsburg, S. & Watling, C. (2018). 'Rising to the level of your incompetence': What physicians' self-assessment of their performance reveals about the imposter syndrome in medicine. *Academic Medicine, 93*(5), 762–768.

are not intelligent or capable enough to do what we're supposed to be doing and we worry about being exposed as a fraud. This is most often experienced by highly motivated and high achieving individuals.[21]

> *I am most afraid that I will end up in a role far beyond my ability and get found out.*
>
> *I am most afraid that I do not have the skillset or confidence that I did before being pregnant and going off on maternity leave.*

Imposter phenomenon may come and go, depending on circumstances,[22] and can cause us to make choices and behave in ways that avoid potential negative outcomes.[23] Unfortunately, this focus on 'playing it safe' to avoid 'being found out' can lead to us making choices that actually take us further away from where we want to be – and what we've set out to accomplish in the first place.

ENTREPRENEURIAL THINKING AND MINDSET IN PRACTICE
DR MARC REID AND IMPOSTER PHENOMENON

The case study is intended to illustrate the following:

- the prevalence of fear (and fear of failure) in professional contexts
- the relationship between fear of failure and the imposter phenomenon
- learning to cope with the (ever present) fear of failure.

This is the case study of Marc Reid. Marc is an organic chemist and founder of the firm Pre-Site Safety which seeks to support innovations in workplace training and accident readiness. He is also a researcher and expert on the imposter phenomenon.

The case is narrated in Marc's own voice.

EDUCATIONAL BACKGROUND AND CAREER

I was born and raised in Glasgow, Scotland. I did both my degrees at University of Strathclyde training as a chemist. And for the longest time, my career

[21]Colman, *A Dictionary of Psychology.*

[22]Warren, R. (2016). Imposter syndrome will kill your business. *Entrepreneur*, 6 April. Available at: www.entrepreneur.com/article/270562

[23]Cowman, S. E. & Ferrari, J. R. (2002). 'Am I for real?' Predicting imposter tendencies from self-handicapping and affective components. *Social Behavior and Personality, 30*(2), 119–125.

path has remained on that trajectory. I have trained and climbed the ladder as an academic scientist becoming a postdoc at Edinburgh, starting my independent career later at Strathclyde, with appointments at Bristol in between and working between departments in the University as well. I have been on a tracked academic path until the last three or four years, and my observations on my own imposter phenomenon in that space have led me to write a book on the subject.

ON IMPOSTER PHENOMENON

Much has been said about feeling like an impostor, feeling like a fraud, feeling like you don't belong in your workplace and that someone is one day going to find you out and chuck you out of the place. In more recent years, I've been more public about my own experiences with the imposter phenomenon as we would call it and indeed more public about some of the research that I've tried to bring together in that field to understand the imposter phenomenon more and why it is that so many of us feel that way.

But the story doesn't begin there. The story begins about five years before any of the research started. It started when I was moving from my PhD position at the University of Strathclyde to my first postdoctoral position at the University of Edinburgh.

There is a specific set of details about where I started and where I was going. But what matters for anyone reading this is that I started off in one professional set of circumstances with a close-knit team, people who I had become intimately familiar with, knew how they ticked, knew how they worked with me, knew what we were all doing. It became comfortable.

Moving from my PhD to my postdoc was the first time that I had moved to a new team, with new people, a new set of projects, a new set of circumstances, and far more unknowns as to where all of these people had come from in this new team. And at that time, with that first large professional move in my career, it was a real first instance that I had ample excuse to compare myself to others in the room, to look at my credentials, my papers, my citations and weigh those up against other people that I was working with.

But not just weigh them up against other people I was working with, but move very swiftly towards a state of panic where I felt that everything that they did was better than what I had achieved. Everything that they had managed to put out in the world was higher ranking than mine. And moving on from that, leading to the outcome of thinking there's one day very soon that one of these people in this new team that I'm working in is going to point their finger at me and say, this guy doesn't know what he's talking about. You're a complete and utter fraud. Get out of the room. You don't belong in this team.

CHILDHOOD AND THE ROOTS OF IMPOSTER PHENOMENON

I grew up in a family with two younger brothers. I, like many of those we've now come across in our research on the imposter phenomenon, was the first person to have that opportunity to go to university straight out of school. Therefore, as exciting as that is, from a family perspective, that can also breed the related pressure of being 'the smart one', someone smart enough to go to university. All of that family-related circumstance is all well-meaning, unconsciously, subconsciously even, it can leave you with the labels of how you assume you have to be. It made me feel like I need to be the smartest person in the room. I am deeply insecure about being in a room where there are people who are further ahead than me, know more than me.

It isn't the only place that impostor experiences come from. Another one relates very much to those moving to different areas within academia or moving to a different level of your training.

WHAT TO DO ABOUT IMPOSTER PHENOMENON

How do I deal with it? How do I get rid of it? How do I overcome it?

That one question from my experience of trying to come to terms with it myself and later experience of running a research program on the imposter phenomenon, asking the question of how to overcome it is not only the most commonly asked question, it's the most poorly framed question. Who's to say that any of us ever overcome it? We see many instances of books and articles where the claim is to overcome imposter experiences, to cure it, to smash it, to get rid of it.

But my belief is that what you're trying to do with impostor experiences is to manage them, so that when you take those risks as your career progresses, as you learn to walk into the unknown, you're ready for the fact that each one of those new instances and new experiences could throw up something that your brain can't predict, might throw up an experience, something scary that you've never come across before and that you have no training and can't possibly be ready for. If you go into that thinking that you've already overcome the impostor experience, then you're setting yourself up for the disappointment for it to come back in a new form.

ON REJECTION AND FAILURE

One other way that I've come to manage that fear myself is looking at rejection and managing failure. The fear of failure is real in the sense that so many people feel it. But it's not real to the extent that it's a physical being, a monster that need cloud everything that you do.

Back in those early PhD and postdoc days when I was moving from one position to another, it was also around the same time that I was trying to put the feelers out with academic fellowships and put together proposals to take my next, more independent step in my career. what I was not at all prepared for at that time was how I would respond to that first rejection email popping up in my inbox to say that, thanks for your application. It was part of a wide and large range of applications that came in. Yours wasn't good enough this time. when that first happened to me, I wasn't at all prepared for the failure.

To manage that fear of failure, to manage that resistance to wanting to try that new thing, that thing that might make you feel like an impostor is to realise not only that you can fail, that more often than not, you will. You will fail on route to what you really want to succeed at.

And what I've realised over that period of going from not being able to handle rejection through to working with it has been to use the word failure less often and use it either alongside or replace failure with the word experiment. Each failure can be viewed as an experiment, a way for you to find out, to get the data in that you need to craft the thing that will eventually become successful.

And to give you one example, an author from around the 1950s who went by the pen name Zora Raeburn. There's a famous image of Zora out there in the world where it shows her plastering a wall in London with 200+ rejection letters from when she tried to have her novels published. In tracking the history of Zora, I found that not only did she try to persevere and continue on past the multiple rejections she received, that at one time she actually was successful.

She got a publisher on board, but it happened to be amidst world war II, and that publisher got bombed out of existence, and she went back to square one but still, she kept trying.

what we can often do when we compare ourselves to other people is to see the instantaneous nature of how they are now, not how they got to now. And indeed, that completely clouds your own view of yourself and where you are today versus where you were yesterday. Realising that if you compare yourself today to being a better version than you were yesterday, that's the only game you can actually ever win, that comparison of you being here now as a slightly better version of yourself than you were yesterday.

what you will never win is comparing yourself to someone else and forgetting that they have had a story to get to where they are. And more often than not, you completely fail to see all of those details.

CV OF FAILURES

Most of us are still very much focused on how we present our successes rather than how we could possibly present our failures. In other words, we are in a professional world very much fixated on how we can decorate our CVs or resumes, how we can add more bullet points to those CVs with more accolades, more competitions won, more qualifications, more things that we feel others will look on positively when we want them to judge us.

Such is that fixation on how to present successes and to work with what we think are the ultimate metrics of our performance being judged that we simply forget that there is a richer story to be told in all the failures, the near misses, the missed opportunities that happened in between each of those bullet points of success on our CVs.

And although it's becoming more popular, I know it's still arguably very rare to hear the terms CV and CV of failures within the same sentence. And the

CV of failures is the powerful underutilised tool of our time with regards to managing failure and being able to celebrate it and learn from it to the best of everyone's potential.

I learned about the CV of failures from a scientist, Melanie Stefan, and an economist, Johannes Haushofer, who each in their own way were among the first in the scientific world to present a CV of failures, with all of the bullet points that don't make it into the CV and that we might often be ashamed to even air, let alone write down in written form for a PDF.

I took inspiration to not just write my own CV of failures but to publish it. Now, I have on my website my CV, my main biography, the traditional thing that everyone is expecting and my CV of failures. In the latter I list all of those bullet points of fellowships I've gone for but weren't successful, jobs I've gone for but did not get, competitions I've entered but did not win, papers I've got rejected, all of those things that don't ever appear on a CV but should be presented in order to bring the full picture, the real context of whatever appears on my CV. I put mine out there to let others close to my world take some motivation from it and realise that we are all human. There are no superheroes in or beyond our work environment. Everyone fails and everyone has these stories of repeated rejection, unless they have never dared to try.

5.5 SUMMARY AND NEXT STEPS

Building on the concepts of persistence and resilience (from Chapter 4), this chapter has considered how our beliefs about ourselves, the world and our place in the word – our *core beliefs* – shape our ability to sustain action under uncertainty. We have explored the link between our core beliefs and our fears, identifying and discussing a number of common fears relating to entrepreneurial action, specifically fear of failure, success, loss of self-esteem and not realising our potential. We have also considered the link between fears and imposter phenomenon. Whilst we will in all likelihood never be without fears, we can manage our fears by addressing them proactively and openly, in the same way that we can challenge our core beliefs and query where they are potentially holding us back from trying new things, making judgements and taking action. We'll explore this issues further in Chapter 6.

WHERE AM I NOW?
FEARS AND CORE BELIEFS

Having worked through this chapter, you have now started to identify your fears. You have also begun to consider what core beliefs underpin these fears and which life experiences may have contributed to you holding these fears in the first place. Spend a few minutes considering how these hold you back from taking action and record your thoughts below.

1. How do these fears (and their underlying core beliefs) hold you back from taking action?

2. What are the consequences of not taking action?

3. Which three fears can you identify as your top priority to work on?

Keep hold of your thoughts – you'll come back to them in a moment for an activity on 'fear-setting' (see Practising entrepreneurial thinking below).

5.6 CONTINUE YOUR LEARNING

The following activities are designed to support you on your learning journey, building on ideas introduced in this chapter. These can be completed at any time and in any order, although you may find it helpful to begin with the 'Check your understanding' activity before moving on.

CHECK YOUR UNDERSTANDING

1. Self-worth and self-efficacy are synonymous.

   ☐ **TRUE**

   ☐ **FALSE** (It's false – self-worth is our belief that we are worthy human beings, whereas self-efficacy is our belief that we can get something done)

2. Fear of failure can stop people pursuing their entrepreneurial ideas.

   ☐ **TRUE** (It's true – please see section 5.4.2)

   ☐ **FALSE**

3. Fear of failure can be a barrier or a motivator, depending on how we respond to it

   ☐ **TRUE** (It's true – please see section 5.4.2)

   ☐ **FALSE**

4. Imposter phenomenon refers to individuals sending their twin sibling to work in their place.

   ☐ **TRUE**

   ☐ **FALSE** (It's false – please see section 5.4.3)

FURTHER READING

1. **Build for Tomorrow** by Jason Feifer

2. **The Procrastination Equation** by Piers Steel

3. **You are NOT a Fraud** by Marc Reid

STOP AND THINK

MARC'S EXPERIENCES

Looking back to Marc's story....

1. where does Marc's imposter phenomenon come from?

2. How does Marc tackle his imposter phenomenon?

3. In Marc's view, what is the link between imposter phenomenon and comparing ourselves to others?

COGNITIVE-BEHAVIOURAL REFLECTION
RESPONSE TO FEARS

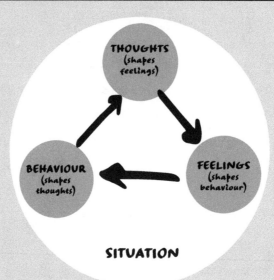

Drawing on the cognitive-behavioural framework introduced in Chapter 1, consider a situation where you felt afraid or even just conscious of failure or any other type of fear described in the chapter (fear of loss, fear of success, imposter phenomenon, etc.)

Why do this? This activity helps you to identify in more detail how fears play out in your daily lived experiences. It will therefore give you a more accurate picture of when, how and through which mechanisms they affect your behaviour.

Step 1. Describe this situation in two to three sentences.

Step 2. Describe the thoughts you had in this situation. [This is your **interpretation** of the situation, so make sure you explore it in sufficient detail. we'd recommend about four to eight sentences.]

Step 3. Describe how you felt in this situation. [These are your **emotions**. Be as specific as you can in your language, avoiding general terms like 'happy' or 'sad' in favour of more nuanced terms.]

Step 4. Describe how you behaved in this situation. Did you go ahead despite the fear? Or did you avoid doing something or changing something? Did the fear make you do something that otherwise you would not have done? [Focus on how you responded, identifying both positive and negative responses.]

Step 5. Looking back on this situation, what sense can you make of it? What do you now better understand about yourself, your feelings and your behaviours? How do these relate to your own frames of reference and worldview?

PRACTISING ENTREPRENEURIAL THINKING
FEAR-SETTING

Having started to consider your own personal fear(s), we want to think about where you can start to address and tackle these. Tim Ferris talks about a technique to address his fears head-on, something he calls 'fear-setting'.

Start by watching the Ted Talk where Tim outlines his approach and how he has applied this in his own life: **www.ted.com/talks/tim_ferriss_why_you_should_define_your_fears_instead_of_your_goals?language=en**

1.   Apply Tim's approach to fear-setting, using the 'define', 'prevent' and 'repair' headings

Define	Prevent	Repair
1.	1.	1.
2.	2.	2.
3.	3.	3.

Consider the **cost of inaction**, over the following timescales:

6 months

1 year

3 years

CHAPTER 6

DEVELOPING AND REFINING YOUR ENTREPRENEURIAL JUDGEMENT

"The emotional tail wags the rational dog."

– Jonathan Haidt,

Thinking Fast and Slow.
Daniel Kahneman (2012)

6.1 INTRODUCTION

As we've explored in the preceding chapters, the way we think and feel shapes how we behave – what we do, or how we act. But what we haven't fully considered yet is the process that occurs before we do something – before we *take action*.

All entrepreneurial action is a result of decisions – decisions to act, not act, or to act in particular ways. When we're operating under uncertainty, our decision making is subject to a degree of *judgement*. We simply don't know what the outcomes of certain choices can or will be, so we need to make a call on what is appropriate given the information that we do have available to us. Have you ever considered the process by which you make decisions? How long does it take you? Do you respond quickly, or does it take you more time to reflect on options and to determine a course of action? How do you then feel once you've made a decision and taken action?

This chapter will start with an introduction to judgement styles, considering the three elements that comprise judgement (speed, relevance and awareness). We will then explore in depth two common judgement styles, the fast and intuitive 'System 1' style and the slower and more deliberate 'System 2' style. These judgement styles also link closely to our tolerance for risk and ambiguity (see Chapter 4) as well as our core beliefs and fears (see Chapter 5). We will then consider the implications of these styles, as well as some of the trade-offs in terms of our entrepreneurial thinking and action, particularly in terms of how we make sense of our own judgements and the outcomes of these decisions.

After working through this chapter, you should be able to:

- articulate the role of judgement in entrepreneurial action
- differentiate between system 1 and system 2 thinking
- consider the impact of your own style of judgement on your own entrepreneurial thinking and behaviour.

6.2 THE BASICS OF JUDGEMENT

Aligned to the myth of the 'hero' entrepreneur (see Chapter 1), when we think about judgement in the context of entrepreneurial activity we often get a mental picture of someone making decisions quickly, decisively and confidently. They seldom pause to wonder if they're doing the right thing – they just go for it!

As we know by now, some of this imagery isn't reflective of what is really going on. We all have different preferences, beliefs, perspectives and experiences, which means that we're all going to make judgements in different ways. We also need to understand that there isn't a right or wrong way to make decisions. Entrepreneurial activity takes place in a huge range of spaces, places and forms and so assuming that one approach to judgement is better than another is inherently problematic. In fact, we'd emphasise that not one style of reasoning is best suited to all entrepreneurial activity. What is important is that we become aware of our own reasoning and judgement style under conditions of uncertainty so that we can become aware of when and how it serves us well and, likewise, when it may be less than ideal.

So what exactly do we mean by judgement? Judgement is a form of thinking and the precursor to decision making (which is itself the precursor to action). It involves us weighing up options based on the information we have available and deciding the likelihood of a certain outcome based on certain actions. You can think of it in in terms of 'if I do X then I am likely to get Y'. Yet, as we have discussed, when we are making entrepreneurial judgements we are usually operating under uncertainty where there is no clear course of action. We may have little information of what to do or what is possible. In these circumstances, we often look back to our past experiences and think about what we can expect given what happened in (similar) previous situations.

As we discussed in Chapter 3, this can be both helpful and problematic as we can potentially fall into established patterns of thinking and action (i.e., the einstellung effect) that are not fit for purpose given our current circumstances. As a result, when considering our entrepreneurial thinking it is particularly important to identify how we personally make judgements and where this could be helpful/unhelpful to our own value creation efforts.

Sometimes it can be helpful to think about what something is *not*. Judgement is not about criticising or condemning someone or something. Rather, it reflects our own style of decision making based on the dimensions of *speed, relevance* and *awareness.*

6.3 DOMINANT JUDGEMENT STYLES

Just as we discussed with regard to mindset in Chapter 2, there isn't a 'right' or 'wrong' judgement style. As you might imagine, every style has its strengths and weaknesses. Judgement styles are built on the three core dimensions of *speed, relevance and awareness:*[1]

> *Speed* refers to how long it takes us to make a judgement. This could range from a few seconds to a few minutes or even hours or days.

> *Relevance* refers to whether we consider all relevant features of the situation at hand, whether we are using only a small number of all the potentially relevant factors, or whether the factors we believe are relevant to the situation are only partially relevant (or even not relevant at all).

> Finally, *awareness* refers to whether (or not) we actively acknowledge both the judgements we are making and the assumptions that are informing our judgements.

---

[1]Jones, M. V. & Casulli, L. (2014). International entrepreneurship: Exploring the logic and utility of individual experience through comparative reasoning approaches. *Entrepreneurship Theory and Practice, 38*(1), 45–69.

Whilst there are a number of judgement styles out there, we will focus on two core ones to get us started – what are known as *System 1 thinking* and *System 2 thinking.*

WHERE AM I STARTING FROM?
IDENTIFYING YOUR JUDGEMENT STYLE

Have you ever thought about your judgement style? The Cognitive Reflection Test[2] was developed to determine whether an individual has the tendency to think intuitively (e.g., System 1) or to be more deliberative (System 2). Work through the following three questions and write down your answers:

1. A bat and a ball cost $1.10 in total. The bat costs $1.00 more than the ball. How much does the ball cost?

2. If it takes 5 machines 5 minutes to make 5 widgets, how long would it take 100 machines to make 100 widgets?

3. In a lake, there is a patch of lily pads. Every day, the patch doubles in size. If it takes 48 days for the patch to cover the entire lake, how long would it take for the patch to cover half of the lake?

If you have answered 10 cents, 100 minutes and 24 days then **you are exhibiting System 1 thinking.**

If you have answered 5 cents, 5 minutes and 47 days then **you are exhibiting System 2 thinking.**

6.3.1 'SYSTEM 1' THINKING

System 1 thinking, also referred to as heuristics-based thinking, is a fast and intuitive style of making judgements. Broadly speaking, System 1 thinking is unconscious and we may not even be aware that we are using it, nor may we be aware of the assumptions we are making while using it!

Heuristics can be thought of as 'rules of thumb', mental shortcuts that allow us to make quick and reasonably reliable judgement calls particularly when under conditions of uncertainty.[3] These quick judgement calls substitute for the lengthy gathering and processing of all relevant

---

[2]Frederick, S. (2005). Cognitive reflection and decision making. *Journal of Economic Perspectives, 19,* 425–442.

[3]Tversky, A. & Kahneman, D. (1974). Judgment under uncertainty: Heuristics and biases. *Science, 185*(4157), 1124–1131.

information, which we tend not to do as individuals[4] and which can be challenging in uncertain, ambiguous and changing situations. Whilst heuristics can help facilitate our judgement, they can also open us up to potential sources of *bias*. We'll now consider a number of the main heuristics in detail, specifically *representativeness, availability* and *anchoring and adjusting*.[5]

THE REPRESENTATIVENESS HEURISTIC

The *representativeness heuristic* is used when making judgements on whether the situation we are currently experiencing, or the object at hand, is a member of a certain category. We do so by reasoning on how similar or typical the situation or object seems to be compared to others of that category.[6]

For example, when we meet a new person, we often try to 'place' or 'explain' this person so that we can better predict what we may expect from them. We may try to judge whether this person is similar to us in terms of values or in interests. In such cases, we make judgement calls about the person on the basis of the few attributes that are visible and available to us. This might include the way the person talks or their physical characteristics and appearance. As we do that, our brain (often unknown to us) is trying to think back to people we previously met that were similar to this person. Put differently, we try to judge how representative this new person is of our stereotyped image of people with the characteristics we are trying to make a judgement about.[7]

The main bias associated with this heuristic is that the features we pick up on and use to make our judgement calls are seldom the whole story. Linked to 'stereotyping', we may make choices based on generalisations (or external features) that do not in fact best depict the situation or object that we are seeking to understand.

FOOD FOR THOUGHT
THE REPRESENTATIVENESS HEURISTIC AND STEREOTYPING

As we've discussed, the representativeness heuristic allows us to make quick judgements based on visible attributes and how these relate to certain categories.

---

[4]Braisby, N. & Gellatly, A. (eds) (2005). *Cognitive Psychology*. Oxford: Oxford University Press Inc.

[5]Tversky & Kahneman, Judgment under uncertainty.

[6]Tversky, A. & Kahneman, D. (1973). Availability: A heuristic for judging frequency and probability. *Cognitive Psychology, 5*(2), 207–232; Kahneman, D. & Tversky, A. (eds) (2000). *Choices, Values, and Frames*. Cambridge: Cambridge University Press; Braisby & Gellatly, *Cognitive Psychology*.

[7]Kort, M. J. J. & Vermeulen, P. A. M. (2008). Entrepreneurial decision-makers and the use of biases and heuristics. In P. A. M. Vermeulen and P. L. Curseu (eds), *Entrepreneurial Strategic Decision-Making: A Cognitive Approach* (pp. 123–134). Cheltenham: Edward Elgar.

Spend a moment looking at the two pictures below. For each, consider:

How would you describe this person?	How would you describe this person?
what attributes stand out to you?	what attributes stand out to you?
what profession do you think this person works in?	what profession do you think this person works in?

Now spend a moment considering why you answered as you did. How has your own representativeness heuristic shaped your judgement?

when we try to classify individuals (or situations, or objects) we tend to simplify what we see and become more fixated on certain attributes. In this example, many people will assume that the person on the left works as an accountant or business professional due to the fact that he is wearing a suit and tie.

THE AVAILABILITY HEURISTIC

The *availability heuristic* is used when we make a judgement on the likelihood or the frequency of an event occurring. When making judgement calls about outcomes which are uncertain, we tend to search our memories for examples of similar situations we can readily recollect.[8] To do so, we use a number of memory search – or 'priming' – mechanisms; the ones we use will determine whether our memory search is more or less accurate.

Generally, these mechanisms result in four main biases,[9] including the *retrievability of instances bias*. Also called the *ease of recall bias*, this bias means that we tend to give a greater sense of importance to things that we can recall easily. The more vivid or recent[10] things are the more likely we are able to recall them.

Source: Pixabay

For example, if we asked you what form of transportation you find the riskiest and therefore scares you the most, you may well say you're more afraid to fly than to take a bus, train or to drive. The data in fact clearly shows that driving is statistically far more dangerous than flying, yet many more of us have a fear of flying than a fear or driving. So why are we more afraid of flying? Generally, air crashes are covered in-depth internationally by news outlets and they tend to stay very vivid in our memories for a long time. Car accidents, because they are so common, are less likely to be reported by national let alone international media, and any coverage they are given is short lived. Thus, the specifics of car accidents don't come to mind so easily unless we have been involved in one ourselves!

---

[8]Braisby & Gellatly, *Cognitive Psychology.*

[9]Tversky & Kahneman, Judgment under uncertainty.

[10]Bazerman, M. H. (2001). The study of 'real' decision making. *Journal of Behavioral Decision Making, 14*(5), 353–355.

The *anchoring and adjustment heuristic* is used when estimating the likelihood or value of something, starting – and adjusting – from an initial 'anchor point'.[11] Perhaps the most familiar situation where this applies is when bargaining at a market or shop. When the vendor quotes us a price, they are providing an anchor point on which the negotiation to follow will hang. We will then make an offer based on that anchor. For example, let's say we are at an antiques fair looking at a porcelain vase. We ask the vendor what price they want for it and they say $100. This is our anchor point. We may then try to bargain down to $80, with the vendor then asking for $95. In the end we may both settle on a price of $90.

The main bias associated with this heuristic relates to the fact that we tend to fixate on the anchor point and that the adjustments we make are usually minor or insufficient.[12] In our example of the vase, when the vendor asks for $100 we are unlikely to counter with an offer of $10. Why? Because we accept that the price quoted by the vendor ($100) is (more or less) the true value of the object. As a result, we tend not to deviate much from an anchor point even when we know that the value of an anchor is completely arbitrary.[13]

6.3.2 'SYSTEM 2' THINKING

If System 1 thinking is characterised by speed and intuition, System 2 thinking is the opposite. Deliberate and effortful, System 2 thinking is a conscious process where we are normally aware that we are engaged in judgement and that we are also aware of the assumptions informing our reasoning. This judgement style is also referred to as *analogical reasoning*.[14]

Just like in System 1's heuristic-based reasoning, in System 2's analogical reasoning we are still trying to make sense of a situation by drawing on previous knowledge and experience. A key difference exists in how we go about doing this. Instead of making quick (and often superficial) comparisons, this thinking style develops an *analogy* – a comparison between two things that helps us to explain or make sense of these things. The construction of these mental analogies takes time and effort and therefore the process is slower and more deliberate.[15] Importantly, to construct a useful analogy we often need to search our memories in a deeper and more detailed way, rather than grasping on to more vivid or recent events as

---

[11]Tversky & Kahneman, Judgment under uncertainty.

[12]Epley, N. & Gilovich, T. (2006). The anchoring-and-adjustment heuristic: Why the adjustments are insufficient. *Psychological Science, 17*(4), 311–318.

[13]Tversky & Kahneman, Judgment under uncertainty.

[14]Holyoak, K. J. (2012). Analogy and relational reasoning. In K. J. Holyoak & R. G. Morrison (eds), *The Oxford Handbook of Thinking and Reasoning* (pp. 234–259). Oxford: Oxford University Press.

[15]Jones & Casulli, International entrepreneurship.

we do in System 1. Importantly, we do not just consider how the current situation is *similar* to those previously experienced, but we also make an effort to consider the ways in which the current situation is *different* from what we have seen before.[16]

As we begin to 'map' our existing knowledge and experiences to the current situation, we do so in three different forms (please see example under section 6.3.3):

- *Attributional mapping.* Here we ask: 'To what extent are the attributes of the current situation similar to the ones I can recall? To what extent are they different?'
- *Relational mapping.* Here we ask: 'How are the relationships between attributes in this situation similar to the relationships between attributes in the situations I can recall? To what extent are they different?'
- *Systemic mapping.* Here we ask: 'How does the system in which the current situation exists function and how is that different from the systems I have previously experienced?'

The main problem associated with System 2 thinking is the time it may take to make a judgement, potentially leading to 'paralysis by analysis' and preventing us from taking action.

DEEP DIVE
THINKING, FAST AND SLOW

Systems 1 and 2 thinking have been popularised by the work of Nobel prize recipient Professor Daniel Kahneman. Professor Kahneman summarises these two judgement styles and their implications for decision making at **https://youtu.be/PirFrDVRBo4**

6.3.3 THE IMPLICATIONS OF SYSTEMS 1 AND 2 FOR ENTREPRENEURIAL THINKING AND ACTION

As we mentioned at the start of this chapter, there isn't a 'right' or 'wrong' judgement style to have – both System 1 and 2 styles have their strengths and their weaknesses.

In early research on entrepreneurial decision making, the prevailing view was that entrepreneurs (in this case defined as the owner–managers of ventures) were more likely to use System 1 thinking than non-entrepreneurs.[17] Later evidence, however, indicated that even

---

[16]Williams, D. & Grégoire, D. (2015). Seeking commonalities or avoiding differences? Re-conceptualizing distance and its effects on internationalization decisions. *Journal of International Business Studies, 46,* 253–284.

[17]Busenitz, L. W. & Barney, J. B. (1997). Differences between entrepreneurs and managers in large organizations: Biases and heuristics in strategic decision-making. *Journal of Business Venturing, 12*(1), 9–30.

non-entrepreneurs disregard factual evidence when making decisions, relying instead on heuristics based on their own experience.[18] Since we now know that value creation can come from individuals from all educational backgrounds (e.g., engineers, software developers, artists, etc.) and occupations, to say that entrepreneurs (or entrepreneurial people) use System 1 thinking over System 2 is likely untrue. Rather, we all use either System 1 and System 2 at some point, depending on our preferred reasoning style, our previous experience, and the task at hand.

System 1 allows us to make fast and intuitive judgements, responding quickly to opportunities as they arise. Yet this form of judgement can result in errors based on our own biases or our 'blind spots'. Those who produce innovative ideas and use heuristic-based reasoning can be so focused on the positives of their ideas that they are blind to the potential pitfalls – a phenomenon known as the *overconfidence bias.*[19] Overconfidence bias is associated with a promotion focus (which we encountered in Chapter 2) and can help when we choose to take the plunge with truly innovative ideas. However, it can be detrimental in later phases of the value creation process.[20] Crucially, we now know that System 1 thinking can also result in *innovator's bias,* a tendency to focus on the value that is being created and neglect the collateral damage that the innovative idea can create.[21]

System 2, on the other hand, allows us to make slower and more considered judgements. In doing so, we might miss opportunities or get caught up in analysis and delay acting. Yet, when we do take action, our judgements are less prone to error.

Consider the following illustrative scenario of System 1 and System 2 at play:

Two health and fitness enthusiasts want to find innovative ways for themselves and their fellow fitness lovers to consume health-boosting vitamins while on the go. Their research suggests that most people in their target market drink coffee daily as a habit, so they decide that tapping into the coffee drinking habit is an effective way to ingest more vitamins regularly. They invent a vitamin enriched cold blend coffee called 'Caffeinate your way to health'.[22] Whilst the drink does not taste quite like straight

[18]Buckley, P. J., Devinney, T. M. & Louviere, J. J. (2007). Do managers behave the way theory suggests? A choice-theoretic examination of foreign direct investment location decision-making. *Journal of International Business Studies, 38*(7), 1069–1094.

[19]Busenitz, L. W. & Lau, C. M. (1996). A cross-cultural cognitive model of new venture creation. *Entrepreneurship Theory and Practice, 20*(4), 25–40; Forbes, D. P. (2005). Are some entrepreneurs more overconfident than others? *Journal of Business Venturing, 20*(5), 623–640.

[20]Trevelyan, R. (2008). Optimism, overconfidence and entrepreneurial activity. *Management Decision, 46*(7), 986–1001.

[21]Reece, A., Eubanks, A. D., Liebscher, A. & Baumeister, R. F. (2022). Enforcing pragmatic future-mindedness cures the innovator's bias. *Journal of Applied Social Psychology, 53*(7), 542–554.

[22]This is a fictitious name given to a real start-up to protect the anonymity of those involved in this illustration.

coffee, the product is successful with the target market because the latter are prepared to compromise on the traditional taste of coffee for the benefit of having their daily fix of immune-boosting vitamins in a single, easy solution.

The start-up now needs further investment to grow so they pitch for funding from an investment syndicate. The syndicate is composed of about six individuals of mixed gender and physical fitness. However, none of the syndicate members is the intended target of the product in that none of them is a health and fitness fanatic. The syndicate gets a briefing on the target market and the product, followed by a tasting of the product. They now have to make a judgement call on whether this product is worthy of their investment, and they have a limited amount of time (in the order of 15 minutes) to make a decision following the pitch and the sampling.

Here is what a decision based on System 1 thinking looks like in this scenario:

One of the investors declares 'this does not taste like coffee. It's actually not particularly pleasant – I would never drink it (representativeness heuristic – failing to see that 'I' is not representative of the target market) instead of real coffee (anchoring and adjustment heuristic – benchmarking on the taste of coffee, which is not the priority for the intended target market), I don't think we should invest'. Then, turning to a fellow panellist, he asks 'What do you think, Rosie, would you drink this instead of coffee?' to which Rosie, who loves coffee more than fitness (confirmation bias – searches for support from someone likely to share his view), responds 'Yeah, I agree, this is not a substitute for coffee, really!'

OUTCOME – PANEL DECIDES NOT TO INVEST.

Here is what a decision based on System 2 thinking looks like in this scenario:

One of the investors declares: 'Personally I prefer the taste of traditional coffee to this. However, I am not the intended target market for this, so my priority on taste may be different from the priority of the target market, which is on the health benefits' (attributional mapping – taste versus benefit as top priority). He continues 'What I think works best in this sort of situation is, instead of going by our preferences, we should consider what evidence the founders have that the market prefers the health factor over the taste factor' (relational mapping – recalling how is it fair to proceed when our own experience is not relevant to making the decision). He adds 'Is there anyone who thinks that the market research in this case is still not telling us what we need to know?' (systemic mapping – could there be anything in how this industry works that makes market research not the whole story). The panel cannot think of anything that market research on preferences for taste versus health benefits could have missed out. Therefore, the panel decides to make the decision based on the market research available from the business founders. The research indeed confirms that health enthusiasts prioritise the health benefits over the authentic taste of coffee.

OUTCOME – PANEL DECIDES TO INVEST.

The examples above illustrate the importance of being aware of the limitations of System 1 thinking in some circumstances – namely, when quick judgement calls lead us to draw on irrelevant or only partially relevant information. However, System 1 and System 2 thinking do not always compete with one another for optimal performance. In fact, research tells us that their collaboration is linked to creative thinking.

The unconscious, mind-wondering, intuitive System 1 can make connections between seemingly unrelated facts and perspectives, thus generating new insights[23] – the so-called 'connecting the dots' that has been associated with entrepreneurial ideas.[24] Importantly, our System 1 thinking does that whilst we are not purposefully working on the problem we may get an idea for. Rather, this mind-wondering aspect of System 1 is active while we rest, sleep, or have our leisure time. System 1 stops at the insight that has been generated and passes the insight to the more effortful System 2 for refining, sense-checking and for turning the insight into a fully-fledged idea.[25]

Therefore, no one system is more important or efficient than the other. The critical thing is that we are aware of the thinking style we tend to gravitate towards and consider how this is going to help (or hinder) us in specific situations. In some cases, fast thinking is helpful, particularly if it taps into relevant information – as we will see from the Deep dive on expert intuition below. Other times, we must wonder whether our intuitive System 1 is biased by previous experiences that are not relevant to the current situation. Other times yet, our two systems will work together to identify and refine ideas.

DEEP DIVE
EXPERT INTUITION

Whilst we think of fast, intuitive System 1 as based on limited information, rapidity can indeed go hand in hand with access to a vast amount of experience-based information. This is called 'expert intuition' and has been observed in fast paced, continuing evolving environments where decisions may need to be made on the spot, yet carry dire consequences for human life, such as in nursing[26] and firefighting.[27]

---

[23]Norris, P. & Epstein, S. (2011). An experiential thinking style: Its facets and relations with objective and subjective criterion measures. *Journal of Personality, 79*(5), 1043–1080.

[24]Baron, R. A. (2006). Opportunity recognition as pattern recognition: How entrepreneurs 'connect the dots' to identify new business opportunities. *Academy of Management Perspectives, 20*(1), 104–119.

[25]Kellerman, G. R. & Seligman, M. E. (2023). *Tomorrowmind: Thriving at Work with Resilience, Creativity, and Connection—Now and in an Uncertain Future.* New York: Simon and Schuster.

[26]Benner, P. & Tanner, C. (1987). How expert nurses use intuition. *AJN The American Journal of Nursing, 87*(1), 23–34.

[27]Klein, G. (2008). Naturalistic decision making. *Human Factors, 50*(3), 456–460.

Daniel Kahneman explains what expert intuition is at **www.youtube.com/ watch?v=ksopQLMQsq8**

6.4 MAKING SENSE OF JUDGEMENTS

Once we've made a judgement and taken action, we try to make sense of our judgements by looking back 'in hindsight' on how events have unfolded. In doing so, we often can't help but evaluate the judgement call we took. Did we do the right thing? Did we miss something? Have we made a *mistake?*

When we are making a judgement call, regardless of whether we are adopting System 1 or System 2 thinking, we are trying to make the best choice we can given the information (or lack of information!) available to us. Generally, we do not set out with the intention to make poor decisions! Yet when we look back on what we have done, our knowledge, insight or perspective has likely changed and thus it becomes tempting for us to question whether we have made the right choice. Whilst reflecting on our thinking and action can be helpful, we do want to be careful about using the word *mistake.*

The word *mistake* implies blame – that we or someone else have done something wrong. This is not only problematic when we're working to create conditions of psychological safety where people feel free to try and potentially fail (see Chapter 8), but also feeds into our own fears of failure (see Chapter 5) and influences our ability to persist and be resilient in challenging situations (see Chapter 4). In situations of uncertainty, where we are exploring possibilities and creating new value, it is very probable that outcomes from our judgement will be what we anticipated. Thus, we need to accept that judgement calls made in good faith – and using the most appropriate information available to us – are the best we can do at the time.

CHALLENGING ASSUMPTIONS
THE DIFFICULTY OF JUDGEMENT CALLS

On 15 January 2009, an aircraft departing from New York City was struck by a flock of birds shortly after take-off. This bird strike caused the plane to lose power in both engines and the plane's pilots, Chesley 'Sully' Sullenberger and Jeffrey Skiles, had to decide what to do next.

Watch the following extracts from the emergency landing on the Hudson River on 15 January 2009. Please watch the videos in the order in which they are listed (1 to 5):

1. **https://youtu.be/wGEblErBJqw** (12:22)

2. **https://youtu.be/N1fVL4AQEW8** (3:30)

3. https://youtu.be/2njLFOOOftQ (3:04)

4. https://youtu.be/-GHYMpmxdaA (3:33)

5. https://youtu.be/A_HtGyOXA4c (3:16)

Now that you have watched the videos, please answer the following questions:

- what thinking style(s) did Sully use when making the judgement on where – and how – to land the plane?

- what did the inquiry simulation do differently to what Sully did in the emergency landing on the Hudson?

- what information did the inquiry simulators have that Sully did not have at the time of making a judgement call on where to land?

- How did this difference between understanding in hindsight and judgement at the time of the incident affect the inquiry's accusations against Sully?

6.5 SUMMARY AND NEXT STEPS

This chapter has considered the issue of judgement, a thinking style that underpins our decision making particularly when operating under uncertainty. We have considered the key elements of judgement – speed, relevance and awareness – and discussed how these manifest in two judgement styles. We've explored the differences between the fast and intuitive System 1 thinking and the slower and more deliberative System 2 thinking, considering both pros and cons when it comes to thinking and acting entrepreneurially. To reiterate, one form of thinking is not better than the other; the important thing is that we are aware of our own preferred style so that we can leverage its strengths or mitigate the potential biases or time-delays that it introduces. We'll revisit these preferences in Section 3, where we start to consider value creation beyond your own personal entrepreneurial thinking and action, exploring the importance of connecting, collaborating and communicating with others to explore possibilities and take action.

WHERE AM I NOW?
SYSTEM 1 VS SYSTEM 2 IN PRACTICE

Having worked through this chapter, you should now have a high-level appreciation of System 1 and System 2 thinking and judgement styles. Spend a few minutes reflecting on your own thinking style and record your thoughts below.

1. In which situations are you more prone to use System 1 thinking? Why? What do you use it for?

2. In which situations are you more prone to use System 2 thinking? Why? What do you use it for?

3. What patterns do you notice in your use of System 1 vs System 2 thinking?

6.6 CONTINUE YOUR LEARNING

The following activities are designed to support you on your learning journey, building on ideas introduced in this chapter. These can be completed at any time and in any order, although you may find it helpful to begin with the 'Check your understanding' activity before moving on.

CHECK YOUR UNDERSTANDING

1. Heuristics are reasoning shortcuts that allow us to make fast judgement calls.

   TRUE (It's true – please see section 6.3.1)

   FALSE

2. When we stereotype, we are using an availability heuristic.

   TRUE

   FALSE (It's false – please see section 6.3.1)

3. Anchoring and adjustment heuristics are often used in bargaining and negotiations.

   TRUE (It's true – please see section 6.3.1)

   FALSE

4. System 2 thinking is fast but sometimes inaccurate.

   TRUE

   FALSE (It's false – please see sections 6.3.1 and 6.3.2)

5. Entrepreneurs use System 1 thinking to respond quickly to opportunities.

   TRUE (It's true – please see section 6.3.3)

   FALSE

6. When entrepreneurs use System 1 thinking, they are especially prone to *overconfidence* and *innovators' bias*.

   TRUE (It's true – please see section 6.3.3)

   FALSE

FURTHER READING

1. **Thinking, Fast and Slow** by Daniel Kahneman
2. **Black Box Thinking: Why Some People Never Learn From Their Mistakes, But Some Do** by Matthew Syed
3. **Predictably Irrational** by Dan Ariely

COGNITIVE-BEHAVIOURAL REFLECTION
YOUR DECISION MAKING

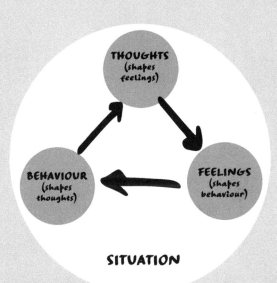

Drawing on the cognitive-behavioural framework introduced in Chapter 1, and the content of this chapter, consider a situation where you are currently in the process of making a significant decision. This could include, for example, deciding whether to buy a house, how to resolve a disagreement at work, choosing a degree programme, deciding whether to change your job or career, etc.

Why do this? This activity helps you to identify in more detail how your reasoning style plays out in a specific situation. Because we forget our reasoning pretty quickly after the fact, doing this activity as you go will give you a much more accurate picture of how you make decisions.

Step 1. Describe this situation in two to three sentences.

Step 2. Describe what factors you are considering to make this decision and why. [This is your **interpretation** of the situation, so make sure you explore it in sufficient detail. We'd recommend about four to eight sentences.]

Step 3. Describe the feelings this situation is generating. [These are your **emotions**. Be as specific as you can in your language, avoiding general terms like 'happy' or 'sad' in favour of more nuanced terms.]

Step 4. Considering this situation, and your cognitive and emotional considerations, where are you using your System 1 thinking and your System 2 thinking?

PRACTISING ENTREPRENEURIAL THINKING
REFINING YOUR JUDGEMENT

By now you will have figured out if you are more prone to System 1 or System 2 thinking.

If you find you are prone to use System 1, you may benefit from practising System 2, particularly in circumstances where you're unlikely to know enough to be able to trust your intuition or 'gut feel'. If you are more prone to use System 2, you may suffer from 'paralysis by analysis' and need to practise how to trust your gut instinct.

If you are prone to System 1, the next time you need to make a meaningful decision at home or at work, go through the following steps:

1. Develop a list of factors that are important in making this decision.

2. Talk to someone who knows more than you about the subject. Check to see if there are any factors that you should be considering that you are not.

3. Decide the relative importance of these factors, rank them in order of importance.

4. Find all information that underpins the factors.

For example, if you are interviewing someone for a new position at your company and were using your default System 1 thinking, you'd likely make a judgement based on your gut-feel about the applicant. To build your System 2 thinking, you can develop a list of attributes and skills that the candidate must have (e.g., years of experience, degree, good references, ability to get along with others). These could act as your initial factors. You would then need to speak with colleagues (for example, the people who will be working with the new hire) to see if there are other factors to be added and what their relative importance would be. You can then find sources of information and data to determine if the factors are met (or not).

If you are prone to System 2, the next time you need to make a meaningful decision at home or at work, go through the following steps:

1. Recognise that you are likely delaying making decisions by getting caught up in too many factors.

2. Limit the research you do and prioritise the top three factors.

3. Avoid seeking too many opinions.

4. Give yourself a deadline to make a decision, whether you feel ready or not.

For example, if you are interviewing someone for a new position at your company and were using your default System 2 thinking, you may build too complicated a list of criteria, take too long to make a decision and thus lose some good candidates (i.e., missing out on opportunities). To build your System 1 thinking, you can start by setting a firm and timely deadline for a decision. You could then decide a list of factors and, with the input of key voices only, prioritise the top three you will look for.

SECTION 3

CONNECTING, COLLABORATING AND COMMUNICATING WITH OTHERS

Having now considered what we mean by entrepreneurial thinking and mindset in Section 1 and the link between entrepreneurial activity and uncertainty in Section 2, we will now turn our attention to how we leverage our own entrepreneurial thinking and mindset to work with others. It is now widely recognised that in our current complex world with fast paced change we need to bring together people with diverse sets of skills, worldviews and experiences if we are to look beyond what is and seek to create new value.

Yet working with others is not always straightforward. When we collaborate, we need to be open to the views and inputs of others, which often requires us to rethink and challenge our assumptions, frames of reference and worldview. We may also need to challenge how we are collaborating, including **how** we are communicating and the assumptions we are making during these conversations. We also want to consider how we build the conditions that allow people to connect, collaborate and communicate as they work together to create value. This is particularly important given that entrepreneurial thinking and action is situated in conditions of uncertainty (think back to Section 2), where to create value we all need to step out of our 'comfort zones' and look at the world in a different way.

CHAPTER 7 will start by exploring what we mean by **entrepreneurial contexts** – the situations and places in which entrepreneurial thinking and action take place. we will consider how these differ from other 'business' contexts due to their inherent novelty, uncertainty and lack of charted paths for individuals and groups to follow. we will then revisit the notion of worldview, considering how our own assumptions and worldview not only shape our own beliefs as discussed in Chapter 3, but also how we think about and approach working with others.

CHAPTER 8 will then build on the understanding from Chapter 7 of entrepreneurial value creation as a collective activity to explore the role of empathy, trust and psychological safety in building productive relations within collaborative settings and with a range of stakeholders and audiences. we will consider the concepts of empathy and trust and discuss how they can manifest in entrepreneurial contexts to support value creation activity, specifically in the form of psychological safety among collaborative groups.

Finally, **CHAPTER 9** will consider the practicalities of how we communicate with others. we will explore in depth two of the main types of communication – verbal and non-verbal. Building on concepts from Chapters 6 and 8, we will consider the nature of verbal communication, including the encoding and decoding of messages, as well as non-verbal communication, particularly the impact that our facial expressions and tone of voice have on how others decode our messages.

CHAPTER 7

COLLABORATING AND WORKING WITH OTHERS IN ENTREPRENEURIAL CONTEXTS

"There's No 'I' in Team"

– Song by Taking Back Sunday

7.1 INTRODUCTION

As we noted in Chapter 1, we often have a mental image of the 'heroic' entrepreneurial individual working alone, having a moment of insight that allows them to create something that revolutionises our lives and the world. Yet, as we've discussed at length, that is not at all representative of reality! When we are looking to create value we are nearly always working with others. These may be people you work with formally (e.g., your employees, people on a team you build), people who will benefit from your value creation activity (e.g., customers, communities) and others in between. This activity may also take place in a range of different contexts.

When you reflect on what value might mean for you either professionally or personally, do you think about the contexts in which this may take place? Do you envision yourself working alone, or are you collaborating with others? In what way? Who might you want to – or need to – work with to achieve your goals?

This chapter will start by exploring what we mean by *entrepreneurial contexts* – the situations and places in which entrepreneurial thinking and action take pace. We will consider how these differ from other 'business' contexts due to their inherent novelty, uncertainty and lack of charted paths for individuals and groups to follow. For clarity, we will also consider what these contexts are *not*. We will then revisit the notion of worldview, considering how our own assumptions and worldview not only shape our own beliefs as discussed in Chapter 3, but also how we think about and approach working with others. We will consider a number of key worldviews and their underpinning assumptions, exploring the implications of collaborative entrepreneurial value creation activity.

After working through this chapter, you should be able to:

- identify a range of common entrepreneurial contexts
- communicate how and why entrepreneurial thinking manifests in entrepreneurial leadership and entrepreneurial teams within these contexts
- consider the impact of different worldviews on collaborative activity for value creation.

7.2 WORKING WITH OTHERS IN ENTREPRENEURIAL CONTEXTS

Whilst many people still associate entrepreneurial thinking and action with the creation of a new venture, the evidence base now shows us that entrepreneurial action takes place in a much wider range of **entrepreneurial contexts**. So what we do we mean by this term? The concept of a context is complex, but in terms of *entrepreneurial context* we consider spatial, temporal, institutional, social and societal elements and how they combine to influence 'where' and 'when' entrepreneurial thinking and action take place and 'who' this impacts.[1] 'Where' might cover physical space (e.g., customer-facing retail space, an industrial warehouse, a community centre), spatial location (e.g., a rural area, a deprived community, an upmarket shopping street, a post-conflict region) or institutional form (e.g., a new venture, an established organisation, a social enterprise, a public-sector institution like healthcare). Each of these elements can combine and intersect, so you may have, for example, an entrepreneurial context that comprises a café in a rural farm setting operating as a cooperative owned and managed by local farmers. In brief, entrepreneurial contexts are highly varied, despite what the media might tell us!

7.2.1 WHAT IS DIFFERENT ABOUT WORKING WITH OTHERS IN ENTREPRENEURIAL CONTEXTS?

Regardless of the specificities of each entrepreneurial context, what is common to all these forms of collective entrepreneurial activity is that there is likely to be a high degree of novelty as we seek to create value. Aligned to this, there are seldom clear guidelines on what to do and how to collaborate as we work together. As a result, we may find that the rules of engagement with others are 'fuzzy' when engaging in entrepreneurial activity.

For example, if we are trying to create new value in the context of an existing organisation, let's say by developing a new service, we might have some existing guidance or policies to draw on (e.g., a strategy document or market research data) but these are unlikely to (a) clearly map out all the potential situations we might encounter or (b) tell us how we should respond to each of these situations if they were to in fact occur. In other words, there is no 'handbook', corporate policy or other system that we can draw on that tells us where we stand, where others stand and what actions to take (or not take). The policies, handbooks, strategies or other guidance that we do have access to have been written based on how things *currently work*, which is fundamentally at odds with entrepreneurial thinking and action – where we seek to think beyond what is and to consider *what could be*, breaking away from the status quo.

---

[1]Brännback, M. & Carsrud, A. (2016). Understanding entrepreneurial cognitions through the lenses of context. In F. Welter & W. B. Gartner (eds), *A Research Agenda on Entrepreneurship and Context* (pp. 16–27). Cheltenham: Edward Elgar; Welter, F. (2011). Contextualizing entrepreneurship: Conceptual challenges and ways forward. *Entrepreneurship Theory and Practice, 35*(1), 165–184.

CHALLENGING ASSUMPTIONS
WHEN THERE IS NO HANDBOOK FOR INNOVATING WITH OTHERS

For those of us coming from environments that are organised and regulated through policies, handbooks and other guidance documents, it may be hard to imagine situations where there is no blueprint for collective entrepreneurial action. Thus, it may help to consider the following scenario:

A medium-sized private organisation wants to introduce significant processes innovation to create economic value for the company as well as personal value for employees by improving productivity and wellbeing on the job. Because there is no in-company expertise to introduce such innovation, the company identifies an opportunity to host an expert in the subject area on secondment from a much larger organisation. The secondee is responsible for developing and delivering the process innovation to the host organisation within the timescale of one year in order to then return to his home organisation. Notably, the secondee remains formally employed and paid by their home organisation for the duration of the secondment, and thus their employment is subject to the policies of their home organisation rather than the host organisation. The host organisation (the medium-sized company that wants to introduce the innovation) has its own employment policies, which are different from those of the home organisation of the secondee. The company cultures also turn out to be very different: the secondee home organisation has a culture based on trust, psychological safety and decentralised decision making. The host organisation, on the other hand, has a culture of suspicion of the unknown, top-down decision making and command and control implementation of decisions. The host organisation has no previous experience of doing similar projects or doing secondments and so there are no policies on how to hire and manage the secondee, and no guidance for them on how to use their time in the host company. Because the host organisation is under continued time pressures, there is never time to design a blueprint for working with the secondee. This leaves the secondee and the members of the host organisation with no alternative but to negotiate the implementation of the project based on interpersonal interactions. The latter prove to be challenging, given the different company cultures and the often-conflicting assumptions on which these are based. Key challenges stem from the different worldviews on working with others, whereby the host organisation is busy guarding itself from potentially opportunistic employees and deploying methods to monitor and control their efforts, whereas the secondee is working under assumption of trust as a guiding principle for introducing innovation. The secondee is also of the view that employee involvement and participation in the changes being introduced is key to the success of the innovation. This seems to be at odds with the host organisation's approach, where often decisions about implementing new processes are made without consulting with staff.

Crucially, there are underlying, opposite assumptions about both how the innovation process is to be approached and what its key outcomes are expected to be in practical terms. Negotiating these differences without the time, space and willingness to unpack the tensions in underlying assumptions and worldviews becomes increasingly strenuous for all involved until the innovation project stalls.

Furthermore, in entrepreneurial contexts we are more likely to work with people who are very different from us. This may be because their job specialisation is different (e.g., people from different functional divisions in an organisation), their educational background is different (e.g., a computer programmer may find themselves working alongside a surgeon on a project for digitisation of patient data), or because they are from different cultures (think of international students collaborating on university projects or company employees from different country offices of a multinational being assigned to a project).

In such scenarios it is more important than ever that we have the competencies that will enable us to work with others in a space without clear-cut written rules, being mindful and respectful of differences all the while remembering that we are all (or, at least we should be) pulling in the same direction. Sounds difficult? It is!

7.2.2 EXAMPLES OF ENTREPRENEURIAL CONTEXTS

Whilst entrepreneurial contexts vary widely, there are a number of contexts that you might encounter – or have already encountered – as you seek to create value. These include *start-ups*, *organisational entrepreneurship* and *entrepreneurial communities*. Despite all being contexts of high novelty and uncertainty, each brings their own opportunities and challenges, particularly when seeking to collaborate and work with others.

Start-ups A start-up is perhaps the most prominent example of an entrepreneurial context with low structure and high uncertainty. In the very early stages of a new venture, there is usually limited or no separation of different organisational functions, with founders taking on nearly all activities such as fundraising, prototyping, market research and so on. This also results in a flat organisational structure to support collaboration and communication, rather than a hierarchical one where a small number of people direct and manage the activities of a larger group of other individuals. A flat structure allows a start-up to respond to fluid and changing circumstances, when the decisions made at any given point may need to be revised or changed at short notice and courses of action altered accordingly.

Organisational entrepreneurship Organisational entrepreneurship refers to entrepreneurial thinking and action that takes place in established organisations. This can include combinations of within-company strategic new projects or spin-outs (*intrapreneurship*), continuous innovation in work practices (*continuous innovation*), and innovative, usually non-hierarchical, organisational structures.[2] It is defined as 'embodying entrepreneurial efforts that require organizational sanctions and resource commitments for the purpose of carrying out innovative activities in the form of product, process, and organizational innovations'.[3] In such entrepreneurial organisations, employees are encouraged to develop and use an entrepreneurial mindset,[4] as opposed to relying on specific instructions (or even micro-management) to tackle their job.

These organisational contexts share some of the features of start-ups. Although the organisation may be more established and its product/services/processes more developed, there are continuous changes to the status quo as both internal processes or external offerings change. Whilst this is the case for any organisation, the frequency and degree of changes to products, services or processes in entrepreneurial organisations is higher than in less

[2]Morris, M. H., Kuratko, D. F. & Covin, J. G. (2011). *Corporate Entrepreneurship & Innovation* (3rd edn). Northampton, MA: South-Western/Thomson Publishers.

[3]Hornsby, J. S., Kuratko, D. F. & Zahra, S. A. (2002). Middle managers' perception of the internal environment for corporate entrepreneurship: Assessing a measurement scale. *Journal of Business Venturing, 17*(3), 254–255.

[4]Kuratko, D. F., Hornsby, J. S. & McKelvie, A. (2023). Entrepreneurial mindset in corporate entrepreneurship: Forms, impediments, and actions for research. *Journal of Small Business Management, 61*(1), 132–154.

entrepreneurial contexts. Also, while established organisations may have separation of organisational functions (e.g., an operations team, a sales team) that start-ups do not, these divisions cannot afford to operate in a vacuum, but rather need to communicate and collaborate effectively because any changes to one function will affect all other functions. Especially in organisations with flatter organisational structures, the chain of command may not be as hierarchical as in traditional organisations.

Entrepreneurial communities We can also think of entrepreneurial contexts beyond the boundaries of an organisation (although there may well be organisations involved!). We can think of entrepreneurial communities, where organisations, individuals and wider groups collaborate to create value. This is particularly common when tackling social issues, which require a wide range of 'stakeholders' to join forces. Such an entrepreneurial context often exhibits a networked structure, encouraging entrepreneurial thinking and behaviour amongst all parties involved. A community may be located in a certain spatial location (see, for example, the Sciacca case in Chapter 11), or can transcend specific geographic boundaries based on core values and objectives as parties work together to tackle pressing issues that are not geographically constrained. When tackling social issues, or other 'wicked problems' that do not lend themselves to simple solutions or 'quick wins' (we'll discuss this further in Section 4), entrepreneurial communities also face significant novelty and uncertainty. Thus, an openness to change and a willingness to invest in the conditions necessary to encourage entrepreneurial thinking and action are critical.[5]

DEEP DIVE
EXPLORING ENTREPRENEURIAL COMMUNITIES

Sometimes entrepreneurial value creation activity doesn't happen within the boundaries of a single organisation, but rather as a result of partnerships or collective action across a range of institutions, organisations and stakeholders.

Consider the example of Trade Right International (TRI), a social enterprise founded by a husband and wife located in an area of significant deprivation just outside of Glasgow, UK that manufactures and sells handcrafted shea butter bath and body products under the label 'Carishea'. Yet the story is

---

[5]Lichtenstein, G. A., Lyons, T. S. & Kutzhanova, N. (2004). Building entrepreneurial communities: The appropriate role of enterprise development activities. *Journal of the Community Development Society, 35*(1), 5–24.

far more complex than it would appear at first. TRI aims to tackle poverty and help 'the world's poor by bringing employment, training and skills to enable them to work efficiently to bring prosperity to their household and community'. They also aim to 'help men from chaotic lifestyles to transition to become valuable contributors to the local community'.

TRI works in partnership with a range of businesses, charities, non-profits and government organisations to deliver on its goal to create value for individuals and communities. For example, they work with local development organisations in Ghana to support local women to collect shea fruits and process them into shea butter, providing income during a time of year when other income can be scarce. This income allows women to support their families, particularly covering education and medical fees. The shea butter produced in Ghana is then shipped to Glasgow where, again working in partnership with institutions such as the Scottish Prison Service and drug rehabilitation charities, the shea butter is turned into bath and body products by men who are recovering from drug or alcohol abuse, or who are reintegrating into the community after serving time in prison. TRI provides them with training and mentoring to build their employability skills, as well as helping build a sense of self as they transition back into their local communities.

Sources: https://traderightinternational.com/site/; www.carishea.com/

WHERE AM I STARTING FROM?
YOUR OWN ENTREPRENEURIAL CONTEXT

Spend a few minutes reflecting on your current thoughts on what value creation will mean for you and what context(s) this is likely to take place in. Record your thoughts below.

1. What are your current thoughts on value creation? What will this mean in your personal life? Your professional life?

....

....

2. what context(s) is this value creation activity likely to take place in?

3. what features of this context do you think will be important in supporting your value creation efforts?

4. what features of this context might get in the way of your value creation efforts?

7.2.3 HOW ENTREPRENEURIAL THINKING AND BEHAVIOUR MANIFESTS IN ENTREPRENEURIAL CONTEXTS

Having considered a number of entrepreneurial contexts – and remembering that this is by no means an exhaustive list – we can now consider how entrepreneurial thinking and behaviour manifests in these contexts characterised by novelty and uncertainty. When considering how this relates to communicating and collaborating with others, we can consider entrepreneurial thinking and behaviour as foundations for *entrepreneurial leadership* as well as *entrepreneurial teams*.

Entrepreneurial leadership is often found in organisations where employees are encouraged and supported to produce solutions and ideas, as well as organise the means to execute them. This could take place in an organisational or community context just as easily as it could in a start-up context! Entrepreneurial leadership places emphasis on removing obstacles and supporting employees to success, rather than more traditional 'command and control' models of leadership. To do so, entrepreneurial leaders make it their priority to boost employees' morale and confidence, which are recognised to lead to better outcomes. Crucially, entrepreneurial leaders have a lot of tolerance for the mistakes that others are likely to make while trying novel approaches and seek to develop spaces in which people can try, fail and learn (we'll discuss the concept of *psychological safety* further in Chapter 8). They reward innovative action over the use of tried and tested approaches and penalise inaction rather than mistakes.

An example often quoted is that of Apple, which is reported to have built its success on entrepreneurial culture and the entrepreneurial leadership it advocates at every level.[6] Think back to Philip's story in Chapter 2, on his own experience of working within Apple's entrepreneurial environment. Entrepreneurial leaders understand that, in order to capitalise on opportunities to create new value, they have to lead their people towards a shared vision whilst, at the same time, empower them to come up with ideas and take initiative towards the opportunity identified.[7]

FOOD FOR THOUGHT
ARE YOU AN ENTREPRENEURIAL LEADER?

In your professional life you may hold – or have held – a leadership role. Have you ever considered your own leadership style and whether you were exhibiting the behaviours of an **entrepreneurial leader**? You could also apply this exercise to your current leader (or boss, or manager)...

Consider the statements below and tick (a) those that you think apply.

I / my leader...

Bolster(s) people's confidence in their creative potential ☐

Take(s) pride in people's work and accomplishments ☐

Praise(s) people's creative work ☐

Publicly praise(s) people's creative efforts even if they aren't successful ☐

Stand(s) up for the innovative efforts of others ☐

Encourage(s) people to collaborate with others at work ☐

Encourage(s) people to communicate openly with individuals in other departments ☐

Stress(es) the importance of sharing ideas among colleagues ☐

---

[6]Lashinsky, A. (2015). Apple's Tim Cook leads different. *Fortune*, 26 March. Available at: http://fortune.com/2015/03/26/tim-cook/

[7]Renko, M., El Tarabishy, A., Carsrud, A. L. & Brännback, M. (2015). Understanding and measuring entrepreneurial leadership style. *Journal of Small Business Management, 53*(1), 54–74.

Encourage(s) people to set goals for innovation and improvements ☐

Encourage(s) people to challenge current approaches as the 'status quo' ☐

Work(s) persistently to secure resources needed for people to be innovative in their work ☐

Reward(s) people for their creative work ☐

Serve(s) as a role model for creative ideas and solutions to problems ☐

Demonstrate(s) a passion for my/their work ☐

Communicate(s) a vision of the future of the business/project/work/task ☐

If you have ticked most of these boxes, you (or your leader) are exhibiting the characteristic behaviours of an entrepreneurial leader.[8]

1. How do you feel about these results?

| |
| |
| |

2. What do they help you to understand about yourself or your leader?

| |
| |

In entrepreneurial contexts entrepreneurial thinking and behaviour may also manifest in *entrepreneurial teams*. An entrepreneurial team is a group of individuals that share a common goal and that achieve the goal by combining individual entrepreneurial actions.[9] Being an entrepreneurial team does not imply that activity is taking place within a particular entrepreneurial context (e.g., a start-up); they can emerge and thrive within, across or outside existing organisations and communities. In order to work effectively together, entrepreneurial teams need to appreciate that the potential outcomes of any

---

[8]Renko et al., Understanding and measuring entrepreneurial leadership style.

[9]Harper, D. A. (2008). Towards a theory of entrepreneurial teams. *Journal of Business Venturing, 23*(6), 613–626.

course of action is not fully predictable (e.g., that they are operating under uncertainty), that any rewards for the team's collective efforts have to satisfy the expectations of all team members.[10] The team also needs to acknowledge 'co-power', which means that individuals in the team understand that through an appropriate combination of actions they collectively can make the desired outcome happen.

This sense of understanding hinges on the worldview of team members (think back to Chapter 3) and how this shapes their worldview when it comes to collaborating with others (we'll come to this shortly in section 7.3). Linked to worldview, team members need to be able to appreciate the perspective of those who see things in a different way. This means taking time to develop *empathy* and *perspective taking* skills, which we will delve into in Chapter 8. It also means ensuring constant and effective *communication*, so that everyone is empowered to understand and act upon the frequent changes required, something we will look at further in Chapter 9.

7.2.4 WHAT WORKING WITH OTHERS IN ENTREPRENEURIAL CONTEXTS IS NOT

As with many of the ideas we have covered thus far, it can be just as helpful to think about what something is *not*. This is particularly important when considering what collaborating and working with others in entrepreneurial contexts entails. Again, we may have a mental image of what we 'should' do, or what entrepreneurial companies 'always do', which may or may not match up to reality.

First of all, working collaboratively to create value does not mean a free-for-all! While the absence of clear-cut rules, policies and procedures and the focus on personal initiative may lead us to think that entrepreneurial behaviour in groups and teams means that everyone can just do what they want, nothing could be further from the truth. Most of the focus on entrepreneurial teams is, in fact, about collaborating effectively within an agreed set of boundaries or structures to create synergies. When those boundaries don't exist, it's up to the team to identify, define and uphold them.

Linked to this, collaborative entrepreneurial thinking and action also does not mean a lack of shared goals or objectives. Quite the opposite! Whilst the means and/or the ends in any entrepreneurial context may not be fully clear at the outset (or even during the process of value creation itself), there must be a 'vision' or a 'purpose' that is shared by everyone involved. When the vision is not 'shared' – that is, not everyone buys into it – the conditions required for entrepreneurial value creation will most likely not be met.

---

[10]Zizzo, D. & Tan, J. (2003). *Game Harmony as a Predictor of Cooperation in 2 X 2 Games*. Oxford University Department of Economics Discussion Paper No. 151.

7.3 HOW PERSONAL WORLDVIEW SHAPES COLLABORATION

When considering how we can collaborate and work with others to create value we need to revisit the idea of worldview. Whilst we spoke about this in relation to ourselves and our frames of reference in Chapter 3, we also need to consider how our assumptions about the world shape how we engage in collaboration. When working in any social context, we as individuals tend to revert to our assumptions and worldview about others, particularly if the people we are working with are new to us or the environment in which we are collaborating is new (think back to the Challenging assumptions box at the beginning of this chapter!). We are not normally aware of this, nor are we aware of any assumptions that this might cause us to (inadvertently) make, including that others view the world in the exact same way that we do! As we discussed in Chapter 3, no worldview is inherently positive or negative. However, we need to recognise that when our own worldview is different from the worldview of others it can create misunderstandings and challenges. We thus want to familiarise ourselves with a range of key worldviews that relate to how we engage and collaborate with others,[11] specifically the *opportunism*, *reciprocity*, *Darwinian* and *collaboration vs competition* worldviews. Once we're familiar with these, we can then consider how they shape the assumptions that we (or even others) might be making about working collaboratively, helping us to develop our self-awareness when it comes to our interactions with others in entrepreneurial contexts.

It is also worth noting that these worldviews are not binary and set. For example, when considering whether we view others as opportunistic, we are unlikely to be opportunistic all the time. Rather, our expectation that others may take advantage may sit somewhere in the middle, and shift depending on different sets of circumstances. We are thus considering the degree to which we identify with each of these worldviews and in which circumstances, rather than if we identify with them or not.

7.3.1 OPPORTUNISM WORLDVIEW

When engaging with others, some of us adopt an 'opportunism'[12] worldview. Originating in the field of behavioural economics, the notion of opportunism describes the need to account for flaws in others' intentions and behaviours and thus the need on our part to exercise a degree of 'circumspection and distrust'.[13] In this sense, it is important to appreciate that

---

[11]Drawing on fields of research, including economics, anthropology, sociology and biology.

[12]Williamson, O. E. (1975). *Markets and Hierarchies: Analysis and Antitrust Implications: A Study in the Economics of Internal Organization.* University of Illinois at Urbana-Champaign's Academy for Entrepreneurial Leadership Historical Research Reference in Entrepreneurship.

[13]Williamson, O. E. (1993). Opportunism and its critics. *Managerial and Decision Economics, 14,* 97–107.

'opportunism' is different from 'seizing opportunities' for value creation. The latter refers to the (usually positive) expectation that an idea can turn into an opportunity for value creation. On the other hand, the opportunistic worldview refers to the expectation that other individuals will take advantage of a situation, usually to the detriment of someone or something else. The latter is, therefore, inherently negative.

Those of us who assume opportunistic behaviour in others are less likely to rely on non-written agreements such as 'taking someone's word', preferring more formal documentation of discussions and agreements. In a work environment, leaders with opportunistic worldviews prefer to adopt 'command and control' methods to track people's efforts rather than trust and delegation methods.

However, as we discussed at the beginning of the chapter, in entrepreneurial context we work in ambiguous spaces where we don't always have written rules or written contracts as to what is to be done or a blueprint for how we are going to get there. Under such circumstances, a degree of trust is necessary to replace formal agreements and to grant individuals in projects the necessary freedom to progress on the project as they see fit. Under assumptions of opportunism, there is likely going to be limited trust. As we will discuss further in Chapter 8, trust is an important foundation of working together on entrepreneurial value creation. We are still to see evidence, therefore, that embracing an opportunistic worldview can ever be conducive to value creation.

FOOD FOR THOUGHT
OPPORTUNISM WORLDVIEW AND REMOTE WORKING DURING COVID-19

When the world went into lockdown during the height of the Covid-19 pandemic, there was a sudden closure of workplaces and many office-based employees switched nearly overnight from working in the office to working from home. Organisations and leaders responded in different ways to this transition.

Those operating under an opportunistic worldview made a number of assumptions about employees' abilities to remain productive and complete work to the expected standard, in many cases assuming that employees would not work as hard from home and would spend their time watching TV. Or, as Elon Musk put it in his infamous tweet, 'pretending to work'. These leaders and organisations started implementing various forms of surveillance and monitoring for remote workers, for example requiring that webcams be on at all times, using software to track time spent away from the keyboard, and expecting employees to be on day-long Skype or Zoom for accountability.

1. How do you think such an opportunistic worldview may affect employees?

2. What effect do you think such a worldview had on employees' willingness to go the extra mile for their company during the Covid-19 pandemic?

3. What effect do you think an opportunistic worldview had on employees' ability to identify opportunities for new value creation?

7.3.2 RECIPROCITY WORLDVIEW

The notion of reciprocity stems from cultural anthropology[14] and refers to the idea of offering goods or labour to others in expectation that the offer will be reciprocated, either immediately or at some other point in time.[15] In modern societies, we may signal to someone that we embrace the reciprocity worldview when we say 'I owe you' in response to an act of service they have done for us. On the other hand, if we do not embrace a balanced reciprocity worldview, or we view the offer as a gift,[16] we may believe that we have not entered a moral obligation with the person and thus will never reciprocate. The other person may, in turn, come to view our lack of reciprocity as ungrateful or even exploitative. This highlights how this worldview, when different from that of others, can create unfavourable conditions in working together, particularly in unstructured entrepreneurial contexts. In such situations, we are already grappling with uncertainty stemming from several other sources and not knowing whether we should expect reciprocity from others can add another layer of uncertainty. In such situations, it's not the reciprocity worldview (or it's opposite) that is detrimental *per se*. Indeed, this worldview is not intrinsically positive or negative for entrepreneurial value creation with others and one may find evidence of both working well in different settings. What may be detrimental is not being aware of working with others who are operating under different assumptions about it and the misunderstandings that are likely to ensue if these assumptions are not explicitly shared and managed.

DEEP DIVE
RECIPROCITY IN CHINESE NETWORKS (GUĀNXI, 关系)

The notion of reciprocity is at the core of the Chinese notion of **guānxi (关系)**, a network of personal connections built on trust and mutual (reciprocal) obligations to help get things done.

The following article in **Forbes** magazine illustrates how, when reciprocity is culturally assumed, someone who does not share this worldview can run into difficulties: **www.forbes.com/sites/michaelcwenderoth/2018/05/16/how-a-better-understanding-of-guanxi-can-improve-your-business-in-china/?sh=acd647a5d85b]**

---

[14]Sahlins, M. (1965). On the sociology of primitive exchange. In M. Banton (ed.), *The Relevance of Models for Social Anthropology* (pp. 139–236). London: Tavistock.

[15]Graeber, D. (2001). *Toward an Anthropological Theory of Value: The False Coin of Our Own Dreams*. New York: Palgrave.

[16]Sahlins, M. (1972). *Stone Age Economics*. Hoboken, NJ: Taylor & Francis.

7.3.3 DARWINIAN WORLDVIEW

Most of us will likely be familiar with Charles Darwin's work on 'survival of the fittest' in the evolutionary biology sphere.[17] We may be less familiar with the notion of Social Darwinism,[18] which draws on Darwin's notions as developed in the biological world and applies them to people in social situations. A Social Darwinist worldview consists of believing that the strongest in society acquire more power and resources, whereas the weak in society have less power and resources.

What being 'strong' or being 'weak' means depends on context and there is no definitive list: being strong in some environments may mean being highly competent at something, having access to networks, or having other characteristics that facilitate an individual or group's success, however that may be defined. When we first meet a new group of people and we find ourselves comparing our strengths to the perceived strengths of others, we are implicitly assuming the principles of Social Darwinism. We are trying to gauge whether, in the group, we are going to be considered a strong link or a weak link.

Those who hold a Darwinist worldview in their interactions with others tend to assume that the weak links in a group or a community hold everyone else back and therefore are best removed if progress is to be made. On the other hand, those who assume a more humanitarian worldview are prepared to compromise on the group outcomes for the benefit of moving forwards together, regardless of individual strengths or weaknesses. The latter worldview believes in prioritising supporting the weak in the group, community or society first and foremost and potentially at the expense of the best possible outcome for a subsection of the group.

What does this mean in entrepreneurial value creation? The very roots of economic theory of entrepreneurship is one of creative destruction,[19] whereby creating innovative solutions that are fitter for purpose compared to the previous will make existing solutions obsolete. Therefore, when looking at entrepreneurial ideas for innovation, a Darwinian worldview seems to hold true. However, when it comes to the people we are working with for value creation, things look very different. It is increasingly acknowledged that innovative ideas can come from the most unlikely individuals. Indeed, diverse sets of abilities, backgrounds and skills are increasingly being recognised as the main ingredients for identifying solutions to ambiguous and complex problems. Seen in this light, there isn't an easily identifiable

---

[17]Darwin, C. (2004). *On the Origin of Species* [1859]. London: Routledge; Claeys, G. (2000). The 'survival of the fittest' and the origins of social Darwinism. *Journal of the History of Ideas, 61*(2), 223–240.

[18]Williams, R. (2000). Social Darwinism. In J. Offer (ed.), *Herbert Spencer: Critical Assessment* (pp. 186–199). London/New York: Routledge.

[19]Schumpeter, J. A. (2013). *Capitalism, Socialism and Democracy*. London: Routledge.

'weak link' that the group should shed because, in order to establish who is best at solving the problem, the problem should have defined parameters. Under conditions of uncertainty and ambiguity that is never the case. Under conditions of uncertainty, the solution to the problem can be anyone's game. Therefore, when we think of collaborating with others for value creation, there is currently no evidence of the value of adopting a Darwinian worldview. On the other hand, there is some evidence that an openness to consider everyone's ideas is conducive to innovation.[20]

7.3.4 COLLABORATION VS COMPETITION WORLDVIEW

Another dimension of our worldview refers to the general assumption we make about whether it is better to *collaborate* or to *compete* with others. Aspects of collaboration versus competition have been theorised in economic game theory,[21] which has attempted to build mathematical models of 'zero-sum games' and 'non-zero-sum games'. What zero-sum games imply is that there can only be one winner out of multiple individuals (or 'agents', in economic terms). Therefore, if one person wins, the others will necessarily all have to lose. The implication of zero-sum games is that individuals are always in competition with one another, and that collaboration is not possible. On the other hand, non-zero-sum games (as illustrated in the famous thought experiment *prisoner's dilemma*[22]) allow for individuals to win together through cooperation. While they may not each get 100% of what they want, they may still get more through cooperating than through competing. This reasoning also aligns to the assumption we make about the resources available to us. Do we assume scarcity of resources and thus are driven by competition, or do we assume sufficient resources and therefore emphasise collaboration? [23]

From a value creation perspective, some would suggest that groups where there is no competition may be driven to groupthink and, therefore, come up with less creative, divergent ideas.[24] On the flipside, as we already mentioned above and will return to in Chapter 8, unhealthy competition leading to lack of trust and psychological safety can undermine the sound implementation of ideas and, ultimately, the creation of the intended value.

---

[20]Østergaard, C. R., Timmermans, B. & Kristinsson, K. (2011). Does a different view create something new? The effect of employee diversity on innovation. *Research Policy*, 40(3), 500–509.

[21]Myerson, R. B. (1991). *Game Theory: Analysis of Conflict*. Cambridge, MA: Harvard University Press.

[22]Poundstone, W. (1993). *Prisoner's Dilemma*. New York: Anchor.

[23]Sahlins, *Stone Age Economics*.

[24]Janis, I. (1972). *Victims of Groupthink: Psychological Studies of Policy Decisions and Fiascoes*. Boston, MA: Houghton Miflin Company.

DEEP DIVE
PRISONER'S DILEMMA

This famous thought experiment challenges two rational players to determine whether to compete or collaborate:

Two criminals, Criminal A and Criminal B, belong to a gang and are arrested and imprisoned. They each could face a sentence of up to ten years in prison. Each criminal is placed in solitary confinement and so are unable to communicate (conspire) about what to say in court.

Unfortunately for the Police, they do not have enough evidence to convict either prisoner to the full sentence of 10 years in prison. The Police thus plan to sentence each prisoner to two years in prison on a lesser charge, but offer each prisoner a bargain: if one criminal confesses to the crime, betraying the other, they will be pardoned and free to leave, while the other criminal must serve the entirety of the full 10 year sentence instead of just two years for the lesser charge.

	B stays silent	B betrays
A stays silent	2 / −2	0 / −10
A betrays	−10 / 0	−5 / −5

Given the scenario, there are four possible outcomes:

1. If A and B both remain silent, they will each serve the lesser charge of 2 years in prison.
2. If A betrays B but B remains silent, A will be set free while B serves 10 years in prison.

3. If A remains silent but B betrays A, A will serve 10 years in prison and B will be set free.

4. If A and B both betray the other, they will share the sentence and serve 5 years each.

Whilst options 2 and 3 would be the best for one of the two prisoners, option 1 would be the best outcome for them together. Interestingly, if each of them attempts to get the best possible outcome for them alone (option 4) by confessing and betraying the other, both of them will be worse off. Under these circumstances, therefore, not knowing what the other prisoner will say, each one of them is better off not betraying and collaborating (option 1).

This principle can be seen in action through the notion of John Nash's equilibrium, as portrayed in the movie 'A Beautiful Mind': https://youtu.be/LJS7lgvkGZM

PRACTISING ENTREPRENEURIAL THINKING
YOUR OWN PRISONER'S DILEMMA

Think of a scenario you are currently facing (at work, in your studies, at home) that has the same characteristics of the Prisoner's Dilemma. This could be, for example a joint project either for coursework (at university) or for a client (at work). The scenario should be such that:

• you cannot anticipate what the other people involved will or will not do

• you are aware that, if they 'betray' – i.e., they do not do what they said they would – you will personally be worse off

• you are also aware that if you 'betray' them by not doing what you said you would do, both of you may potentially be worse off, unless they stick to the plan and do what was agreed.

1. Map out all the possible outcomes for this scenario based on those illustrated above for the prisoner's dilemma.

....

....

....

2.   Which option do you feel most comfortable taking? Which one will you choose?

....

....

....

3.   In making this choice, are you working under assumptions of:
- collaboration (choosing the option where you maximise overall win and minimise overall loss) or
- competition (choosing the option that potentially maximises your own personal win, risking potential loss)?

....

....

....

7.4 OTHER FACTORS THAT AFFECT HOW WE WORK WITH OTHERS

As you have been thinking about your own worldview when it comes to working with others, you may have observed that your thoughts and assumptions are not clear cut; they may vary depending on the circumstance or situation, or the specific group of people you are engaging with. Generally, our assumptions may vary depending on a number of factors including how familiar we are with the people involved, our understanding of their cultural norms, the time available to support collaboration and how any 'rewards' resulting from collaborative activity are structured.

When we have prior shared history or *familiarity* with the people involved in a project or other endeavour, we have some information to go by when starting on a new collaborative activity. For example, we know whether there is shared trust or, vice versa, whether there is a history of broken trust. We may also understand a person's unique skill set, how they like to work, what they consider their strengths to be, etc. Importantly, familiarity does not just come from knowing a specific person – it can also be felt when we meet people that we consider to be 'like us'. Consider, for example, the immediate sense of connection that you feel with someone from your same country or hometown that you meet in an international setting, or when you meet someone on your course who has the same education or training that you do (e.g., an accountancy degree, or experience in coding using Python or C++), perhaps unlike everyone else in the room.

Thinking back to Chapter 6, we discussed the role of heuristics such as 'representativeness'. When we meet new people, we are quickly trying to establish whether they are 'like us' or different from us. In the absence of lots of information on the person, we look for cues from them (the way they talk, what they say, how they present themselves, what we know of them, perhaps from their CV) to establish whether they are 'representative' of our 'in-group'. Are they also an engineer? Are there things we have in common (e.g., nationality, education, interests)? Do we live in a similar area? Do they also have children? A lack of familiarity may lead to *othering*, when we deem the person we just met 'not one of us'. Entrepreneurial endeavours will often require working with people who are different from us – people from other countries, cultures, professional specialisms, socio-economic background, etc. Thus, being able to build connections and develop familiarity with people we initially perceive as being 'not like us' or 'others' is an important foundation of entrepreneurial action, something we'll come back to further in Chapter 8 when we look at the concept of empathy.

An element to consider as we seek to develop familiarity rather than 'othering' is that of *cultural norms*. Every culture has a different focus when it comes to value creation based on whether it prioritises the *collective group* (*collectivism*) or the *individual* (*individualism*).[25] In collectivist cultures, the priority is holding the community together and striving for the benefit of the group. In individualistic cultures, the focus is on the rights, freedoms and concerns of each individual person. Because collectivist countries strive for unity, selflessness and altruism are encouraged and rewarded. On the other hand, individualistic cultures value personal freedom, self-determination and individual achievement.[26] The implications of collectivism and individualism are far reaching and span international politics, economic policy and many other areas that go well beyond the remit of this book. When it comes to creating value together though, cultural norms can impact the assumptions we make about working with others and what the outcomes of that work are if not addressed at the outset of any collaborative activity.

DEEP DIVE
COLLECTIVISM VS. INDIVIDUALISM

As we discussed in Chapter 4, much of our understanding of national cultural and related cultural preferences, perceptions and behaviours stems from the work of Professor Geert Hofstede. From this, we have a better understanding of national preferences in terms of collectivism and individualism.

---

[25]Hofstede, G. (1984). *Culture's Consequences: International Differences in Work-Related Values* (Vol. 5). London: Sage.

[26]Ibid.

COLLABORATING AND WORKING WITH OTHERS IN ENTREPRENEURIAL CONTEXTS

Visit the Country Comparison function of the Hofstede Insight webpage, available at **www.hofstede-insights.com/country-comparison/**. Here you can type in the name of your own national context as well as other countries you want to compare with. Of the dimensions shown on the graph, pay particular attention to the one labelled 'Individualism'.

Is your context of operation highly individualistic?

Does your experience in this context match the Hofstede scores?

Note that, within the broader context of country attitudes to individualism vs collectivism, the specific group of people you are collaborating with may well have a different attitude than what is reflected in country-level attitudes!

Given the complexity of working with people with different assumptions, worldviews and cultural norms, it can often take considerable time to establish effective collaborations (think of the classic forming, storming, norming and performing stages of group formation).[27] Thus *time availability* becomes a critical factor when thinking about how we work with others in entrepreneurial contexts. In our current society, many of us lament our lack of time – we have so much to do and so few hours in which to do so! Research now talks of 'time famine'[28] in modern organisations and highlights that our perceptions of lack of time are the main predictor for failing to adequately consider the needs of others in our interpersonal interactions. In theory, we generally understand the importance of taking the time to understand others' needs and helping them when necessary. Yet in practice, we often feel that we can't 'afford the time' in the moment.[29] But how much time do we actually *need*? And what is the (time) cost to us of not spending adequate time at the start of our collaborations? After all, we hardly ever stop to think of the amount of time we spend in untangling misunderstandings, bad feeling or other issues arising from not taking time 'in

[27]Tuckman, B. W. (1965). Developmental sequence in small groups. *Psychological Bulletin, 63,* 384–399.

[28]Perlow, L. A. (1999). The time famine: Toward a sociology of work time. *Administrative Science Quarterly, 44*(1), 57–81.

[29]Riess, H., Kelley, J. M., Bailey, R. W., Dunn, E. J. & Phillips, M. (2012). Empathy training for resident physicians: A randomized controlled trial of a neuroscience-informed curriculum. *Journal of General Internal Medicine, 27*(10), 1280–1286.

the moment', for example getting to know our fellow team members, their assumptions and worldview.

Part of these conversations should consider how any 'rewards' resulting from collaborative activity are structured. Linked to collaboration vs competition worldview, the *structure of the reward* is an important and often paradoxical aspect of working with others,[30] particularly in western societies. Is the reward being created for the whole group, or for specific individuals within the group? The answer, of course, depends on what we consider to be the *reward*. Consider the example of a football match. The reward is a clear one: winning the match. Is the reward of value to everyone in the team? Yes, we may argue. However, on closer inspection, beyond the winning and losing of the match, there are other factors at play. Who gets the 'credit' for winning the match? All the team or a few individuals in particular? It would be fair to say that the post-match press coverage will focus on the person who scored the most goals or made the successful penalty kick, as opposed to all of the other players who facilitated the goal scoring (and prevented goals from the opposing team) throughout the match.

Similarly, in many organisations, career progression, pay and other 'rewards' are at the individual level, yet the immediate reward of creating value through a project (e.g., a new product) requires everyone to work collaboratively.[31] In many workplaces, people achieve new value by working in teams, yet the preference remains to pick out the 'star players' and reward them individually, resulting in what is known as the team paradox.[32] Thus, aligning broader reward structures when seeking to encourage collaboration to support the creation of value is an important consideration when we ask people to work together.

7.5 SUMMARY AND NEXT STEPS

In this chapter we have considered entrepreneurial thinking and action for value creation as a collaboration between individuals in a range of entrepreneurial contexts. These contexts can include structured organisations such as start-ups or established firms, as well as network-based collaborations that exist across institutions, organisations and spaces. When we work in these contexts we continue to face inherent novelty and

[30]Bamberger, P. A. & Levi, R. (2009). Team-based reward allocation structures and the helping behaviors of outcome-interdependent team members. *Journal of Managerial Psychology, 24*(4), 300–327.

[31]Mossholder, K. W., Richardson, H. A. & Settoon, R. P. (2011). Human resource systems and helping in organizations: A relational perspective. *Academy of Management Review, 36*(1), 33–52.

[32]Yang, T., Bao, J. & Aldrich, H. (2020). The paradox of resource provision in entrepreneurial teams: Between self-interest and the collective enterprise. *Organization Science, 31*(6), 1336–1358.

uncertainty (see section 7.2) and need to reconcile our own preferences, beliefs, attitudes, assumptions and worldviews with those of others. We need to be aware of, and consider, how the worldviews of others shape their beliefs about – and approaches to – working

with others and we have explored a number of key worldviews and related factors. These considerations will form the foundation for our discussions on empathy and psychological safety, which we'll explore in detail in Chapter 8.

WHERE AM I NOW?
WORLDVIEW

Having worked through this chapter, you have had a chance to consider value creation as a largely collaborative activity that takes place in a range of different entrepreneurial contexts. As we've discussed, however, how we engage in collaboration stems from the worldview(s) we hold about working with others. Spend a few minutes to reflect on your own assumptions and record your thoughts below.

1. Do you operate based on the assumption of survival of the fittest (Darwinian worldview) or by a sense of moral obligation to the weaker (humanitarian worldview)?

2. Where do these beliefs stem from?

3. How do these beliefs influence how you approach working with others?

7.6 CONTINUE YOUR LEARNING

The following activities are designed to support you on your learning journey, building on ideas introduced in this chapter. These can be completed at any time and in any order, although you may find it helpful to begin with the 'Check your understanding' activity before moving on.

CHECK YOUR UNDERSTANDING

1. A start-up is one of many contexts for entrepreneurial value creation.

   ☐ **TRUE** (It's true – please see section 7.2.2)
   ☐ **FALSE**

2. An opportunistic worldview refers to someone who identifies entrepreneurial opportunities.

   ☐ **TRUE**
   ☐ **FALSE** (It's false – please see section 7.3)

3. If you have a Social Darwinist worldview you believe that the strongest in society acquire more power and resources, whereas the weak in society have less power and resources.

   ☐ **TRUE** (Its's true – please see section 7.3)
   ☐ **FALSE**

4. A non-zero-sum game implies that if one wins everyone else loses.

   ☐ **TRUE**
   ☐ **FALSE** (It's false – please see section 7.3)

5. In entrepreneurial organisations there shouldn't be shared goals.

   ☐ **TRUE**
   ☐ **FALSE** (It's false – please see section 7.2.4)

FURTHER READING

1. **Failure is Not an Option** by Gene Kranz
2. **Maverick: The Success Story Behind the World's Most Unusual Workplace** by Ricardo Semler
3. **The Five Dysfunctions of a Team** by Patrick Lencioni

COGNITIVE–BEHAVIOURAL REFLECTION
EXPERIENCING OPPORTUNISM

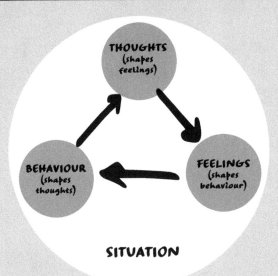

SITUATION

Drawing on the cognitive–behavioural framework introduced in Chapter 1, and based on the notion of opportunism covered in this chapter, consider a situation where you experienced opportunistic behaviour from your employees, colleagues or superiors in the workplace.

Why do this? This activity helps you to identify in more detail how opportunistic behaviours play out in your daily lived experiences. It will therefore give you a more accurate picture of when, how and through which mechanisms they affect your future responses to others.

Step 1. Describe this situation in two to three sentences. Who was being opportunistic and in which context?

....

....

....

....

....

....

Step 2. Describe the thoughts you had in this situation. [This is your interpretation of the situation, so make sure you explore it in sufficient detail. We'd recommend about four to eight sentences.]

....

....

....

....

....

....

....

Step 3. Describe how you felt in this situation. [These are your emotions. Be as specific as you can in your language, avoiding general terms like 'angry or 'sad' in favour of more nuanced terms.]

....

....

....

....

....

....

Step 4. Describe how you behaved (i.e., acted) in this situation. [Focus on how you responded, identifying both positive and negative responses.]

....

_____

_____

_____

_____

Step 5. Looking back on this situation, what sense can you make of how it affected your expectations (both positive and negative) of others? How do these relate to your own frames of reference and worldview when working with others?

_____

_____

_____

_____

_____

_____

PRACTISING ENTREPRENEURIAL THINKING
ASSEMBLING YOUR OWN ENTREPRENEURIAL CONTEXT

As we've discussed, entrepreneurial contexts can take many shapes and forms. They can have formal boundaries (e.g., new ventures, established organisation) or loose structures based on partnerships, agreements or wider collaboration (think back to the example of Trade Right International in section 7.2.2).

Thinking about the value you want to create, what entrepreneurial context will best suit and how can you assemble it? Work through the following prompts to get started.

WHAT – what value is being created? For whom?

_____

WHERE – Are existing organisational structures suitable, or are new organisational structures required? Do these need to be formal (i.e., new ventures, corporate spin-outs, special projects) or informal (i.e., personal networks, community relationships)?

WHO – What should the group look like? Who needs to be involved and why? Who should be involved and why?

WHEN – Is this the right time for each group member? Can everyone contribute and commit fully? If no, then when?

HOW – How will the group organise itself? How will everyone be incentivised to collaborate? How will the reward work for the group and the individuals? How will everyone be motivated?

CHAPTER 8

BUILDING EMPATHY, TRUST AND PSYCHOLOGICAL SAFETY

"IF THERE IS ANY ONE SECRET OF SUCCESS, IT LIES IN THE ABILITY TO GET THE OTHER PERSON'S POINT OF VIEW AND SEE THINGS FROM HIS ANGLE AS WELL AS YOUR OWN."

— HENRY FORD

8.1 INTRODUCTION

As we've discussed, entrepreneurial value creation is generally a collective rather than individual activity. We as individuals have limited information/knowledge – there is only so much information we can collect and retain on a particular topic. To overcome this, when we think about *what could be rather than what is,* we can work with others to build on a greater range of skills, knowledge or experience that we may have ourselves. Yet, as we've just discussed in Chapter 7, this collaboration is not always straightforward, particularly when individuals hold different worldviews on collaboration and the outcomes from the collaboration.

So how then can we support individuals to work together, particularly in uncertain and changing entrepreneurial contexts? How can we encourage the entrepreneurial thinking and behaviour of those around us? What might make people want to collaborate? What makes you personally feel open to collaboration? Equally, what puts you off or prevents you from collaborating with others?

Building on the understanding from Chapter 7 of entrepreneurial value creation as a collective activity, this chapter will explore the role of empathy, trust and psychological safety in building productive relations within collaborative settings and with a range of stakeholders and audiences. We will consider the nuances of these concepts, as well as how we can apply them in practice. This chapter will start by exploring the concept of empathy, considering the role that it plays in entrepreneurial thinking, what empathy is (and is not) and how to build our ability to empathise. We then consider the concept of trust and discuss the foundational role that empathy plays in developing trust relationships between individuals. We then consider how empathy and trust can manifest in entrepreneurial contexts to support value creation activity, specifically in the form of psychological safety among collaborative groups.

After working through this chapter, you should be able to:

- articulate the role empathy plays in supporting entrepreneurial thinking and action in entrepreneurial contexts
- explain the cognitive and emotional dimensions of empathy, differentiating empathy from kindness or trust
- consider the impact of empathy and trust on building psychological safety to support collaborative activity for value creation.

8.2 THE ROLE OF EMPATHY IN ENTREPRENEURIAL THINKING

When we think of our stereotypical images of entrepreneurs, we may not necessarily conjure up people who we could define as highly empathetic individuals. In fact, the opposite might well be the case! Many of the 'heroic' entrepreneurial figures featured in the media are often described as 'single-minded', 'determined', or 'go-getters', rather than focused on the feelings and needs of others. Think of Amazon founder Jeff Bezos or Tesla founder Elon Musk. How would you describe them? Would you think of them as being *empathetic,* able to understand and appreciate the feelings of others?

Yet the notion of empathy and entrepreneurial activity are fundamentally interlinked. When seeking to create value, a critical first task is to consider how this will relate to potential customers/users – they *empathise* in order to determine how well their needs and wants are met. These needs and wants may be practical, but there is often an emotional component as well, particularly in relationship to needs. Just as we need to empathise with customers or users, we also need to consider how we can engage with our peers, superiors, subordinates, clients and stakeholders more broadly in an empathetic manner. For example, when seeking external investment, empathy can help us to better appreciate what the priorities of investors may be and, thus, alignment to the entrepreneurial activity we are undertaking.[1] Equally, putting ourselves into the shoes of those we manage helps us to empower them to work effectively in contexts that may be increasingly complex and beyond their comfort zone or current skill set. Empathy towards our superiors may allow us to better understand their decisions, however unpopular, as well as empower us to make a case for any innovation or change we may want to introduce.

Empathy is thus a foundational piece in our ability to work with others, particularly to cooperate for problem solving, idea generation, conflict resolution and value creation.[2] Yet, despite recognition of its importance, it is not something that often we spend time seeking to cultivate and develop. This can stem from our own frames of reference (think back to Chapter 3), or the nature of the environment in which we are currently working or studying. Some educational environments, like the famous 'crucible' of Harvard Law School for example, give limited importance to empathy and prioritise aggressive dominance over others above collaboration.[3] Indeed, in a study where MBA students were asked to rank what they considered the ten most important leadership competencies, empathy was consistently ranked in the bottom three![4]

[1]Neck, H., Brush, C. & Greene, P. (2014). *Teaching Entrepreneurship: A Practice-Based Approach.* Cheltenham: Edward Elgar.

[2]Bacigalupo, M., Kampylis, P., Punie, Y. & Van den Brande, G. (2016). *EntreComp: The Entrepreneurship Competence Framework.* Luxembourg: Publication Office of the European Union.

[3]Cain, S. (2012). *Quiet: The Power of Introverts in a World That Can't Stop Talking.* London: Penguin Books.

[4]Holt, S. & Marques, J. (2012). Empathy in leadership: Appropriate or misplaced? An empirical study on a topic that is asking for attention. *Journal of Business Ethics, 105,* 95–105.

WHERE AM I STARTING FROM?
BELIEFS ON LEADERSHIP QUALITIES

Spend a few minutes reflecting on your current personal assumptions about the qualities that make a good leader. Record your thoughts below.

1. Start by ranking the following qualities[5] in order of importance, where 1 is what you consider the most important and 10 is what you consider the least important.

Leadership quality	Rank in order of importance (1 = most important and 10 = least important)
Authenticity	
Charisma	
Commitment	
Courage	
Drive	
Empathy	
Experience	
Intelligence	
Service	
Vision	

2. What qualities made your top three? Why?

....

....

[5] Ibid.

3. what qualities made your bottom three? why?

4. where in your ranking did you place empathy? why?

When we are working with others to create value, empathy is an important part of building collaborative relationships through *trust as well as collaborative group beliefs like* **psychological safety** that allow us to imagine what *could be.*

8.3 UNDERSTANDING EMPATHY

When we speak about *empathy,* or being *empathetic,* what exactly do we mean? As empathy is an innate human ability and naturally occurring part of human life,[6] we often take the word empathy for granted and use it without being specific about what it means and, equally, what it does not! Once we understand the boundaries of empathy as a concept, we can then consider how we can foster it and embed it in our own personal and professional lives.

Empathy has been defined in many ways, but a good place to start is with an understanding in the entrepreneurship domain of empathy being the 'cognitive and affective process fostering the capability of understanding and appreciating the feelings, thoughts, and experiences of others'.[7] This definition usefully separates out what are two distinct dimensions of empathy that can be developed independently of each other – the emotional dimension and the cognitive dimension.

The emotional (or affective) dimension of empathy is akin to 'compassion'. Stemming from the Latin 'passio' (suffering) and 'com' (with), compassion is defined as 'feel[ing] another's suffering as keenly as one's own'.[8] When we think of empathy, this is likely

---

[6]Decety, J. & Jackson, P. L. (2004). The functional architecture of human empathy. *Behavioural and Cognitive Neuroscience Reviews, 3,* 71–100.

[7]Korte, R., Smith, K. A. & Li, C. Q. (2018). The role of empathy in entrepreneurship: A core competency of the entrepreneurial mindset. *Advances in Engineering Education, 7*(1), n1.

[8]Oxford English Dictionary (2023). Available at: www.oed.com/

what comes to mind first. This form of empathy has been named 'emotion-matching', as it rests on the ability to feel what another person is feeling.[9] For example, when we see someone else suffering and we feel that knot in our stomach, we are experiencing emotional empathy.

The cognitive dimension of empathy, on the other hand, views empathy as an ability to *understand,* as opposed to *feeling,* the experience of others from their own viewpoint. More specifically, it entails developing an awareness and knowledge of the feelings, thoughts and experiences of others as experienced by them.[10] This view of empathy focuses on 'perspective taking', which is the ability to consider another's perspective without necessarily having experienced it ourselves.

These two dimensions of empathy can manifest in what are recognised as eight different psychological states;[11] people can experience one – or many – of these in a single situation.

- Knowing another person's internal state, including thoughts and feelings.
- Adopting the posture or matching the neural responses of an observed other.
- Coming to feel as another person feels.
- Intuiting or projecting oneself into another's situation.
- Imagining how another is thinking and feeling.
- Imagining how one would think and feel in another's place.
- Feeling distress at witnessing another person's suffering.
- Feeling for another person who is suffering.

FOOD FOR THOUGHT
IDENTIFYING EMPATHETIC STATES

Nearly every day presents us with opportunities to practise empathy. This might be with our family, our friends, our colleagues or with total strangers. Yet when was the last time you stopped to think about how you've responded in these kinds of situations?

---

[9]Packard, M. D. & Burnham, T. A. (2021). Do we understand each other? Toward a simulated empathy theory for entrepreneurship. *Journal of Business Venturing, 36*(1), 106076.

[10]Ibid.

[11]Decety, J. & Ickes, W. (2009). *The Social Neuroscience of Empathy*. Cambridge, MA: MIT Press.

Drawing on the list of empathetic psychological states above as a starting point, reflect on a situation in the last week that required an empathetic response from you. Consider:

1. What was the nature of the situation? Can you describe it in a sentence?

2. Looking back, did you respond to this with cognitive empathy? Emotional empathy? Both?

3. Which state(s) from the list above did your response manifest in? Why do you think this was?

8.3.1 HOW TO BUILD EMPATHY

It is generally accepted that all humans (and some animals too!) are hardwired to be empathetic, albeit some more than others. Yet, as with many of the competences we've discussed thus far, the evidence shows that empathy is something that can be developed and strengthened through practice, building the closeness and respect needed to foster trust (we'll look at trust more in section 8.4).

Importantly, empathy is not a single response or way of behaving. Rather, it is a complex response that we each engage in that can be shaped by a number of different elements[12] including our *emotional intelligence, shared experience* and ability to engage in *perspective taking.*

EMPATHY THROUGH EMOTIONAL INTELLIGENCE

One element influencing our ability to empathise cognitively and emotionally is *emotional intelligence.* Built on our ability as human beings to think abstractly, it is one of the three forms of 'hot' intelligences (along with personal and social intelligence). Emotional intelligence is considered a 'hot' intelligence because it deals with 'hot' information, that is cues about motives, feelings and other factors that are of direct relevance to an individual's wellbeing.[13]

We can gauge our emotional intelligence based on the following four components:[14]

1. how accurately we can perceive emotions, both in ourselves and in others
2. to what extent we integrate emotions in our information processing (e.g., are we able to describe our emotions in the same way we are able to describe other physical sensations)
3. to what extent we understand the meaning and implications of emotions and appreciate how they combine and evolve over time
4. how well we can monitor and regulate emotions for both personal and wider social growth and wellbeing.

Whilst some of evidence indicates that emotional intelligence may be impacted by early life experiences in addition to some inborn personality traits,[15] there is a general consensus that it can be learned as a set of competences based on the four components above.[16]

For example, to practise how we perceive our emotions, we can look at photos showing different facial expressions and try to gauge what emotions these may represent.

---

[12]Decety, J. & Holvoet, C. (2021). The emergence of empathy: A developmental neuroscience perspective. *Developmental Review, 62,* 100999.

[13]Mayer, J. D. & Mitchell, D. C. (1998). Intelligence as a subsystem of personality: From Spearman's g to contemporary models of hot processing. In W. Tomic and J. Kindma (eds), *Advances in Cognition and Educational Practice* (Vol 5, pp. 43–75). Greenwich, CT: JAI.

[14]Mayer, J. D. & Salovey, P. (1997). What is emotional intelligence? In P. Salovey & D. Sluyter (eds), *Emotional Development and Emotional Intelligence: Educational Implications* (pp. 3–31). New York, NY: Basic Books.

[15]Zeidner, M., Roberts, R. D. & Matthews, G. (2002). Can emotional intelligence be schooled? A critical review. *Educational Psychologist, 37*(4), 215–231.

[16]Di Fabio, A. & Kenny, M. E. (2011). Promoting emotional intelligence and career decision making among Italian high school students. *Journal of Career Assessment, 19*(1), 21–34.

FOOD FOR THOUGHT
EMOTIONAL INTELLIGENCE

As we've discussed, emotional intelligence can help us to empathise cognitively and emotionally with others. Part of this is being able to perceive emotions and to make sense of them as we process information.

Spend a moment looking at the picture below.

Source: Pixabay

1. Looking at this person, what feeling is most expressed in their face?

2. What other emotions might they be feeling?

You may have observed that the person in this photo appears to be sad. Perhaps wistful, or resigned as well.

To better understand your own emotional intelligence, you may want to complete the MSCIET[17] test of emotional intelligence. This is a comprehensive test that will take about 60 minutes and is available at: https://testyourself.psychtests.com/testid/3979

3. What were your results?

4. How did these results make you feel?

EMPATHY THROUGH SHARED EXPERIENCE

Another way to develop empathy is to go through the same experience of another person or group of people. This shared experience can help us appreciate the physical and emotional sensations another goes through. For instance, the fasting practice of people of Muslim faith during Ramadan allows them to have empathy towards those who do not have enough to eat. In organisational settings, shared experiences to foster empathy can be simulated. At Ford, the American car manufacturing company, a special 'third age suit' is worn by members of the design team to simulate the troubles with mobility and eyesight that elderly drivers often face.[18] This allows designers to develop a greater awareness and understanding of what it feels like to be an elderly driver in one of Ford's vehicles.

It is important to note, however, that building empathy through shared experience can be challenging, particularly when we consider emotional empathy. In some professions, such as hospice and end of life nursing where individuals are often expected to exhibit selfless

---

[17]Mayer, J. D., Salovey, P., Caruso, D. R. & Sitarenios, G. (2003). Measuring emotional intelligence with the MSCEIT V2.0. *Emotion, 3,* 97–105.

[18]https://agirlsguidetocars.com/fords-third-age-suit/

compassion, emotional empathy can lead to what has been called 'compassion fatigue'.[19] In these circumstances, individuals go beyond 'feeling' for others and develop so-called 'excessive empathy' where they begin to sacrifice their own needs and wellbeing in favour of helping others. This is where cognitive empathy comes into play. We want to not only try to 'feel', but also to *understand* the experiences of others (which we'll come to in just a moment). As with most things, this is a difficult balance to strike and is likely to vary depending on the specific situation and circumstances you find yourself in.

CHALLENGING ASSUMPTIONS
THE PROBLEM WITH EMPATHY SIMULATIONS

Despite the importance of building our ability to empathise, there are challenges with 'simulating' situations to build empathy. Just as Ford's design team wears the 'third age suit' to empathise with elderly drivers, many organisations adopt similar approaches to help their teams and employees better understand their customers or those they are trying to help. For example, Médecins Sans Frontières (Doctors without Borders) held an exhibit in Washington where 'participants climb onto rafts (on dry land) and go through a series of ordeals, having to give up their possessions one by one until they ended up, empty-handed, in front of faux refugee camps'[20] to simulate the experience of a forced migration journey.

Whilst these simulations are usually done with good intentions, they only take us so far. We may get a sense of our own experience of what it feels like (momentarily) to be pregnant if we wear a 'pregnancy suit',[21] or what it feels like to have no sight if we are blindfolded and given an activity to complete. But this understanding is partial and we tend to fixate on the sudden physical change (e.g., suddenly having a heavier tummy) or physical loss (e.g., suddenly not being able to see) rather than developing an empathetic understanding of these as lived experiences.

Developing empathy is therefore not just about how we feel in someone else's shoes, but taking the time and effort to understand how others feel in their own shoes, through the act of perspective taking.

---

[19] Waytz, A. (2016). The limits of empathy. *Harvard Business Review*, January-February.

[20] www.theatlantic.com/technology/archive/2017/02/virtual-reality-wont-make-you-more-empathetic/515511/

[21] www.empathybellyrental.com/

www.theatlantic.com/technology/archive/2017/02/
virtual-reality-wont-make-you-more-empathetic/515511/
www.bustle.com/p/disability-simulators-dont-work-but-there-are-
other-ways-to-be-able-bodied-ally-75727

EMPATHY THROUGH PERSPECTIVE TAKING

Finally, we can build our own ability to empathise through perspective taking. Perspective taking is a form of cognitive empathy that allows us to understand the lived experiences of others from their own point of view. Perspective taking requires investing time and effort in gathering information about others, asking how it feels for them without necessarily expecting to share or know the feeling. This helps us to build an understanding of how others experience specific circumstances. Our ability to perspective take is built on the competence of 'imagination', which gives us the ability to build an abstract mental model of the experience of others by imagining 'what it must be like'.[22]

In order to gather information on another person's experience we can use *empathetic listening*.[23] Empathetic listening, whether with a friend, colleague, employee or family member, should involve:

1. Allowing the person to whom we are listening to *dominate the conversation,* without interruptions and without gestures (of approval or disapproval) from us.
2. *Asking open questions* and only asking questions when the speaker comes to a natural pause. Open questions are questions framed in such a way that the answer cannot be a simple 'yes' or 'no'. For instance, asking 'How did that make you feel?' is an open question, whereas 'Did that make you feel uncomfortable' is a 'closed' rather than open question.
3. *Repeating back what you have heard* so that you can check if your understanding is correct. Hearing their words spoken back to them allows the speaker to check whether what they said was what they really meant, or if they actually meant something slightly different.
4. Finally, *allowing for long moments of silence.* This gives the speaker extra time to gather their thoughts and add detail that they may have just remembered.

Empathetic listening, in addition to supporting perspective taking, also helps us to prevent rash decisions and judgements about individuals (think back to Chapter 6 on System 1 and 2 thinking). By allowing more time for information and insight to emerge, we are more likely to be able to see things from other people's perspectives and to make more informed judgements.

---

[22]Packard & Burnham, Do we understand each other?
[23]Bodie, G. D. (2011). The Active-Empathic Listening Scale (AELS): Conceptualization and evidence of validity within the interpersonal domain. *Communication Quarterly, 59*(3), 277–295.

PRACTISING ENTREPRENEURIAL THINKING
EMPATHETIC LISTENING

As we've discussed, the principles of empathetic listening can help us to develop our cognitive and emotional empathy through perspective taking. This type of questioning may feel 'natural' to you, or it may feel strange. Either way, it is useful for us to practise and develop our listening skills.

To build your own empathetic listening, we'd encourage you to arrange a **life story** conversation. This can be with someone you know very well on a personal level (e.g., a grandparent or spouse), or someone you don't know very well on a personal level (e.g., a colleague or a teammate).

So as not to rush, you'll need at least 20 minutes to conduct this conversation. Base your lines of questioning around the following themes:

- background
- interests
- needs
- problems

Consider:

1. How did you feel at the start of this conversation? Was it easy/difficult, awkward/fun? Why?

2. What have you learned about this person that you didn't know before?

....

....

3.   How has this helped you to better understand this person?

....

....

....

....

4.   How has this changed how you feel toward/about this person?

....

....

....

....

8.3.2 WHAT EMPATHY IS NOT

Just as with other concepts and ideas that we have discussed, it can be helpful for us to think about what empathy is not. As empathy has become more entrenched as a key competence for business and entrepreneurial action, the term has become broader and more all-encompassing. It is no wonder, then, that people have started to ask 'how much empathy is too much?' and 'how can I have any empathy left at home once I've used it all up at work?'.[24]

Some of this links back to our discussions of frames of reference (Chapter 3) and your worldview (Chapter 7) in relation to working with others. Do you tend towards collaboration or competition? Do you value reciprocity? Do you think about working with others as a 'zero-sum game' or 'non-zero-sum game'? If you tend toward 'zero-sum' competition, you are more likely to view empathy as a fixed resource, something that can be depleted if you give too much away. If you value collaboration and reciprocity, you may have a different perspective and see empathy as something infinite over time and space.

Regardless of your worldview, it is important to clarify that empathy is not always about saying 'yes' to others – whether you want to or not! It also does not mean always being

---

[24]Waytz, The limits of empathy.

able and willing to accommodate other people's needs. In fact, sometimes accommodating individual needs beyond the boundaries required of the specific situation or task at hand may be detrimental to the ultimate value we are trying to create and unfairly impact other people's own needs.

In the same vein, empathy is not the same as 'kindness' or 'altruism', even though they are interlinked. We may feel or know the experience and needs of others, but may not necessarily also be *friendly, generous and considerate* towards them[25] with no expectation of reciprocity – being 'kind for kindness' sake.[26] Having said that, people who experience strong emotional empathy often feel the urge to act upon their understanding of the needs of others. If they don't, these individuals may experience *cognitive dissonance* where they feel that they aren't fully embodying their own personal values if they don't do all they can to help.

To summarise, empathy alone stops at the ability to either feel or know the feelings, needs and experiences of others. This does not necessarily imply that empathy will be followed by *acting on the needs and wants of others*. The actions we subsequently take will likely depend on our mindset, worldview and the nature of the relationships we have with individuals.

8.4 BUILDING TRUST

As with empathy, the concept of **trust** has long been considered critical to business and management, particularly within entrepreneurial contexts.[27] Trust can be thought of as a person's willingness to be vulnerable toward another person and, as a consequence, to take the risk that they may get hurt.[28] In many ways, empathy is the precursor to trust. If people don't empathise with us, either cognitively or emotionally, we cannot open up to them and potentially make ourselves vulnerable – and vice versa!

As with empathy, trust also has cognitive and emotional components. Our cognition-based trust is grounded in how we think about another person, where we make assumptions about a person's reliability, dependability and whether or not they have good intentions towards us. Our emotion-based trust is grounded in assumptions of reciprocity (think back to Chapter 7),[29]

---

[25]Oxford English Dictionary.

[26]Peterson, C. & Seligman, M. E. (2004). *Character Strengths and Virtues: A Handbook and Classification* (Vol. 1). Oxford: Oxford University Press.

[27]Welter, F. (2012). All you need is trust? A critical review of the trust and entrepreneurship literature. *International Small Business Journal, 30*(3), 193–212.

[28]Mayer, R. C., Davis, J. H. & Schoorman, F. D. (1995). An integrative model of organizational trust. *Academy of Management Review, 20*, 709–734.

[29]Lewicki, R. & Brinsfield, C. (2011). Trust as a heuristic. In W. A. Donohue, R. G. Rogan & S. Kaufman, *Framing Matters: Perspectives on Negotiation Research and Practice in Communication.* New York: Peter Lang Publishing.

where we make assumptions about how both parties will have care and concern (i.e., empathy) towards one another.[30] When we first trust another person, we take a 'leap of faith'[31] that our cognitive and emotional assumptions will be met.

Generally, interpersonal trust exists as a relationship between two people, based on a mutually shared understanding. Yet, we can also observe trust at the collective or group level as well, as groups are made up of different people who all have interpersonal trust relationships. We can see this, for example, within our families. Parents will trust one another, as well as their children; the children will have their own trust relationships with one another as well as with their parents. Thus, personal trust is critical in fostering trust at the collective or group level.[32]

When we consider entrepreneurial thinking and action – for us, and for those we are working with to create value – trust is a critical foundation of effective collaboration. It allows us to develop strong relationships with others in pursuit of common interests or goals,[33] which in turn help us keep going and persist (think back to Chapter 4) when things get difficult and when we are tempted to give up.[34] It also allows us to cultivate entrepreneurial contexts that support ideation, creation and experimentation through trying, failing and learning.

DEEP DIVE
THE BUILDING BLOCKS OF TRUST

As mentioned above, trust is crucial to building new value together. In the (rather entertaining!) TED Talk below, Harvard Business School Professor Frances Frei takes us through the building blocks of Trust: www.ted.com/talks/ frances_frei_how_to_build_and_rebuild_trust?language=en

---

[30]McAllister, D. J. (1995). Affect-based and cognition-based trust as foundations for interpersonal cooperation in organizations. *Academy of Management Journal*, 38(1), 24–59.

[31]Luhmann, N. (1979). *Trust and Power*. Chichester: Wiley

[32]Welter, All you need is trust?

[33]Uzzi, B. (1997). Social structure and competition in interfirm networks: The paradox of embeddedness. *Administrative Science Quarterly, 42*(1), 35–67.

[34]Davidsson, P. & Honig, B. (2003). The role of social and human capital among nascent entrepreneurs. *Journal of Business Venturing, 18*(3), 301–331.

8.5 THE ROLE OF PSYCHOLOGICAL SAFETY IN SUPPORTING ENTREPRENEURIAL THINKING AND ACTION

When we think about supporting collaborative entrepreneurial thinking and action, we want to consider how we can harness empathetic communication and trust relationships to build a group belief of *psychological safety*.

Psychological safety is a group-level phenomenon that gives people a feeling of safety and makes them more capable of learning new behaviours, overcoming ingrained routines, speaking up, acting proactively and taking risks.[35] We can define it as 'a shared belief that the team is safe for interpersonal risk taking … a sense of confidence that the team will not embarrass, reject, or punish someone for speaking up'.[36] Psychological safety is built on empathy, trust and mutual understanding.

When looking at group collaboration and performance, psychological safety has been found to be a critical success factor[37] in entrepreneurial contexts. For example, in the early 2010s, Google started 'Project Aristotle'[38] to explore what made the perfect 'high performing' team. What they found was that it didn't matter so much who was on the team – what mattered much more was how members of a team treated each other. They found that psychological safety played a critical role in creating an environment in which to encourage innovation, risk taking, trying new things and building a tolerance for making mistakes. When high levels of empathy and trust exist within a group, we are more likely to speak up, to take turns and to be more sensitive towards one another's perspectives and feelings.

To be clear, psychological safety is not a 'shield from accountability', an excuse for poor performance or a way to be seen as politically correct.[39] It's not about being 'nice', but rather building an environment that supports collaboration, which is particularly important when we're navigating entrepreneurial contexts laden with uncertainty, ambiguity or risk. In addition to helping teams perform better, psychological safety allows us as individuals to thrive.

---

[35]Edmondson, A. C. (2002). The local and variegated nature of learning in organizations: A group-level perspective. *Organization Science, 13,* 128–146.

[36]Edmondson, A. (1999). Psychological safety and learning behaviour in work teams. *Administrative Science Quarterly, 44,* 350–383.

[37]Duhigg, C. (2016). *Smarter Faster Better.* New York: Penguin Random House.

[38]https://rework.withgoogle.com/print/guides/5721312655835136/

[39]Clark, T. R. (2021). What psychological safety is not. *Forbes,* 21 June. Available at: www.forbes.com/sites/timothyclark/2021/06/21/what-psychological-safety-is-not/?sh=12a75d656452

FOOD FOR THOUGHT
GOOD VS BAD TEAM EXPERIENCES

Spend a few minutes reflecting on some of your experiences working in a team. This could be in the context of your professional role, in a sport that you play, or perhaps a formative experience when you were growing up. Consider the following and record your thoughts.

1. Identify and describe one example of a good team experience. What made it 'good'?

2. Identify and describe one example of a bad team experience. What made it 'bad'?

3. How did these two different experiences make you feel? Why?

4. How did you react (i.e., behave) in response to these two different experiences? What helped you to contribute/prevented you from contributing?

5. what lessons have you taken from these two different experiences?

When we are working in situations that feel psychologically safe, we are more likely to be able to:[40]

- *Experience more opportunities for personal learning.* We are less likely to fear admitting that we have made a mistake or that something hasn't gone the way we thought it would. We are also more likely to ask others for help and to be more open to feedback and suggestions for improvement.
- *Make change happen.* In being able to speak freely, we are able to challenge the status quo and discuss what is working and what isn't working. We can then identify areas for change and start putting ideas into action for ourselves, for others and for our organisations or entrepreneurial contexts.
- *Challenge beliefs and behaviours.* When we can speak openly, without fear of conflict or breaking up our group or team, we can discuss attitudes, beliefs, frames of reference and worldviews. This allows us to challenge our own perspectives and gives us the space and freedom to change our mind and develop new perspectives and linked behaviours.

DEEP DIVE
REMOVING PSYCHOLOGICAL SAFETY AT BOEING

Boeing has been at the centre of innovation in aviation for decades. Its approach to innovation had always been coupled with uncompromising safety standards. Being first to introduce innovation to market was never more important as being the best at quality control in manufacturing, leading to the highest possible safety standard. The quality control team in engineering at Boeing had always had a culture of psychological safety: if something wasn't spot on, everyone and anyone was encouraged to speak up and the engineering team would have the freedom to deploy the needed time and resources to fixing the problem before it could ever become a safety concern. Reportedly, however, after the merger with XX, the focus changed and

---

[40]Goller, I. & Bessant, J. (2017). *Creativity for Innovation Management*. Abingdon, UK: Routledge.

top-management rewarded speed over quality and started silencing those who spoke up[41] — psychological safety was dead, as eventually were the passengers who flew on two of the new Boeing 737 Max jets produced under the new company culture. A case of soft skills with hard consequences?

Psychological Safety expert Amy Edmondson discusses the case in the article 'Boeing and the Importance of Encouraging Employees to Speak Up': **https://hbr.org/2019/05/boeing-and-the-importance-of-encouraging-employees-to-speak-up**

The investigative documentary by Al Jazeera 'The Boeing 787: Broken Dreams' considers similar issues in the introduction of the innovative 'Dreamliner' by Boeing: **https://youtu.be/rvkEpstd9os**

ENTREPRENEURIAL THINKING AND MINDSET IN PRACTICE
NIGEL LOCKETT ON LEADING WITH EMPATHY

The case study is intended to illustrate the following:

- the role of empathetic listening and perspective taking in leaders
- the link between leader–follower trust and organisational change
- the link between empathy and creating a shared vision.

This is the case study of Nigel Lockett, Professor Emeritus at the Hunter Centre for Entrepreneurship at the University of Strathclyde. Before academia, Nigel launched and grew a successful healthcare supplies business in addition to being involved in a number of social and community enterprises.

The case is narrated in Nigel's own voice.

I'm really a biologist by training, my first degree was in biology, but I've never used my first degree. I went straight into business as soon as I had graduated and, for a very short period of time, I was an administrator in someone else's business before I set up my own first business. My first business was a healthcare supplies business. It was all about buying in bulk –

---

[41]www.forbes.com/sites/kathymillerperkins/2019/10/31/3-things-you-must-know-to-avoid-a-culture-calamity-lessons-learned-from-boeing/?sh=649d93b76c6f; www.nbcnews.com/news/us-news/former-boeing-manager-says-he-warned-company-problems-prior-737-n1098536; www.bloomberg.com/news/features/2019-05-09/former-boeing-engineers-say-relentless-cost-cutting-sacrificed-safety?leadSource=uverify%20wall

health products and medical cleaning products – into a big warehouse, splitting that down and delivering it in smaller packs into the community. So it's the simplest type of business in the world but, in fact, it became more complex, particularly in the UK as the community care market expanded, our business grew substantially. But I've also been an entrepreneur in other settings. I set up a social enterprise in the north of England dealing with excluded groups, including ex-offenders coming out of prison. The business was about delivering organic vegetables and was set up as a cooperative. In such settings, you really cannot do it all by yourself. You need to be a leader, rather than a solo-preneur. Because my educational background is not in leadership, I've learned on the job.

I think there's a myth particularly in the media whereby the focus is on one key individual in the enterprise. But in fact, to me it's all about teams. I alone simply don't have enough knowledge, enough expertise, enough time to do everything and to be all things to all people. I've never wanted to run a business called 'Nigel'. I've also always wanted to run businesses which can scale and make big impact, whether that's social or financial. Therefore, to me, it's all about building teams.

START BY LISTENING

How do I build a team? What I would say is that I think the start of it is all about listening. If you are going to build a team, particularly one that already exists within an organisation when you're the new leader, then of course you've got to listen to people to understand what people really want. It's no good imposing a solution on any team. You've got to work with a team to develop a new solution and you have to start by listening. You're listening, but you're also playing back what you've heard, so you're reaffirming all the time with someone that what you've heard is what they've said. The knowledge that you acquire doing that may be unique because there aren't many people who take the time to talk to everyone in a team. Empowered with that knowledge, you can then start your own reasoning process of developing solutions in response to opportunities or challenges. Then, of course, you have to engage with the team again but this time to share your thoughts and be open to them commenting on your proposed solution. For me it works well and it's fascinating, it's fun but it also has really serious implications in how you build effective teams.

EMPATHY IN LEADERSHIP

Empathy is difficult to put your finger on but I think it's the ability to put yourself in someone else's shoes. I think as an entrepreneurial leader that ability is really important, but it's also really important as an entrepreneur. If I just look at being an entrepreneur, which I've been, I would say the advantages are that I understand my customer so I can empathise with my customer and I begin to understand what their needs are. It's a bit like short circuit market research.

As a leader, it's really important because I always work on the approach that everyone comes to work to do the best job they can. Therefore, if they're not doing the best job they can I assume that there's a reason. It's not because they're being awkward or lazy, it's because something isn't working. Therefore, you need to listen to them and understand what life is like for them and be prepared to respond to that and support them. In doing so, you're using your empathy to build high levels of trust between you and the person, but also you're building a collective response to any situation. When you get it right your team performs really well and your organisation performs really well so you know it's a win-win. It's a win for the individual, but it's also win for the organisation.

You could be a bit cynical about it and say, well, actually I do this to get the organisation to perform but actually in order to do that, you've got to help individuals first. The two go hand-in-hand.

BUILDING TRUST AND PSYCHOLOGICAL SAFETY

Crucially, you need to build up a trusted relationship with each individual. If you're in a team and your manager or leader makes you feel that you can trust them, you're much more likely to share your opinion. This is really important in decision making because I don't think one individual, no matter how clever, can think of everything and is aware of everything, has every perspective available. So it's really important to create an environment where people feel they can share an opinion, even tell you about a mistake or tell you about a problem. You as a leader need to be able to understand what they're saying without any judgement whatsoever and appreciate how their perspective might help you. Also, if there are problems, you've got to get on and deal with them and sometimes you don't have much time. Therefore, investing the time and effort at the beginning to building trust in teams is critical to you to get that two-way communication going, otherwise you're trying to run things with blinkers on, where you can't see everything. You've got to get your blinkers off by letting other people tell you about what's going on, what they think, what they feel. And that way you become much more entrepreneurial in your response to a problem or an opportunity.

I mean, it's not always easy. When you get it right, you know you've got it right because you feel so positive in your work environment and other people feel positive as well. Equally, once you've had that experience, you also know when it's not working. You do have a constant challenge to create that environment and maintain that environment. Life isn't easy. It will constantly throw challenges and disruptions because that's what life is. You've got to be ready to respond to those challenges. I can think of situations where I've been involved in a big team and the team is failing. I've gone into that team and my job is to turn it around. You've got to work so hard to do that. I can think of this one organisation where I inherited a team of 60 people. The organisation didn't know where it was going, it was losing money, people were demoralised and it took me many months of graft and also it took three years to turn the organisation round. So that to me was probably the biggest challenge I've ever faced as a leader.

In the end, we went from 60 to 70 people, we went from loss making to profit making, but the most important thing was that people started to enjoy their work. They enjoyed coming to work and we started doing some amazing things. It's much more rewarding working in that sort of organisation than one that's failing. So maybe it's a bit selfish of me, but I like to create positive teams because it's more fun to be there!

I went in and started listening, then played back what I had heard, and then I would present a new vision. What I tried to do was to create a vision and I wouldn't get it right first time, but by putting it out there, if people trust you, they will tell you where they think it's wrong and will help you. You then recreate a vision which has got buy in. It's almost a formula: you listen, you create a solution, you present the solution, you listen again and then you create a shared vision. When you get that shared vision, you press the Go button – you start to make decisions and then you manage. You transition from leading to managing. You get your head down and start the hard graft and others around you will see that and start behaving the same way.

8.6 SUMMARY AND NEXT STEPS

This chapter has built on our understanding from Chapter 7 of entrepreneurial value creation as a collective activity to explore the role of empathy, trust and psychological safety in building productive collaborations to support value creation in entrepreneurial contexts. We have explored the cognitive and emotional dimensions of empathy, observing that empathy whilst an inherent human ability is also something that can be fostered and strengthened through our emotional intelligence, shared experience and perspective taking. We have also differentiated between empathy and trust, observing that both are critical foundations upon which we can build the group shared belief of psychological safety. Psychologically safe environments allow us try, fail and learn, which is essential when we think about creating value in uncharted and uncertain situations. They also support collaboration and open communication, which we'll explore next in Chapter 9.

WHERE AM I NOW?
COGNITIVE AND AFFECTIVE EMPATHY

Having worked through this chapter, you now have a better understanding of empathy and your own ability to empathise with others. Take a few minutes to complete the following test, which measures both your cognitive empathy and affective empathy, and reflect on the results. Record your thoughts below.

Complete the test available at **https://greatergood.berkeley.edu/quizzes/ take_quiz/empathy.** This should take about 10 minutes, but spend as long on the test as you need/wish.

1. what was your score (out of 110)?

2. what did your results show?

3. How do you feel about the results? Are they reflective of the views you hold about yourself and how you engage with others?

....

....

....

8.7 CONTINUE YOUR LEARNING

The following activities are designed to support you on your learning journey, building on ideas introduced in this chapter. These can be completed at any time and in any order, although you may find it helpful to begin with the 'Check your understanding' activity before moving on.

CHECK YOUR UNDERSTANDING

1. Empathy can be improved through practice.

   ☐ **TRUE** (It's true – please see section 8.3.1)

   ☐ **FALSE**

2. Empathy means always acting on the needs of others.

   ☐ **TRUE**

   ☐ **FALSE** (It's false – please see section 8.3.2)

3. One of the components of trust is empathy.

   ☐ **TRUE** (It's true – please see section 8.4)

   ☐ **FALSE**

4. Psychological safety refers to not worrying that we may get physically hurt at work.

   ☐ **TRUE**

   ☐ **FALSE** (It's false – please see section 8.5)

5. Change is more likely to happen in psychologically safe environments.

   ☐ **TRUE** (It's true – please see section 8.5)

FURTHER READING

1. **Emotional Intelligence** by Daniel Goleman

2. **The Fearless Organization: Creating Psychological Safety in the Workplace for Learning, Innovation, and Growth** by Amy Edmondson

3. **The Outward Mindset: Seeing Beyond Ourselves** by The Arbinger Institute

STOP AND THINK
NIGEL'S PERSPECTIVE

Looking back to Nigel's discussion ...

1. What form of empathy does Nigel use in organisations?

2. Why does Nigel not believe in imposing solutions?

3. According to Nigel, what are the factors that make people happy and productive in work?

COGNITIVE-BEHAVIOURAL REFLECTION
EXPERIENCING LACK OF EMPATHY

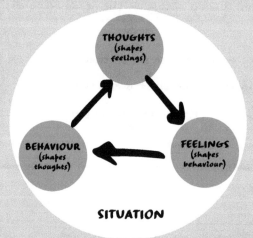

Drawing on the cognitive-behavioural framework introduced in Chapter 1, and based on the content of this chapter, consider a recent situation where your colleagues or line manager showed lack of understanding and appreciation of the challenges you were experiencing in the job.

Why do this? This activity helps you to identify in more detail how it feels to be on the receiving end of lack of empathy. It will therefore give you a more accurate picture of when, how and through which mechanisms lack of empathy can affect others too.

Step 1. Describe this situation in two to three sentences. What challenges were you experiencing? How did your colleagues or line manager respond?

Step 2. Describe the thoughts you had in this situation. [This is your **interpretation** of the situation, so make sure you explore it in sufficient detail. We'd recommend about four to eight sentences.]

Step 3. Describe how you felt in this situation. [These are your **emotions.** Be as specific as you can in your language, avoiding general terms like 'happy' or 'sad' in favour of more nuanced terms.]

....

....

....

....

Step 4. Describe how you behaved (i.e., acted) in this situation. [Focus on how you responded, identifying both positive and negative responses.]

....

....

....

....

....

....

....

Step 5. Looking back on this situation, what sense can you make of it? Consider your own response to the needs of others. What do you now better understand about yourself, your feelings and your behaviours?

....

....

....

....

....

....

....

PRACTISING ENTREPRENEURIAL THINKING
THE JOHARI WINDOW

Building an empathetic understanding of others can be challenging. we have spoken about the importance of perspective taking (see section 8.3.1) to get a sense of how others think and feel about their own lives and experiences, yet anything can be difficult when information and insight is not forthcoming.

The Johari window[42] **is a tool to help us understand how we relate to other people in terms of our own self-awareness; we can also 'flip' this to consider what it is that others may know (or not know) about themselves.**

JOHARI WINDOW

	KNOWN TO SELF	NOT KNOWN TO SELF
KNOWN TO OTHERS	*Arena*	*Blind Spot*
NOT KNOWN TO OTHERS	*Façade*	*Unknown*

Start by organising a one-to-one chat with a handful of colleagues, peers or classmates and try to determine **what elements fit within each of the four quadrants.**

---

[42]Luft, J. (1984). *Group Processes, An Introduction.* Mountain View, CA: Mayfield.

When all the chats are complete consider:

1. How might you be able to uncover things that may be in the 'Blind spot', 'Façade' or 'Unknown' quadrants?

2. How do we deal with the limitations of these quadrants when trying to understand the needs, wants and desires of others?

CHAPTER 9

COMMUNICATING VERBALLY AND NON-VERBALLY

"REAL COMMUNICATION STARTS WHEN WE UNDERSTAND
WHAT THE WORLD LOOKS LIKE TO THOSE IN FRONT OF US".

9.1 INTRODUCTION

As we've explored in the preceding chapters of Section 3, entrepreneurial thinking and action is a collaborative task to create value, *something new, improved, or in a novel space that an individual or group of individuals considers to have worth.* However, during much of this process we are creating a vision of the future – of what is possible – rather than something more tangible. We thus need to consider how to create this vision in a collaborative manner, communicating with a range of individuals to create a shared understanding in pursuit of a common goal.

Have you ever considered how you communicate with others? Are you aware of how you make sense of what others are saying? Or how they are making sense of what you say? What about the things you don't actually say?

This chapter will consider the practicalities of how we communicate with others, be it through verbal or non-verbal communications. It will begin by considering the important role that communication plays in entrepreneurial thinking and behaviour within entrepreneurial contexts. We will then explore in depth two of the main types of communication – verbal and non-verbal. Building on concepts from Chapters 6 and 8, we will consider the nature of verbal communication, including the encoding and decoding of messages. We will also consider how analogies and metaphors can help to explain intangible concepts and visions of the future, particularly where we might experience problems with message coding/decoding. We will then look at non-verbal communication, particularly the impact that our facial expressions and tone of voice have on how others decode our messages, before considering what we can do to improve communication and avoid potential biases.

After working through this chapter, you should be able to:

- articulate the link between effective communication and entrepreneurial value creation
- understand and explain the nature of verbal communication, both the encoding and decoding of messages
- assess key forms of non-verbal communication and their link to potential forms of misunderstanding and bias
- consider how to overcome potential sources of misunderstanding and bias when communicating with others in entrepreneurial contexts

9.2 THE ROLE OF COMMUNICATION IN ENTREPRENEURIAL VALUE CREATION

As we've been discussing, creating value requires us to work with others to create a shared purpose and vision of what *can be*. But this can be harder to achieve than it may seem at the outset. As we discussed in Chapters 7 and 8, the entrepreneurial context in which we're operating, the worldview of those we are working with and our shared understanding of how to collaborate (or not) in a manner that supports empathy, trust and psychological safety all influence how we collaborate with others. A key part of this is how we *communicate*.

Communication plays a central role in entrepreneurial value creation for a number of reasons. First, it is an essential part of creating a shared vision of what can be achieved.[1] Such visions only work when they are effectively shared and everyone is committed to their execution. Effective communication is important to allow others to 'picture' what it is that we are thinking of – a new process, a new service, a new product, or a way of tackling social or 'wicked' problems (which we'll tackle further in Section 4). Second, effective communication can replace the role of policies and guidelines, which often do not (yet) exist in entrepreneurial contexts (think back to Chapter 7), and help to create a set of rules of engagement for collaborative activity. Not only will this require an exercise in *perspective taking* (as discussed in Chapter 8), but it also requires that we understand how to communicate an idea with a form of words that is interpreted in the desired manner by others.

WHERE AM I STARTING FROM?
COMMUNICATING YOUR IDEAS

Consider a recent situation where you have put forward an idea for something new or different. How did people respond to you when you did this? What did you notice about this communication? Record your thoughts below.

1. Did you get a sense that the other person understood your idea? What did they do and/or say that made you think this?

2. Did you have to change how you communicated your messaging? Why/ why not?

---

3. Do you generally feel that you can make yourself understood, particularly when speaking to people from different walks of life?

4. Do you generally feel that people take what you say seriously?

We also need to recognise that communication does not only mean the words you say – there are non-verbal components of communication at play which shape how our messages are received and interpreted by others. In particular, our facial expressions and our tone of voice influence how our message is perceived. In the same way, whether we are aware of it or not, the non-verbal behaviour of others shapes how we perceive and respond to their own messaging. It is worth becoming aware of these unconscious perceptions so that we can minimise bias and maximise effectiveness in communication, particularly within the uncertainty of entrepreneurial contexts.

DEEP DIVE
PERSUASION WITHOUT DECEPTION

Persuasion is key in entrepreneurial endeavours: we are trying to persuade others of the value of our ideas in order to get their buy-in. All too often, however, persuasion has been synonymous of manipulation and deception. Communication expert Michael Collender offers a fresh take on persuasion at www.youtube.com/watch?v=UxSwQOpxLkc

9.3 VERBAL COMMUNICATION IN ENTREPRENEURIAL CONTEXTS

As with other activities, we may not give too much thought to how we communicate verbally – how we speak to others in the process of sending and receiving messages. Yet effective verbal communication is the foundation upon which successful collaboration is built! As experts in team communication note:

Talk is cheap. I'm not meaning that figuratively – I mean it literally. Paying attention to talk and communication is literally one of the cheapest improvements that can be made for a team. If a team dispenses with the idea that talk is just some 'secondary characteristic' of getting the job done, it can unlock the full potential of talking.[2]

9.3.1 THE BASICS OF VERBAL COMMUNICATION

So what precisely do we mean by verbal communication? When we communicate verbally with another person, we assume we are entering in an exchange of sentences with them – that we say something and then they respond. However, verbal communication is much more complex than that. Before we even speak, whether we are aware of it or not, we go through the following series of steps:[3]

1. We think of what message we want to convey.
2. We choose the words that, in our opinion, will best convey the message.
3. We compose (encoding) and deliver (through speech) the message.

In turn, the person we are speaking with also follows a series of steps:

1. They receive the message.
2. They match the words they have heard to the associated meaning that these words have for them.
3. They interpret the message (decode).
4. They then proceed to respond following the three steps of message coding above.

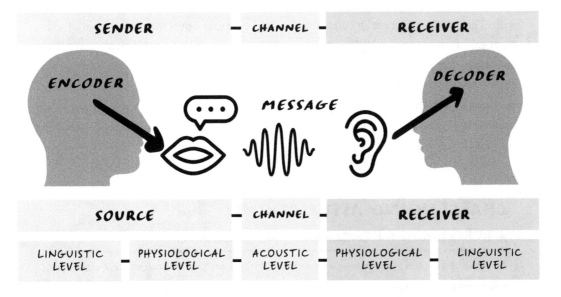

[2]MacLaren, A. C. (2022). *When you talk to each other, you're DOING teamwork*. Available at: www. linkedin.com/pulse/when-you-talk-each-other-youre-doing-teamwork-dr-andrew-maclaren/

[3]Based on Hall, S. (1973). *Encoding and Decoding in Television Discourse*. CCCS Stencilled Paper no. 7; also in During, S. (ed.) (1993). *The Cultural Studies Reader*. London: Routledge.

Normally, we don't have to actively think of these steps because with the people we communicate with regularly (our so-called 'reference groups') we have developed established patterns of behaviour where the underlying meaning of messages is assumed to be shared. Therefore, when we code or decode messages, we know that the other person will understand what we mean. Consider the following example:

Person A: Excuse me, Sir, would you *be able* to tell me what time it is?

Person B: Sure, it's 12:03pm.

Technically, Person A has not asked Person B for *the time* – they have in fact asked whether Person B has *the ability* to tell the time. Person B's logical response would have been 'Yes, I am able to' or 'No, I am not able to'. However, because Person B knows what Person A is really asking despite the form of words used (i.e., what the time is), they answer the question in the way Person A expects.

We have lots of exchanges of this sort every day, where our verbal communication is logically flawed but an underlying shared understanding of meaning allows us to communicate effectively.

9.3.2 POTENTIAL PROBLEMS IN VERBAL COMMUNICATION

These logical flaws in verbal communication become an issue, however, when a shared understanding of 'what we mean' is not there. This occurs when we talk to people from different backgrounds, contexts or who use forms of language that we are not familiar with. This is often the case in entrepreneurial contexts, as novel ideas in pursuit of value creation often involve people with very different specialisms, abilities, worldviews and so on. A classic example of this challenge is the use of acronyms. These tend to be either industry or organisation specific and can be a source of confusion as 'outsiders' may not know what the acronym means or – even worse – they may misinterpret it because they also have the same acronym but in their line of work it means something completely different!

CHALLENGING ASSUMPTIONS
A BREAKDOWN IN ENCODING AND DECODING

As we've discussed, communication exists based on the encoding and decoding of a message. When a disconnect exists between what we encode and what the receiver decodes, our message can get lost.

Take, for instance, the following short video clip from the film The **Pink Panther Strikes Again**: https://youtu.be/SnXtuktNdlM

These kinds of missed communications happen when we make assumptions about contexts, situations and others. Consider the following situation:

Andy has placed an order online with a sports retailer for a new peaked tennis cap that he will collect in store. When he receives the notification that his order has arrived, Andy visits the store to collect it. He walks to the collection counter and, after saying good morning, engages in the following communication with the sales associate:

Andy: I am here to collect a package for an order I placed online.

Sales associate: Sure. How big is the package?

Andy: I don't know - I've never seen it!

Sales associate: [Laughs out loud]

Clearly something went wrong in the encoding and decoding process between Andy and the sales associate. Can you describe in which step of the process the communication broke down and why?

Even when we're working with people from the same industry, from a similar educational background or our own organisation, we still need to bear in mind the possibility for problems in interpreting messages. Individuals interpret words and sentences differently depending on their own personal meaning attached to words. These interpretations can make the difference between agreement or disagreement and, in turn, can make or break a shared vision or purpose.

Take, for example, the following situation:

In his capacity as a consultant, Robert was asked to help a company improve their 'productivity'. The management team believed that addressing some operational inefficiencies would help improve productivity without having to ask their employees to work more or harder. Robert decided that the first step would be to gather the views of employees on the matter, however as soon as he mentioned the word 'productivity' he experienced hostility. It later became clear that the employees assumed that the word 'productivity' meant that they were not working hard enough (in direct contrast to how the management team viewed things). This assumption then created resentment among staff who believed they were already working exceptionally long hours and trying their absolute best.

9.3.3 FACILITATING COMMUNICATION THROUGH ANALOGY AND METAPHOR

As we discussed in Chapter 6 when we talked about System 2 thinking, we may make sense of information by drawing on analogies. Linked to this, we may also use analogies to communicate with others, particularly when we're working in situations where we lack shared understandings or face challenges in communication. This is also particularly relevant when we have an image in our mind of how to create value. These mental images are not necessarily 'speakable' – we may not know what words to use or how to construct sentences that can help others to understand and accept our ideas! To try and communicate what we're thinking (and the mental images that we have) we may draw on 'analogies' or 'metaphors'. When we use analogies, we are showing how what we are thinking of is 'like something else' that already exists and that others can picture. In the movie *Forrest Gump*, he explains 'Life is like a box of chocolates – you never know what you're going to get!'.[4]

When we use **metaphors**, we are using a figurative rather than literal comparison with something that already exists. As Shakespeare famously wrote, 'All the world's a stage, And all the men and women merely players',[5] comparing the world to a stage and people to the actors playing their parts. A metaphor often used for business success is the image of a trophy.

Consider the following example:

Engineers PLC is a UK-based engineering services company where engineers are constantly on the move around the country. The coordination of where each engineer goes depends on matching their technical skills to the client's problem, combined with where in the country they currently are if they are currently with a client. One of the engineers proposes to have an employee that oversees all the daily coordination activities. When he explains what he is thinking of to the board of directors, he says 'we need an air traffic controller'. This is a metaphor borrowed from a different industry altogether (aviation) that helps him to convert his mental image into a message that others can quickly grasp.

Generally, analogies are considered to be more accurate and specific than metaphors. With the former, we are giving our listener a more precise idea of what we mean, one that is less subject to personal interpretation. However, as an analogy requires us to know enough about what else currently exists it is more likely to be used by experienced individuals. The use of analogy also requires that our audience knows enough about the industry or context that we are using to draw similarities with. When either us or the people we are communicating with do not have sufficient knowledge, then we may rely on metaphors more than analogies. Metaphors may also be more suited to disruptive ideas, that are completely new and unrelated to anything that already exists in the specific industry or place where we are trying to introduce our idea.

---

[4]*Forrest Gump* [film] (1994). Directed by Robert Zemeckis. USA: The Tisch Company.

[5]Shakespeare, W. (1954). *As You Like It*, Act 2, Scene 7. New Haven: Yale University Press.

9.4 NON-VERBAL COMMUNICATION IN ENTREPRENEURIAL CONTEXTS

In addition to verbal communication, we also want to consider non-verbal communication that impacts how others decode and respond to our messages. Non-verbal communication includes our facial expressions, tone of voice, movement and posture, physical characteristics and attire. Most of the time we are unaware that these are impacting how we interpret messages, or how others are interpreting our own messages! Yet these (and their related unconscious biases – think back to Chapter 6) are constantly at play in situations where we are trying to persuade others – whether they will be persuaded will depend on whether they perceive that we are up to the task at hand.

9.4.1 FACIAL EXPRESSIONS

Our facial expressions also play an important part in our communication with others, particularly when it comes to our emotions and how others interpret those. When we're collaborating with others to create value we are likely to work with people who do not know us very well.[6] As a result, our facial expressions may be the only source of information available about how we are feeling in a situation!

Research has found that facial expressions of emotion are largely consistent across cultures; we are all programmed to be able to identify key emotions such as being happy, sad or scared no matter where we are from.[7] However, we may interpret what we see in different ways depending on our worldview and frames of reference.

Generally, when we appear happy or excited others can interpret this as enthusiasm or passion for the task at hand. This passion can even be 'contagious' to the people around you, persuading others to follow along.[8]

---

[6]Davis, B. C., Hmieleski, K. M., Webb, J. W. & Coombs, J. E. (2017). Funders' positive affective reactions to entrepreneurs' crowdfunding pitches: The influence of perceived product creativity and entrepreneurial passion. *Journal of Business Venturing, 32*(1), 90–106.

[7]LaFrance, M. & Mayo, C. (1978). Cultural aspects of nonverbal communication. *International Journal of Intercultural Relations, 2*(1), 71–89.

[8]Cardon, M. S., Post, C. & Forster, W. R. (2017). Team entrepreneurial passion: Its emergence and influence in new venture teams. *Academy of Management Review, 42*(2), 283–305; Cardon, M. S. (2008). Is passion contagious? The transference of entrepreneurial passion to employees. *Human Resource Management Review, 18*(2), 77–86.

Some facial expressions, called 'communal' expressions of emotions,[9] convey to others that we are seeking to be part of the group, that we are seeking social affiliation rather than dominance. In fact, communal facial expressions including sadness, happiness, and fear convey lack of dominance.[10] Expressing both happiness through smiling as well as expressing sadness (e.g., through crying) are perceived as signs that we want to involve others in what we are saying or doing – it's a call for action. When we show emotions such as sadness or fear, we are communicating to others that we want their help. Equally, when we smile, we encourage others to support us rather than fight us.

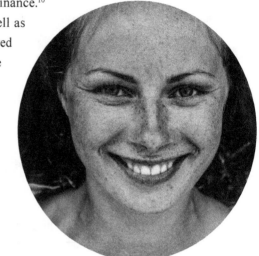

Source: Pixabay

On the other hand, expressions of anger and disgust are taken as a sign of social dominance and are referred to as 'agentic'. These characteristics are associated with independence and aggressiveness,[11] such as the ability to stand one's ground.

---

[9]Hess, U., Adams, R. & Kleck, R. (2005). Who may frown and who should smile? Dominance, affiliation, and the display of happiness and anger. *Cognition & Emotion, 19*(4), 515–536.
[10]Ibid.
[11]Powell, G. N. (2011). *Women and Men in Management* (4th edn). Los Angeles: Sage; Powell, G. N. & Butterfield, D. A. (2015). Correspondence between self- and good-manager descriptions: Examining stability and change over four decades. *Journal of Management, 41*(6), 1745–1773.

These implicit expectations based on facial expressions play a role when people pitch their ideas to potential investors. For example, in a large study of investors' evaluation of business pitching, expressions of sadness (regardless of gender) were interpreted as a sign of weakness and of inability to do what it takes.[12] Interestingly, though, the same study found that some (though limited) expressions of fear are not detrimental to getting investment[13] but, rather, can convey a sense of realism about the task ahead.

FOOD FOR THOUGHT
HOW WOULD YOU RESPOND?

Consider how you would respond to a new colleague who seems troubled by an aspect of a project you are both assigned to work on. Imagine that this colleague shows signs of distress on his/her face when they are asking you for clarification on the project.

Source: Pixabay

---

[12]Warnick, B. J., Davis, B. C., Allison, T. H. & Anglin, A. H. (2021). Express yourself: Facial expression of happiness, anger, fear, and sadness in funding pitches. *Journal of Business Venturing, 36*(4), 106109.

[13]Ibid.

1. In what way does this affect your perception of your colleague?

2. In what way does this affect your perception of your colleague's ability?

3. In what way does this affect your perception of your colleague's commitment to the project?

4. How does this make you feel?

5. What do you do? (e.g., help them, tell them to figure it out, etc.)

9.4.2 TONE OF VOICE

Just like our facial expressions, our voice also influences – and potentially biases – the perceptions of others. This matters not only for what we have to say, but also whether the listener is persuaded by our message. Tone of voice includes characteristics such as speed (whether we speak slowly or quickly), pitch (whether our voice is heard to be 'high' or 'low'), volume and control over our tone of voice.

Just as with our facial expressions, different aspects of our tone of voice can be interpreted by those we are speaking with. For example, faster speakers are often judged as being more competent, intelligent and truthful – perhaps because we assume that it takes more time to think of lies than to speak the truth! Similarly, lower pitch voices are also perceived to be a sign of competence and trustworthiness. This can be in many ways be a potential source of bias, as low pitch is characteristic of adult male voices and high pitch of children and female voices.[14]

More recently, research has found that a controlled tone of voice is perceived by others as more competent. Within entrepreneurial contexts, it has also been found to help persuade investors. A stressed or emotional voice, on the other hand, is found to convey low competence and deters investors and other stakeholders from 'buying in'.[15]

DEEP DIVE
TONE OF VOICE

As we've just discussed, our tone of voice is an important part of our non-verbal communication. With lower pitch voices considered to be more competent and trustworthy, individuals often seek to modulate their own natural voice to convey a sense of authority, competency or power. This is particularly the case in competitive business situations, such as during pitches to investors.

Elizabeth Holmes, once the founder and CEO of health technology start-up Theranos and now convicted for fraud, reportedly worked to change her voice

[14]William, A., Streeter, L. A. & Krauss, R. M. (1979). Effects of pitch and speech rate on personal attributions. *Journal of Personality and Social Psychology, 37*(5), 715–727; Cheng, J. T., Tracy, J. L., Ho, S. & Henrich, J. (2016). Listen, follow me: Dynamic vocal signals of dominance predict emergent social rank in humans. *Journal of Experimental Psychology: General, 145* (5), 536–547; Oleszkiewicz, A., Pisanski, K., Lachowicz-Tabaczek, K. & Sorokowska, A. (2017). Voice-based assessments of trustworthiness, competence, and warmth in blind and sighted adults. *Psychonomic Bulletin and Review, 24*(3), 856–862.
[15]Wang, X., Lu, S., Li, X. I., Khamitov, M. & Bendle, N. (2021). Audio mining: The role of vocal tone in persuasion. *Journal of Consumer Research, 48*(2), 189–211.

from high to low pitch in order to be more persuasive and to sound more competent: https://youtu.be/PLGLd4qDKNl

In a dramatisation of the Theranos case, actor Amanda Seyfried (playing Elizabeth Holmes) practises changing her voice: https://youtu.be/zj_qlgGbLgY

9.5 IMPROVING COMMUNICATION TO AVOID MISUNDERSTANDING AND BIASES

We have already highlighted the importance of communication in entrepreneurial endeavours – communicating effectively helps create a shared vision, persuades others and articulates what's 'in it' for everyone involved. On the flipside, issues of communication – both verbal and non-verbal – can create misunderstandings, biases and potentially lead to outright conflict, all of which make it improbable that we will all be on the same page, let alone create value together. Yet, far too many times we spend insufficient time and effort in improving our communication to prevent pitfalls and maximise value creation. Improving communication will require a combination of:

- Clarifying understanding – good communicators always check that what they understood was what the speaker intended to say (verbally) or convey (non-verbally).
- Voice concerns – if something that is said (verbally) or implied (through tone of voice or facial expression) is perceived as unpleasant or concerning, voicing our concerns (in a psychologically safe environment – see Chapter 8) can help dispel the risk of misunderstandings. Our concerns may stem from biased interpretations of the message rather than from real instances of, for instance, disrespect or bad intentions.
- Giving everyone a voice – because not everyone will be able to communicate through the means available (for example, during a meeting), offering different platforms for communication ensures that everyone has a voice.

All of the above add significant time and require a lot of deliberate effort, so we need to be able to appreciate the value of doing so – and the pitfalls of not doing it. The illustrative case below illustrates the primacy of putting effort into good communication.

DEEP DIVE
COMMUNICATION ACROSS CULTURES

Communication conventions range widely across countries. Not only do different languages use different forms of words but the very balance of what is said and what is not can vary substantially. Equally, the use of body language can be very different from one country to another. INSEAD Business School Professor Erin Meyer gives us an insight into these differences at www.youtube.com/watch?v=zQvqDv4vbEg

ENTREPRENEURIAL THINKING AND MINDSET IN PRACTICE
ANGELA ON COMMUNICATION IN A DIVERSE ORGANISATION

The case study is intended to illustrate the following:

- the challenges in communication, both within the organisation and with external stakeholders
- the importance of verbal and non-verbal communication in a diverse group of employees
- strategies for inclusive communication and their value to organisational performance.

This is the case study of Angela Prentner Smith, Founder and Managing Director at This is Milk. Angela and her team at This is Milk specialise in human-centric design for digital, user research and strategy service design. Her organisation also provides training and public speaking.

The case is narrated in Angela's own voice.

BUILDING A BUSINESS ON HUMAN-CENTRIC DESIGN

This is Milk is a human-centric design consultancy. The essence of everything we do is about solving human problems by engaging with people and understanding them. Over the last 10 years we've seen a real awakening to changes in what organisations need to do for their customers and digital has forced that because you can't hide from your customers. They interact with you through digital. Everything has to be based on real insights and user research and testing. From an internal business perspective, there has been a real drive towards diversity and inclusion. And you can't be inclusive if you're not listening to your employees in the first place, and they don't have a place to speak up. All these different drives are taking us to a place where human-centric is becoming increasingly more adopted. These practices are being baked into operational processes.

RECRUITING DIVERSE EMPLOYEES

To carry out these projects I have a diverse team in terms of skills, because you need to look at things from a multidisciplinary approach. The type of people that deliver our projects are a mix of culture change specialists, user researchers, designers, strategists and trainers and we put the team together based on what the client needs.

Our team is truly diverse in any way you can imagine. We have a 50/50 split in terms of gender. At one point we had 20% ethnic minority. The age range of staff is from 29 to 55 and we are actively working on bringing in a younger group of interns. We have French team members, Polish team members, American team members. I am a Canadian, we have got a couple of English people, a Romanian.

We have always had a very international team.

At one point the team was 50% neurodivergent. We have about 50% of people in the team with an acknowledged disability from a legal perspective. Whether they consider themselves disabled is a different story. I've been on quite a journey of grappling with neurodiversity in the organisation and what I have come to understand is that being truly inclusive doesn't mean that every type of person will fit in your organisation, and will fit into the jobs that you have, and hiring somebody for a job or for a team they're not best suited to is actually quite detrimental to you and to them. Imagine that we had a vacancy in communications and someone with a particular neuro developmental difference that makes communication hard for them was to apply. Because the job requires them to be a good communicator, but that is not a strength of theirs and it cannot be changed because it is neurologically wired, we are not being inclusive by giving them an opportunity to do that job. It is cruel. Therefore, I have concluded that the make-up of your team can only be as diverse as the skills that you need.

It's difficult to create and foster an environment for inclusion and diversity. It's not as simple as just virtue signalling and platitudes. Actually, there are some stark realities where one person's needs are going to be counter to another person's needs or counter to what you need to achieve as a business. One should start with the question: 'what is it that we are trying to achieve?' and then design your initiatives around the goal. If your business is predicated on everybody doing the same thing, you probably do not really need a diverse team. You need people with the same skills that are going to get on. If you are in a place where you are trying to change the world, then yes, you need multiple, different lived experience. **Innovation is predicated on different points of view, different skills, people coming at a problem from a variety of places.**

So, if you're trying to do something innovative, yes it is worth taking on the challenge of diversity. It's also worth it from a societal perspective. Do we want to live in a world where there's inequity everywhere? I don't think most people do. We are a long cry from anywhere that could be considered equitable, but we can all be trying. And until we get multiple different voices and different lived experiences and marginalised people into decision-making places, nothing is going to change.

CREATING A SHARED UNDERSTANDING WITH CLIENTS

When you get into an organisation, they may be so engrossed in that setting that they can talk their own language, a language that somebody coming from the outside-in will not know or understand. We see that a lot and so sometimes, when we go into a project, we must do that decoding. It may happen that, if we are doing a research strategy or an interview script, we are asked to put the document to review by the project team at the client, and they will reword it based on their internal language!

Equally, sometimes clients have trouble understanding what we mean by our own terminology. Sometimes when we pitch for work, we will use what we assume is standard industry terminology, yet we have on occasion been told that we used a lot of jargon, so it can work both ways. An example would be the word 'user journey', which some clients may think of as something entirely different to what we are going to produce. So, at the start of projects, we always try and do a bit of sense-checking. We ask what they mean when they are asking for something and we clarify what we mean when we say a 'persona', for example. What we believe is an effective use of terminology is a conversation that we have at the start of projects.

CREATING INCLUSIVE, DEMOCRATIC COMMUNICATION

Regardless of whether it is about team dynamics, or whether it is about client work, I am passionate about making sure that we have created a variety of methods for people to share information. It is important, for example, to provide places where people can write instead of speak and to use facilitation techniques to give everybody a space to speak if they so wish. I use a variety of methods and tools to make communication more democratic. I am fond of EasyRetro, because you can hide what everybody says and then expose it all at the same time. Everyone gets space to have their say and it is anonymous. You do not get extrovert bias, whose ideas will always get pushed through purely by being the loudest voice or the most articulate, or the best at debate. Sometimes there is a place for debate but even at that you have to make sure that you are getting everybody else's contribution and sometimes that is about having to tell some people to shut up!

THE IMPORTANCE OF COMMUNICATION IN A DIVERSE TEAM

A diverse team is not an easy team. It takes work every single day, and there's conflict, and there's debate. Some people can be hypersensitive to anything that is said and there are things taken the wrong way and taken out of context. What I have also seen is that certain voices are such that, when they share an idea, it is almost taken as an instruction even if the speaker does not mean it that way, whereas some other voices can be dismissed altogether.

The way I navigate it is constant communication. I will give you an example. We did have a member of the team that identified with autism. Some of the things this person did in meetings other people found deeply offensive and really upsetting. I explained to the team that what this person was doing was stimming. It had nothing to do with the team. This person whistling in a meeting was stimming, not them being disrespectful of others or ignoring others.

One has to be aware of these interpretations going on and it has happened to me on quite a few occasions that I have been blind to how people have perceived other people's behaviour, or other people's communication, style, etc. When it is raised, we immediately start that conversation. But you must provide people with the ability to raise these concerns with you without judgement, or you cannot even have the conversations. Whether people can feel that they can come and say anything speaks volumes about the culture of your organisation. And I mean ANYTHING, even when they may think that it is a small issue and do not want to bother you with it. I have various ways for people to unobtrusively let me know that something is going on, or they can let someone else in the team know. I also use technology for this. I use a tool called Your FLOCK where people can simply say 'I need some help right now. I'm not that happy'. I also do staff surveys so I can pick up on issues. We do monthly team retros where we go through everything, and it's all anonymous, and then we discuss it. I'm constantly encouraging us to reflect on what we are doing and raise issues. Sometimes, even changing slight trivial things that remove the space where a problem could be raised caused real issues. I do not think that you can over ask for reflection and feedback. It has to be constant, and it has to be through various methods, because you cannot assume that people are going to tell you. In my experience, survey fatigue comes when you keep asking the same questions and you do not do anything with the answers.

As the team has grown, I have introduced one-to-one meetings with everybody, particularly with hybrid working and multi locations. Albeit they take up an awful lot of my time, I just do not ever cancel them. They must happen.

DIGITAL COMMUNICATION – WHAT IS DIFFERENT?

You genuinely do not notice people's energy the same way when you are communicating digitally. And if people write stuff down, there is always one million ways that that can be interpreted. That could be the same with verbal communication as well. You know you could say something to me, and I could take that a different way than five other people would. The difference is, with in-person communication, there's physical energy between people. You feel an energy in a room. You do not get that online, and you have to facilitate much more in online communications than in in-person. In-person happenstance can be relied on a lot more, just going with where the conversation goes. In person, that's all okay because you are reading people's body language. You can go off-piste.

When you have people online, you do not necessarily know what they are doing. They could be doing something completely different, just not listening. So, you have got to be much more curated in how you are extracting information from people, and how you are presenting that information as well. There are lots of benefits to it, too. I do a monthly team broadcast and we record it, and we have it transcribed through teams. It means that if you cannot be there at that point to listen, you can listen back to it when you can. You can read the transcription if listening is not ideal for you. Therefore, there are benefits to it, and I do think you could be more democratic online than you can be in person using digital tools.

9.6 SUMMARY AND NEXT STEPS

This chapter has considered the practicalities of how we communicate with others, through both verbal or non-verbal communication, and the important role that communication plays in entrepreneurial contexts to support value creation. We have also raised a number of biases that can arise when we make judgements based on what we hear people say – and equally what they don't say! Whilst we can't eliminate bias completely, it is important to be aware of where bias may affect communication, both our own bias and that of others. This allows us to adjust our communications to ensure that we don't miss out on the important insights, perspectives and contributions that allow us to create value and tackle challenging or 'wicked' problems, which will come to next in Section 4.

WHERE AM I NOW?
VERBAL AND NON-VERBAL MESSAGING

At the start of the chapter you reflected on your experience of communicating a new idea. Now, having worked through this chapter, how do you make sense of this experience based on what you now know about verbal and non-verbal communication? Record your thoughts below.

1. What form of words did you use to communicate your idea?

2. Did you use a metaphor or analogy (think back to section 9.3.3) to help explain your idea? If so, what was it?

3. Did you get a sense that your message was received in the way you intended or not? Why?

4. What elements of non-verbal communication do you think affected how your message was received? (Think back to section 9.4.)

9.7 CONTINUE YOUR LEARNING

The following activities are designed to support you on your learning journey, building on ideas introduced in this chapter. These can be completed at any time and in any order, although you may find it helpful to begin with the 'Check your understanding' activity before moving on.

CHECK YOUR UNDERSTANDING

1. 'Analogies' or 'metaphors' can help communicate abstract, entrepreneurial ideas.

   ☐ **TRUE** (It's true – please see section 9.3.3)

   ☐ **FALSE**

2. Metaphors are more literal representations of the idea, whereas 'analogies' are more abstract representations of the idea.

   ☐ **TRUE**

   ☐ **FALSE** (It's false – please see section 9.3.3)

3. Communal facial expressions indicate that we are seeking dominance.

   ☐ **TRUE**

   ☐ **FALSE** (It's true – please see section 9.4.1)

4. We tend to associate lower pitched voices with competence.

   ☐ **TRUE** (It's true – please see section 9.4.1)

   ☐ **FALSE**

5. In order to avoid misunderstandings, good communicators always check that what they heard was what the speaker intended.

   ☐ **TRUE** (It's true – please see section 9.5)

   ☐ **FALSE**

FURTHER READING

1. **Simply Said** by Jay Sullivan

2. **Smart Brevity** by Jim VandeHei, Mike Allen and Roy Schwartz

3. **Culture Map** by Erin Meyer

STOP AND THINK
ANGELA'S APPROACH

Looking back to Angela's story ...

1. What is the role of communication in the projects that This is Milk delivers for clients?

2. Why is communication important when working within a diverse team?

3. What tools does Angela use to ensure that everyone communicates?

COGNITIVE–BEHAVIOURAL REFLECTION
YOUR OWN DECODING OF MESSAGES

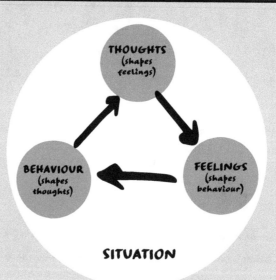

Drawing on the cognitive-behavioural framework introduced in Chapter 1, consider a situation where someone said something that you perceived as confrontational.

Why do this? This activity helps you to identify in more detail how your own decoding of messages, often taken for granted, can sometimes be biased. It will therefore give you a more accurate picture of when and through which mechanisms you may jump to conclusions about the communication from others.

Step 1. Describe this situation in two to three sentences.

- what exact words did the person use?
- what was their facial expression?
- what tone of voice did they use?
- If they said nothing at all, what was their body language?

Step 2. Describe the thoughts you had in this situation. [This is your interpretation of the situation, so make sure you explore it in sufficient detail. we'd recommend about four to eight sentences.]

Step 3. Describe how you felt in this situation. [These are your emotions. Be as specific as you can in your language, avoiding general terms like 'happy' or 'sad' in favour of more nuanced terms.]

Step 4. Describe how you behaved (i.e., acted) in this situation. [Focus on how you responded, identifying both positive and negative responses.]

Step 5. Looking back on this situation, what sense can you make of it? what do you now better understand about yourself, your feelings and your behaviour that can explain how you interpreted the person's communication? How do these relate to your own decoding of communication?

PRACTISING ENTREPRENEURIAL THINKING
IMPROVE THE EFFICIENCY OF YOUR COMMUNICATION

Having worked through this chapter, you will have considered some of the challenges in communicating new ideas, verbally and non-verbally, particularly in the context of working with others to create value.

You can build your communication skills and the skills of those working with you to try to overcome misunderstandings and potential sources of bias by practising the following:

- **Clarifying understanding** – when someone puts forward their ideas, instead of assuming that you (and everyone else) understands what the speaker means, seek clarification. Simple questions like 'do you mean ...' or 'I'm hearing you say that ...' can help give the speaker the opportunity to clarify their thinking and address any misinterpretations.

- **Examine body language** – as we have seen, people respond to communication with non-verbal cues. This might mean smiling, nodding, frowning, fidgeting and so on. Instead of assuming what these cues mean (i.e. nodding meaning agreement or frowning disagreement), spend time questioning them. Spend some time researching different gestures and what they mean for different people and in different cultures. For example, in some countries, people shake their head side to side to indicate agreement rather than disagreement. Equally, a colleague fidgeting may in fact be evidence of them processing your message rather than being bored or uninterested.

- **Giving everyone a voice** – recognise that everyone has different needs when it comes to communication. Some people need more time to think before speaking; others prefer to write instead of speaking. Think about what tools you can use to give everyone an opportunity to share ideas in the time, space and medium that works best for them.

SECTION 4

HARNESSING YOUR ENTREPRENEURIAL THINKING AND MINDSET FOR VALUE CREATION

The fourth and final section of this book will bring together your observations, reflections and learning from the first three sections to consider how your entrepreneurial thinking and mindset will support you in creating value yourself and for others. The focus throughout this section is on how you can apply the concepts and ideas we have discussed in your own life as a creator of value.

CHAPTER 10 will start by revising the notion of 'value' from Chapter 1, broadening it further to consider additional forms of value relevant to our personal and professional lives. It will cover a number of examples of value creation in action, both to provide inspiration as to what is possible but also a chance for you to reflect on what might be relevant for you. It will then consider the link between value creation and self-determination, discussing how our aspirations and priorities play an important role in the actions we take (or do not take) and the outcome for our own personal **flourishing**.

In **CHAPTER 11** we will move from value creation for yourself to consider how you can directly (or alternatively **obliquely**) create value with and for others. It will start by considering the importance of problem identification and exploration, in order to determine and act on the root cases rather than symptoms of problems. This is particularly the case when looking to create value that addresses the world's 'wicked problems', many of which are aligned to the United Nations Sustainable Development Goals (see **https://sdgs.un.org/goals**). Again, a number of examples of value creation for others are provided for both insight and inspiration into how we can create value for others, now and into the future.

Finally, in **CHAPTER 12** we will conclude this book by considering what your next steps are to put your entrepreneurial thinking and mindset into action. It will start by summarising what you've covered throughout this book, before considering how you can determine your 'next steps' through goal-setting and habit formation.

CHAPTER 10

UNLOCKING YOUR ABILITY FOR PERSONAL VALUE CREATION

"TRY NOT TO BECOME A MAN OF SUCCESS,
BUT RATHER TRY TO BECOME A MAN OF VALUE."

— Albert Einstein,
LIFE (1955)

10.1 INTRODUCTION

Throughout the previous sections and chapters of this book, we have considered how important entrepreneurial thinking and action is for us all, regardless of the entrepreneurial context we're working in. We have explored how having an entrepreneurial mindset and related competences is essential in enabling us to support our own personal development and to take action and charge of our lives[1] to *create value* in a way that is meaningful to us.

But what will this mean to you personally? Having now worked to develop your own entrepreneurial thinking and competences, how can or will you apply these to support your own life? What value can/will you create and why?

This chapter builds on our discussion of **value** from Chapter 1 and starts by exploring how different forms of value may be relevant in our own personal and professional lives. To do so, we will look at examples of what value creation has meant for others, to provide insight and inspiration as you determine what is relevant for you. We will then consider how, at a personal level, value creation shapes – and supports – our own **self-determination** and ultimately personal flourishing.

After working through this chapter, you should be able to:

- explain the difference between perceived value, exchange value and value in use and articulate their relevance to selecting what value you may/will create for you
- articulate the role that wellbeing and accomplishment play in supporting creating value for you as an individual
- consider the impact of multiple dimensions of human flourishing in composing your own balance for value creation for you.

10.2 REVISITING 'VALUE'

As we talked about in Chapter 1 (see section 1.7), we often talk about *value* in monetary terms – how much something costs, what financial return we will get, how much utility it will yield and so on. Yet as we've discussed, such *economic value* is just one form of value. We can also consider:

- *social value,* where we seek to help others to reduce their suffering or to make their lives better or happier
- *mental value*, where we derive enjoyment, happiness or a sense of accomplishment from our own entrepreneurial thinking and action

---

[1]Bacigalupo, M., Kampylis, P., Punie, Y. & Van den Brande, G. (2016). *EntreComp: The Entrepreneurship Competence Framework.* Luxembourg: Publication Office of the European Union, 10, 593884.

- *environmental/ecological value*, where we address or solve problems occurring within natural ecosystems or spaces
- *aesthetic value*, where we identify or cultivate feelings of pleasure when looking at or experiencing something that we consider to have beauty or attractiveness.
- *cultural value*, where we seek to preserve or support cultural heritage.

These forms of value are not mutually exclusive; we can create different kinds of value (including economic value) at the same time.

As a reminder, value creation generally consists of three elements:

- *perceived value* (i.e., the benefit I think I will have from something)
- *exchange value* (i.e., what I am willing to give up in order to obtain that something, often measured in terms of money)
- *value in use* (i.e., the benefits I get from using/consuming, which may or not be what I had originally perceived).

WHERE AM I STARTING FROM?

REVISITING VALUE

In Chapter 1, we asked you to consider what value might mean for you, both in terms of your personal life and your professional life. Record your thoughts below.

1. From Chapter 1, what did 'value' mean to you in the context of your personal life?

2. From Chapter 1, what did 'value' mean to you in the context of your professional life?

Now, having discussed a range of entrepreneurial competences underpinning entrepreneurial thinking and action for value creation, consider where your thinking is at now.

3. Does your current thinking reflect what you recorded at the start of this book? why/why not?

....

....

4. How are you currently thinking about value creation for yourself?

....

....

Identifying different forms of value is much easier than considering what value is relevant to us and how we are going to go about creating it. This is because entrepreneurial value creation requires *taking action to change the status quo and thus trading the 'known' for the 'unknown'*. This brings us back to the conversations we've had about uncertainty. Whilst our *perceived value* may be strong, we cannot be so sure about *value in use* as it's hard to know how things will work out in reality. As a result, we often think about our *opportunity cost* – what else we could be doing with our time, effort, money, etc. – and wonder whether our course of action will be '*worth it*' or if we should just stick with the status quo.

Consider the following example:

Tim Smit, founder of the UK's 'Eden' conservation project, previously had a very successful career as a musician. He describes the burning desire to become a musician and the exciting process of writing his first single. The dream of every musician is for their song to be top of the charts and this happened for Tim. In fact, his song stayed at the top of the charts for several weeks. Instead of being happy, however, he describes this success as unexpectedly underwhelming and recalls feeling empty and dissatisfied. He goes on to reflect that this wasn't because he didn't like the song, or that he wasn't happy about the fast car he could now drive with the earnings. He now realises that this 'success' wasn't something that deep down he really wanted, but rather something that he felt he should aspire to because it was considered the ultimate success for anyone in the performing arts. When describing the difference between his perceived value and his value in use, he said:

> '*The problem with getting THERE (i.e., becoming a top-of-the-chart musician) is that when you get there (i.e., when you do become a top-of-the-chart musician) there may be no THERE there*'.

When we make judgements on how we engage in value creation, we may be influenced by what *others* think. Yet value is inherently personal to us – what we consider to be important or to *have worth* may not be the same as others. We often become conditioned to believe that our career and life aspirations should align with societal standards and ideals. In most societies there are 'higher status' and 'lower status' occupations, often aligned to higher and lower rates of pay and other benefits. We often assume that we should all aspire to higher status (and higher paid) careers or positions – and why wouldn't we! But the reality is more complicated. We may have two individuals in the same occupation with the same status and financial rewards, yet one of them may be extremely satisfied, happy and fulfilled while the other is detached, unfulfilled and miserable. This highlights the importance of understanding that *value* means different things to each of us. Our ability to recognise what value means for us personally allows us to think and take action in ways that help us to build a life that is meaningful, fulfilling and allows us to flourish.

10.3 CREATING VALUE TO SUPPORT PERSONAL FLOURISHING

There is general consensus that a happy and fulfilling life requires a fine balance of both **wellbeing** and **achievement**. Wellbeing relates to being both physically and psychologically healthy and therefore experiencing life positively. Achievement relates to goal striving and ambition, usually aligned to our own personal interests, inclinations and potential. Our lives are thus considered to be '*flourishing*' when both wellbeing and achievement are high.[2] This is important when it comes to thinking about value creation for ourselves, as our needs as well as our aspirations and priorities play an important role in the actions we take (or do not take).

While a number of models of human flourishing exist, they largely converge in the core dimensions that compose a life well lived,[3] which we will now discuss.

10.3.1 AUTONOMY AND SELF-DETERMINATION

Self-determination is defined as a person's ability and freedom to manage themselves, to make choices, and to think for themselves.[4] Self-determination and autonomy have long been

---

[2]Green, S. & Palmer, S. (eds) (2019). *Positive Psychology Coaching in Practice.* Abingdon, Oxon: Routledge.

[3]Franklin, J. (2018). Achieving success and happiness: The relevance of theories of well-being and flourishing in positive psychology coaching practice. *Positive Psychology Coaching in Practice,* 21–36.

[4]Deci, E. L. (1971). Effects of externally mediated rewards on intrinsic motivation. *Journal of Personality and Social Psychology, 18,* 105–115.

associated with entrepreneurial activity;[5] many individuals who start their own ventures state 'self-determination' as one of the primary reasons – they want to be in charge of how and when they work. Autonomy and self-determination are core dimensions in theories of human flourishing.[6] When we have discretion on how we go about our life, we experience more life satisfaction, creativity and wellbeing.

Self-determination has also been recognised as a core enabler of individual performance as well as job satisfaction in organisations.[7] Individuals who can decide how to go about their work are found to derive more job satisfaction, are happier and more productive. The recognition that self-determination can increase employee productivity and retention is also linked to the notion of entrepreneurial leadership that we discussed in Chapter 7. Entrepreneurial leaders not only allow their subordinates a higher degree of autonomy, but they also support them and praise them for the initiative that they take (even when the employee's initiative does not result in a success).

Degrees of autonomy in organisations vary, and it is useful to consider the distinction between *structural autonomy*[8] and *strategic autonomy*.[9] When a group has structural autonomy, it can make decisions about what means to use to achieve set ends (whereby the ends are decided by the organisation). On the other hand, when a group has *strategic autonomy*, it has decision-making power over the ends (that is, the goals) and not just the means. Some hold that, in order for an organisation to be entrepreneurial, they have to grant strategic autonomy.[10]

An example of how a degree of structural autonomy can be granted even in the most regulated of industries (aviation) is presented below.

---

[5]Lumpkin, G. T., Cogliser, C. C. & Schneider, D. R. (2009). Understanding and measuring autonomy: An entrepreneurial orientation perspective. *Entrepreneurship Theory and Practice, 33*(1), 47–69.

[6]Deci, E. L. & Ryan, R. M. (2008). Self-determination theory: A macrotheory of human motivation, development, and health. *Canadian psychology/Psychologie canadienne, 49*(3), 182; Ryff, C. D. & Keyes, C. L. M. (1995). The structure of psychological well-being revisited. *Journal of Personality and Social Psychology, 69*(4), 719.

[7]Hackman, J.R. & Oldham, G.R. (1975). Development of the job diagnostic survey. *Journal of Applied Psychology, 60,* 159–170.

[8]Gulowsen, J. (1972). A measure of work-group autonomy. In L.E. Davis & J.C. Taylor (eds), *Design of Jobs* (pp. 374–390) ([1st] edn). Harmondsworth: Penguin.

[9]Bouchard, V. (2002). *Corporate Entrepreneurship: Lessons from the Field, Blind Spots and Beyond.* European Entrepreneurial Learning: Cahiers de Recherch ed' E.M. LYON, N°2002/08.

[10]Lumpkin et al., Understanding and measuring autonomy.

CHALLENGING ASSUMPTIONS
AUTONOMY AT SOUTHWEST AIRLINES

Southwest Airlines is known for allowing its flight attendants to use their initiative and creativity to perform their duties in a way that works for them and for the passengers on each flight. The aviation industry is indeed a heavily regulated one and not one where one would think that individual initiative would be easy to implement!

Some Southwest flight attendants are reported to have found a way to use the freedom of initiative that the company allows to put their comedic skills to use during the normally rather predictable and boring safety briefing once all passengers are on-board. For example, they have told passengers that:

'This is a non-smoking flight. Passengers wishing to smoke are kindly requested to step on the right-hand side wing of the plane during the flight.'

Have a look at some of the briefings recorded by passengers, available on YouTube, including: **https://youtu.be/WbNySCc7GL8**

where is the value creation here? For the flight attendants, the value comes from both their ability to use their personal strengths such as their sense of humour (we'll speak more about personal strengths in a moment), which in turn can create **entertainment value** for the passengers improving passenger satisfaction, wellbeing and even diminishing a fear of flying.

Additionally, the humour engages passenger attention more than a traditional safety briefing would do, which heightens their listening and retention of the safety briefing (higher safety).

10.3.2 BELONGING, CONNECTION AND POSITIVE RELATIONSHIPS

While we need autonomy, we are also social beings and, as such, we have a need for belonging, connection and positive relationships for a successful life. Connection refers to having secure social bonds and feeling respected, appreciated and loved.[11] This definition overlaps with Maslow's notion of *belonging*[12] in his now classic 'Hierarchy of needs'.

---

[11]Franklin, Achieving success and happiness.

[12]Maslow, A. H. (1943). A theory of human motivation. *Psychological Review, 50*(4), 370.

This is a broad category that encompasses personal relationships (friends, spouses, blood relatives) as well as connections at work (a place where we now spend a large portion of our time). Belonging to a group means that the group recognises us as one of their own. In an organisation, belonging may mean that we share the views, values, work practices and goals of those we work with and thus, we feel 'right' and accepted. When we find that our ways of doing things, or our values and objectives do not align with those of the reference group, we may fear being an 'outcast' and not belonging, thus our self-esteem may suffer as a result.[13]

10.3.3 POSITIVE EMOTION

Positive emotions relate to feeling joyful, content, passionate, confident, etc. Positive emotions can stem from the pleasures that the world has to offer us, such as good food, vacations, houses, cars, fashion and time relaxing with friends. This isn't about luxury or extravagance – it's about the momentary experience of something pleasant to us. When we pursue positive emotions, we seek to maximise what are called 'hedonic states' (perception of sensorial pleasure) whilst minimising pain.[14]

The search for positive emotions and the 'pleasant life'[15] may be enabled by career progression and the higher income that often comes with it. Whilst there is no hierarchy of importance in what we do to experience positive emotions, it is also important to be aware that our priorities may shift over time, depending on where we are in our life cycle.[16] Often, life stage determines whether we are going to prioritise experiences that give us hedonic states or shift towards prioritising meaning (as we will see in the next section) over pleasure. Julie's example below is an illustration of such transition.

CHALLENGING ASSUMPTIONS

JULIE'S CHOICE

Julie* did well at school and graduated top of her class with grades that allowed her to study any subject she wanted at university. She was encouraged

---

[13]Tajfel, H., Turner, J. C., Austin, W. G. & Worchel, S. (1979). An integrative theory of intergroup conflict. *Organizational Identity: A Reader, 56*(65), 9780203505984-16.

[14]Ryan, R. M. & Deci, E. L. (2001). On happiness and human potentials: A review of research on hedonic and eudaimonic well-being. *Annual Review of Psychology, 52*, 141–166.

[15] Seligman, M. E. P. & Royzman, E. (2003). Happiness: The three traditional theories, *Authentic Happiness Newsletter, July.* Available at: www.authentichappiness.org/news/news6.html

[16] Levinson, D. J. (1986). A conception of adult development. *American Psychologist, 41*(1), 3.

to study law, graduated top of her class, and went on to secure a highly sought after place in the graduate programme at a Top Three international legal firm.

Julie quickly proved to be an important asset to the organisation. Over the next five years, she was promoted to increasingly senior roles, making her one of the youngest people to achieve these positions in the history of her organisation. She was well rewarded financially. She bought and renovated a home in the most desirable part of her city, enjoyed spa days and shopping at designer boutiques with her friends and enjoyed going on exotic holidays to different part of the world to tick places and experiences off her 'bucket list'.

Julie then got married and took a year off for maternity leave to start a family, returning to work and shortly thereafter receiving a promotion to Partner. In the past she would have been thrilled by this, but upon receiving the offer Julie felt something was wrong. She no longer felt passionate about her job or her organisation, despite her continued successes and the financial rewards. As she explained, 'I didn't love my job, but my job loved me'. Julie realised that her sense of what was important to her had shifted after having her baby and she realised that she no longer found her work meaningful. She wasn't excited to go to work every day, or proud of what she had accomplished at the end of each day.

Julie was faced with a critical choice – to stay in the career which treated her well and would continue to do so, or leave and do something she felt more passionate about.

What does Julie's choice reveal about her path to happiness (pleasure, engagement or meaning)?

In the end, Julie chose to leave her job and to use her skills and knowledge in an organisation that she felt was 'making a difference' in peoples' lives. She took on a senior management role that not only paid well comparatively but offered her more flexibility to organise her work around her family's needs.

*Name has been changed

10.3.4 MEANING AND PURPOSE

Meaning and purpose are fulfilled when we use our strengths and abilities in pursuit of a goal or purpose that is bigger than ourselves and that matters to us. This could be something ranging from family to community, from service in politics to the pursuit of knowledge and innovation. When we pursue the meaning and purpose, we seek to maximise what is called 'eudaimonia' as opposed to 'hedonism', That is, we don't expect to experience pleasure and reduce pain. Rather, we are prepared to endure discomfort or pain (psychological or mental)[17] for a cause that is important and meaningful to us. A common example of this is the transition into parenthood. Not many parents would describe raising young children as a fully pleasurable and painless pursuit, but most parents would describe it as purposeful and meaningful. Notably, when we pursue happiness through meaning, the creation of value for ourselves also creates value for others (the cause that we pursue and gives us meaning).

Consider the illustrative case of Tony O'Neill below. Tony finds his purpose in supporting others achieve wellbeing. In his case, value creation is created by engaging with something bigger than himself.

ENTREPRENEURIAL THINKING AND MINDSET IN PRACTICE
TONY O'NEILL ON FINDING HIS PASSION

The case study is intended to illustrate the following:

* the role of meaning and purpose in creating value for oneself and others
* the link between physical health, mental health and wellbeing.

This is the case study of Tony O'Neill. Tony is the founder and managing director of Animalia Apparel (**https://animaliaapparel.co.uk/**), a high-performance clothing line for combat sports such as kickboxing, Mixed Martial Arts, BJJ, Boxing, Judo and Muay Thai that supports community programmes to build mental resilience.

The case is narrated in Tony's own voice.

---

[17]Seligman, M. E. P. (2002). *Authentic Happiness.* New York: The Free Press; Seligman, M. E. P., Parks, A. C. & Steen, T. (2005). A balanced psychology and a full life. In F. Huppert, B. Keverne & N. Baylis (eds), *The Science of Well-Being* (pp. 275–283). Oxford: Oxford University Press.

EARLY YEARS AND MENTAL HEALTH STRUGGLES

In high school, I really liked Drama, Physical Education and Art. But I only took up Art, I never took Physical Education and never took up Drama. At the time, I was very much a quiet person. I wasn't interested in formal education but I liked to be creative. I'm also colour-blind, which I find quite funny but some things are a challenge.

I tried to take my own life by overdosing at age 15 and I ended up in hospital. In the lead up to it, I had been desperately unhappy but only opened up to my mum about it, nobody else. Once released from hospital and after a few sessions with the psychiatrist, that was the end of that incident.

When I finished high school, I didn't have a plan to go to college, I certainly wasn't entrepreneurial back then. I didn't know what I wanted to do. I wish someone had told me then that one should do the things one likes doing, one shouldn't be doing things because you think society or people think it's cool. That has changed now. I know what my intrinsic motivation is, I know what comes from the heart and I know that when I do these things I love doing I am just far healthier and happier and that then comes out in work, even if you are doing a job that might not be something you really like. However, if you're able to be creative and express yourself in any way in the job, then you're able to do anything.

Working for an industrial electrician at 18 and realising the industrial side and the making side was quite hard graft and also something that I didn't want to do. And again, being colour-blind and working with an electrician, I was very limited in what I could do.

At age 21, I was free to drink and do drugs as an adult. One night I found myself climbing onto the railway tracks, though I pulled myself away just before a train came. I recall going immediately to see my brother, being terrified by how close I had come to darkness one more time. I was prescribed antidepressants, didn't really take them for long, didn't talk to anyone. I was ashamed and worried that people would think I was mad if they knew. I didn't understand anything about mental health at the time, nor about the connection between physical health and mental health. I felt lost, I compared myself to others and they seemed to know where they were heading, whereas I wasn't. I was looking at others for approval, for validation. I never had an inner sense of my worth. I drank too much and was angry most of the time. It wasn't until I started to open up about it that things improved. I went through counselling, voiced how I felt and started by getting myself healthy. The best part of it was developing self-awareness – I learned about what triggers me, what I need to function better, I learned not to be a slave to my anger, to control my emotions. I learned that I should not apologise for turning down things I don't want to do. I learned how to play to my strengths and not compare myself negatively with others for my weaknesses.

By age 23, I decided to go to college and I completed a qualification in 'health fitness and exercise'. I learned to become a Personal Trainer, learned about nutrition, health and wellness. Then I applied to go to university for a degree in 'sport and active lifestyle promotion'. I learned about the power of sport, what sport can do for people, but also for communities. Part of the learning involved a lecturer who is also a cardiac rehabilitation specialist, who taught us that exercise and looking after your mind and your body can make the difference between not just surviving but thriving, living longer and happier lives. Following graduation, my first job was as a 'children and young people sport development officer'. That job taught me about working in communities, working with people and the challenges in financing the charity sector. I learned a lot there about how hard it is to bring money in, how hard it is to get funding applications done.

At the same time, I worked in America for four summers with children with disabilities. I always wanted to work with people with disabilities because I grew up next door to Kerry Ann, who had disabilities. As children, we were taught to understand people, to have empathy towards people. That camp was a massive turning point for me because, even though I was 23 or 24 when I went, I was probably 18 years of age mentally. When I came back, I'd matured greatly. Previously, I was very shy and didn't have much confidence. I didn't really have a voice, I felt that nobody got me. When I went to Camp, I found my voice. People understood who I was and when I came back I understood my role in society. At camp you were responsible for vulnerable people's enjoyment. You had to really step up and look after people, you had to do one-to-one care, showering, wiping, feeding. It's a massive responsibility and then, when you see how people respond to you doing that, how relaxed they are although they are so vulnerable, it's humbling. What I learned at Camp was that there are people in life that don't have others to hold their hand and I was lucky that

I did have such people. I came back feeling very fortunate but also learned a lot from different people from the campers and from the staff. I realised that you could be of service to someone and that gave me a sense of purpose. I felt that was fulfilling me.

When I came back from summer camp, as I continued to work with the young people and the adults in the community, I realised that I was good at talking to people, I liked to communicate with people, I liked to try and understand them. Especially when one wants to help people, you can't presume you know what they need. You have to allow them to tell you what they need and what they want.

ANIMALIA: HEALING COMMUNITIES THROUGH PHYSICAL ACTIVITY

And that led me to what I'm doing, the reason why Animalia was set up. I saw services disengaged from the communities they are trying to serve. If you're trying to make a difference, there's no point going in with a big 'I am', you have to have a bit of humility and humbleness. What I found was that some organisations I looked up to turned out to be not as inclusive as they claimed to be.

In sports specifically, there's a lack of support for athletes, whereby some are funded well but others aren't. In disadvantaged communities, a lot of young people look up to athletes for role models. If everyone who could be an athlete gets funding, then we could have more of these athletes as role models in different communities. If we can give young people as well as adults someone to look up to, someone they can relate to that can make them believe, then maybe we could make a difference in society.

The trigger for funding Animalia came from a personal life event. My brother phoned me and had to pass on the news that my dad had died from a heart attack. My dad was only 53 but had developed diabetes and respiratory issues. He was classed as obese when he passed. However, when he was younger, he was a very talented footballer, a golf player and a tennis player. He was a very fit man, and a very giving man also. That had a massive impact on me in setting up Animalia because I believe that he was trying to get himself healthy but he had just run out of time, unfortunately.

That consolidated my belief in giving people an opportunity to make their life a little bit healthier and happier. It doesn't need to be athletes; it can just be ordinary people who need a bit of support in improving their wellbeing. I knew from my studies that people in their 70s and 80s, after having had a heart attack, can, not only survive but thrive through a combination of exercise and social interaction. That shows you that the human body can be quite resilient, it just needs a chance to do that. I also learned that childhood trauma can have serious implications on your health later on in life, unless you are supported to overcome such traumas.

For me, Animalia is a personal mission. Mental health and physical health are a big part of my life. Helping communities though also helps me. I work with people who are great at what they do so that I don't have to be the face or the main person in the organisation, because that is not what I want, it is not what makes me happy.

Since starting Animalia, I have continued to challenge myself physically and mentally. I have climbed Ben Nevis four times since, each time being faster and more efficient. I have also taken other people with me to climb, and that has boosted mine and their ability to be resilient. This is what keeps me going, what brings me joy.

10.3.5 ENGAGEMENT AND FLOW

Engagement in this context is intended as engaging with an activity or a task, as opposed to social engagement (i.e., connection). When we are extremely engrossed in an activity and time seems to stop, we are said to be in a *flow state*.[18] We are in flow when we achieve an optimal balance between our abilities and the demands of the situation so that we are neither bored (our abilities are not stretched enough) nor anxious (we are out of our depth).[19]

Flow states are best achieved when we play to our strengths, which have been defined as the 'natural capacities that we yearn to use, that enable authentic expression, and that energise us'.[20] There are many classifications of personal strengths, depending on the context of application and the field or research in which they are studied.[21] One classification

---

[18]Csikszentmihalyi, M. (1990). *Flow: The Psychology of Optimal Experience.* New York: Harper & Row.

[19]Csikszentmihalyi, M. (2002). *Flow: The Classic Work on How to Achieve Happiness.* London: Rider.

[20]Govindji, R. & Linley, P. A. (2007). Strengths use, self-concordance and well-being: Implications for strengths coaching and coaching psychologists. *International Coaching Psychology Review, 2*(2), 143–153 – citation p. 144.

[21]Lomas, T., Hefferon, K. & Ivtzan, I. (2014). *Applied Positive Psychology: Integrated Positive Practice.* London: Sage.

of strengths is based on virtues that are valued across cultures and that have helped over history.[22] These encompass six overarching strengths of *Wisdom and Knowledge, Courage, Humanity, Justice, Temperance* and *Transcendence* and can be appraised through the Values in Action (VIA) framework[23] in the reflection box below. These strengths enable flow not just by 'doing' but also by 'being'. Other strengths that can enable flow states may stem from our inclinations and abilities. The best-known classification of such abilities is perhaps that by Gardner,[24] who distinguished between *spatial reasoning, musical ability, linguistic ability, logical-mathematical ability* and *bodily-kinesthetic ability*. Beyond broad abilities, we each have *specific skills* that have direct applications, such as teaching, public speaking and so on.[25] Finally, strengths may come from our interests and passions (which may or may not be the same as our skills and abilities) as well as our broader resources (networks, family support, and so on). Taking time to understand what our signature strengths are is important because using them will allow for engagement and flow as well as productivity and wellbeing.

The state of flow itself is gratifying. It gives us joy and motivates us to pursue the activity that induces flow. The pursuit of engagement does not necessarily give us pleasure in the moment, and it may, in fact, be uncomfortable. Think, for instance, of a rock climber experiencing the state of flow while she is completely engrossed in climbing a steep wall – she is not necessarily experiencing positive emotions (hedonism) and may be so immersed that she may not be attuned to emotions at all.

FOOD FOR THOUGHT
YOUR SIGNATURE STRENGTHS

Flow states are enabled by using our signature strengths. Many free tools exist to assess your strengths. Below are a few to get you started.

---

[22]Peterson, C. & Seligman, M. E. (2004). *Character Strengths and Virtues: A Handbook and Classification* (Vol. 1). Oxford: Oxford University Press.

[23]Peterson, C. & Seligman, M. E. (2006). The values in action (VIA) classification of strengths. In M. Csikszentmihalyi & I. S. Csikszentmihalyi (eds), *A Life Worth Living: Contributions to Positive Psychology* (pp. 29–48). Oxford: Oxford University Press.

[24]Gardner, H. E. (2011). *Frames of Mind: The Theory of Multiple Intelligences.* New York, NY: Basic Books.

[25]McQuaid, M., Niemiec, R. & Doman, F. (2018). A character strengths-based approach to positive psychology coaching. In S. Green & S. Palmer (eds), *Positive Psychology Coaching in Practice* (pp. 71–79). London: Routledge.

1. Your character strengths

The Value in Action (VIA) toolkit allows you to take a self-assessment questionnaire to learn about your Strengths of Character: **www.viacharacter.org/**

2. Your strengths of ability

The self-assessment test at the link below allows you to identify your ability-based strengths based on Gardner's classification: **www.literacynet.org/mi/assessment/findyourstrengths.html**

3. Your strengths of skills, resources and interests

Please list any other skill (something specific and applied that you can do well) that you have.

....
....
....

Please list your resources, including tangible (capital, assets, etc.) and intangible ones (networks, family support, etc.).

....
....
....

Please list your interests (if different from your abilities and skills above).

....
....
....

10.3.6 ACHIEVEMENT, PERSONAL GROWTH AND FULFILMENT OF POTENTIAL

Achievement is intended as putting our abilities and inclinations to fruition so that we can fulfil our potential and achieve competence or mastery at something.[26] We may understand

---

[26]Forgeard, M. J. C., Jayawickreme, E., Kern, M. L. & Seligman, M. E. P. (2011). Doing the right thing: Measuring wellbeing for public policy. *International Journal of Wellbeing, 1,* 79–106.

our achievements as both *intrinsically* or *extrinsically* motivated. Intrinsic motivation for our achievements means that we have an inner sense of satisfaction in achieving competence regardless of whether this is recognised externally. Extrinsically motivated achievement relates to obtaining status, accolades, titles or other recognitions that symbolise external recognition of our competence.[27]

While we often think that more wealth (economic value) means greater life satisfaction and achievement, the data would indicate that it's not quite so straightforward. What it shows is that as our wealth increases, we judge that our circumstances are improving, but this does not translate into whether our wellbeing, achievement or overall satisfaction with life are improving.[28] This highlights that when we are creating value for ourselves, *economic value* may be only one part of the picture. Simply, making money may not be the end in itself, but rather the route to something else. This is where achievement in the larger sense of competence and mastery comes in. Consider the case of Lorenzo Conti below. Lorenzo did not start a business in order to make more money than he would have made as an engineer. Rather, his drive is one of achieving mastery in his engineering creations, which eventually led (indirectly) to the creation of a robot that has potential for commercial applications.

ENTREPRENEURIAL THINKING AND MINDSET IN PRACTICE
LORENZO CONTI ON ACHIEVEMENT AS ENGINEERING MASTERY

The case study is intended to illustrate the following:

- the role of personal preference in achievement
- the importance of collaboration (see Chapter 7) in achievement
- the role of playing to one's strengths in collaborative pursuits.

This is the case study of Lorenzo Conti. Lorenzo is the founder and managing director of Crover (**www.crover.tech/**), a robotic grain monitoring device with potential for multiple applications and winner of the Scottish Enterprise Smart Awards.

The case is narrated in Lorenzo's own voice.

PLAYING WITH ENGINEERING IDEAS

My original background is in civil engineering and I was doing my PhD in an engineering department in Scotland, working in geotechnical engineering and then soil mechanics project.

---

[27]Wigfield, A., Muenks, K. & Eccles, J. S. (2021). Achievement motivation: What we know and where we are going. *Annual Review of Developmental Psychology, 3,* 87–111.

[28]Biswas-Diener, R. & Diener, E. (2001). Making the best of a bad situation: Satisfaction in the slums of Calcutta. *Social Indicators Research, 55,* 329–352.

Every so often I had some crazy ideas, most of them didn't turn out to work out. One day I got this intuition about something inspired by a paper. To move forward with the idea I set to run some simulations, some kind of experiments in my living room, and did so religiously. I even filled the room with sand to try to test this out! I went through two or three weeks where I did simulations and experiments on my own, without telling anyone. I had gone to my supervisor quite a few times before with crazy ideas and each time he'd tell me to go back to focusing on the PhD. Eventually, I summoned the courage to present the thing confidentially to my supervisor. He said absolutely nothing while I was presenting for about an hour. In the end he was just silent and I just thought he was considering what words to use to tell me that this wasn't going to work. I was still convinced that he would come up with some reason why my idea was wrong, as he normally does. I asked 'what do you think?' and he said 'I've never seen anything like this' – the kind of words that he never said before.

START-UP AS FULFILLING OF ENGINEERING POTENTIAL

I was coming to the end of the PhD and I had to decide what to do next. I just wanted to get something that would be significant out of the PhD, rather than just having yet another set of resources that no one really cares about. I wanted to make an impact on the scientific spectrum. There's a lot of room in the granular materials field to make impact. We can't model any kind of real world scenarios and environments. We have to use computationally expensive simulations, but more complex systems are impossible to simulate and fully understand because it would take too much computer time and it's not really feasible so that's why we try to develop better models and this thing was one of my curiosities that I ended up working on.

I mean, I was really at the point where I decided that academia was not for me. I was tired of having to deal with academics that just want to destroy someone else's ideas but I wasn't sure what the alternative would be.

I had absolutely no plan to have a start-up, it was the kind of thing that never even crossed my mind. However, now we had something that we had to do something with. Also, I was quite keen on having something that could deliver practical benefits, rather than just produce scientific theory. So the start-up opportunity just fell quite nicely.

THE TEAM

The main challenge was still the fact that I needed a team, so I started putting more and more time into looking for a co-founder. I realised that it was impossible for me to do everything and also, I knew the theory but I tried to build a robot myself and it's the kind of stuff that I didn't really know how to do. I realised I kept on trying to put aside time to slowly learn how to do those things and build them and I tried to build the first prototype itself but I did not have enough time to do everything on my own. I realised that if I kept on going at that rate we'll never get there.

It took a long time to identify the right person, because I learned the hard way that a lot of people make a lot of promises and don't deliver. Eventually, I was lucky enough to meet my co-founder and our technical director. He is absolutely amazing — he's our engineering superstar. We call him the 'mechanical magician' because he's really the one who built the robot from the ground up. He can design anything he sets his mind to.

That was a big cornerstone because that's when our team came together. We eventually managed to start building prototypes and we started getting more and more successful at competitions and grants and have cash. Then we were able to start getting some interns and then slowly form a proper team.

A NEW TECHNOLOGY IN SEARCH FOR A CAUSE

At that point, we didn't really have any idea what to do with the technology. We could use it to collect samples on Mars and other planets, such as underground exploration.

I was looking for people to help. I organised a meeting with some advisors — I didn't really know who they were and what they would do. I just went to this meeting with Ross. I just walk into this meeting as a crazy looking scientist with this crazy theory and he started asking me, 'what would you do with this?'. I said 'I don't know!'. I started talking about the MARS stuff and other things, and he said 'we need to look at other things'. He started sending me some reading materials about different topics and after about two or three months, reading into stuff I realised that a start-up was the natural way to go, so that's our initial story.

Lorenzo is also an example of 'obliquity'. That is, he did not set out to have a start-up with his earning potential. Rather, he focused on what he did best and enjoyed most, yet extrinsic success and achievement followed. This indirect way to achieve has been theorised by economist John Kay.

DEEP DIVE

WHAT IF OUR GOALS ARE BEST REACHED THROUGH 'OBLIQUITY'?

Whatever our personal objectives and goals, we often think that the best way to reach them is to act on them directly. Economics Professor John Kay makes a compelling argument for why, in a complex world, our goals are best achieved in indirect ways at www.youtube.com/watch?v=_BoAtYL3OWU

So what does all this mean for you? How might all the elements we've just discussed shape the value you can create for yourself? What can you do and what actions can you take? While value will look different for all of us, personal value creation for you might include (but is certainly not limited to):

- career progression (for example, being promoted, moving to the next pay scale or point, taking on new roles or responsibilities, taking on people management responsibilities)
- change of career (for example, moving into a new sector, moving from employment to self-employment or vice versa)
- making work more meaningful (for example, taking on new roles, working on new projects, mentoring others, being mentored)
- improving the work–life balance (for example, spending more time with family, being more disciplined about work hours, building in opportunities for physical and mental wellbeing)
- improving health (for example, exercising, eating well, getting sufficient sleep, laughing more)
- taking on new challenges (for example, running a marathon, learning a new skill, moving to a new country).

The list above is not exhaustive by any means. What it means is that, whatever the circumstances we face, there is always a way we can create value for ourselves (and others) by choosing to do so and leverage our entrepreneurial competences of perseverance (as seen in Chapter 4) and working with others (Chapters 7 and 8). Noreen's example below offers a powerful illustration of how even tragedy can be turned into an opportunity for value creation.

ENTREPRENEURIAL THINKING AND MINDSET IN PRACTICE
NOREEN PHILLIPS ON OVERCOMING PERSONAL TRAGEDY

The case study is intended to illustrate the following:

- the power of flourishing after personal tragedy
- the link between creating value for oneself and creating value for others
- the role of meaning and purpose in overcoming adversity.

This is the case study of Dr Noreen Phillips, PhD in Educational Psychology and His Majesty's Inspector of Education for Education Scotland.

The case is narrated in Noreen's own voice.

It all started when my husband Gordon began to feel really knocked out and he was losing weight. We made the appointment with the GP who sent him right to the hospital where they identified that he had a tumour. We started researching it and there was a 98% chance of death, so it wasn't really a good prognosis. Our children were aged six and three, so they were pretty young at the time and I was working so it was a juggle. Gordon kept getting worse and worse and worse all the time, nothing seemed to be working. Then he died, which was a huge shock because you never think it's going to actually happen, you always hope ...

Talking to the doctors during the time Gordon was in hospital I realised that this particular form of cancer of the oesophagus was on the increase for young people, around 40 years of age. It used to be a disease that was affecting those who smoked and drank heavily but there seemed to be a lot of people that were dying and there was an idea that it was because of really strong, hot, black coffee that can burn the oesophagus. Lots of professionals were being affected by it. The doctor asked me if I would help raise awareness of oesophageal cancer? He thought that we would be a good model to show people. The other thing I realised at the time was that there was no scanner available in Glasgow to diagnose this form of cancer. There was one in Edinburgh but not in Glasgow. It was crucial that Glasgow got its own scanner to speed up the waiting list for diagnosis.

I decided then that I was going to find a way to raise funds to buy a scanner for Glasgow. When I look back, to be honest, at the time I wasn't actually well. I was just functioning. I think this gave me a focus, a resemblance of normality in some ways. It helped because I was out and about and doing things.

The price of a scanner at the time [1999] was £100,000, so it was a lot of money. So, I knew I'd need a committee of friends and other people willing to help me raise the money. I started thinking of the specific skills I needed in that committee: I needed someone to take the minutes, someone who could action plan, and so on. I put together the committee – there was 14 of us and quite a mix of working and non-working women. Many were mums from my kids' school. With children of the same age we became friendly. As a psychologist, I was used to chairing meetings and to be very careful to give everybody their place in a role that played to their strengths. There were some great cooks there, so they would decide on menus because I know nothing about food, my late husband did all the cooking. There were people good at organising balls and at asking people for favours, getting people in their networks to donate things. Others could write really well, so we had them write the materials for publications and publicity. There was a guy who knew a publisher and we published a **Gordon Phillips Scanner Appeal** book. I suppose it is an entrepreneur's skill to give people jobs to do based on what they are good at and enjoy doing. I could see that it was working because they were very involved; this was giving them meaning too.

We had lots of events and I don't know how but the money came in and eventually we got £200,000. We had a final party just for those who had been involved in the fundraising over the previous nine months. At that party, everyone got a memory book that we had assembled with photos from all the organising committees and all the events we had run. These books were given as a 'thank you' and they were really touched by this. Everyone was really disappointed that we were stopping because there had been really good, really fun events.

Later, I got a lot of letters from people who went to the doctors and, because of the new scanner in Glasgow, they could now do something about their diagnosis, so that felt nice.

See press release: **www.heraldscotland.com/news/12149251.widows-abc1-cancer-battlephone-call-from-a-stranger-gives-momentum-to-familys-scanner-appeal/**

As both Noreen and Tony's stories demonstrate, while we may take action to create value for ourselves, in doing so we often indirectly create value for others. This touches on the principle of *obliquity* (see Deep dive box above). Sometimes, in our pursuit to create value for ourselves, we end up creating more than we could have imagined at the outset.

10.4 SUMMARY AND NEXT STEPS

This chapter has built on our discussion of *value* from Chapter 1, reiterating that *economic value,* what we often think of when we speak of value in the context of entrepreneurial thinking and action, is just one form of value that we can create for ourselves. As the cases in the chapter have demonstrated, value looks different to each of us. You might want to help others by creating *social value,* build your own *mental value* to support your personal flourishing, or even work to create or sustain *environmental, aesthetic* or *cultural* value. Ultimately the value we seek to create supports our own *self-determination* and ultimately personal flourishing, linked to the dimensions that compose what we each consider to be a 'life well lived'. These include: autonomy and self-determination; belonging, connection and positive relationships; positive emotion; engagement and flow; meaning and purpose; and achievement, personal growth and fulfilment of potential. As we've discussed, these are not mutually exclusive – you make seek to create value for yourself in a range of spaces to support your own personal flourishing.

WHERE AM I NOW?
FOUNDATIONS FOR PERSONAL FLOURISHING

Having worked through this chapter, consider the current composition of elements of personal flourishing. Take a few minutes to reflect on how these relate to you and your life. Record your thoughts below.

AUTONOMY AND SELF-DETERMINATION

On a scale from 1 (none) to 10 (complete autonomy) how much autonomy and self-determination do you have in your personal life? Please explain the reason for your score.

On a scale from 1 (none) to 10 (complete autonomy) how much autonomy and self-determination do you have in your professional life? Please explain the reason for your score.

....
....
....

BELONGING, CONNECTION AND POSITIVE RELATIONSHIPS

On a scale from 1 (disconnected) to 10 (extremely connected) how connected do you consider yourself in your personal life? Please explain the reason for your score, focusing on the aspects of human connection that are important to you (e.g., quantity versus quality of friendships and family bonds, being accepted, belonging in your reference group, etc.).

....
....
....

On a scale from 1 (disconnected) to 10 (extremely connected) how connected do you consider yourself in your professional life? Please explain the reason for your score, focusing on the aspects of human connection that are important to you (e.g., quantity versus quality of professional connection, being accepted, belonging in your professional circle, etc.).

....
....

POSITIVE EMOTION

Reflecting on the past two to three weeks, what experiences of pleasure or enjoyment (hedonic state) can you recall? How much (10 = very) or little (1 = not at all) do you value and seek such experiences? Please explain the reason for your score.

....

....

ENGAGEMENT AND FLOW

Reflecting on the past two to three weeks, how often (10 = very often; 1 = never) have you experienced states of flow (full engagement in an activity so that time stops)? Please explain the reason for your answer, paying particular attention to the type of activity that engages you most. Describe the characteristics of the flow-inducing activity as well as what strengths of yours this activity allows you to use.

....

....

MEANING AND PURPOSE

what currently gives your life its main purpose? If you can think of multiple sources of purpose and meaning, both from your personal and professional life, can you rank them in order of priority for you?

....

....

10.5 CONTINUE YOUR LEARNING

The following activities are designed to support you on your learning journey, building on ideas introduced in this chapter. These can be completed at any time and in any order, although you may find it helpful to begin with the 'Check your understanding' activity before moving on.

CHECK YOUR UNDERSTANDING

1. **Exchange value** represents what you are prepared to give up in order to obtain something.

    ☐ **TRUE** (It's true – please see section 10.2)

    ☐ **FALSE**

2. Ultimately, the main form of value creation is economic value.

☐ **TRUE**

☐ **FALSE** (It's false – please see section 10.2)

3. Achievement usually refers to accolades, titles and other markers of success.

☐ **TRUE**

☐ **FALSE** (It's false – please see section 10.3.6)

5. We achieve flow states when we are in the sweet spot between boredom and anxiety.

☐ **TRUE** (It's true – please see section 10.3.4)

☐ **FALSE**

6. The need for belonging and connection is as true in our professional life as it is in our private life.

☐ **TRUE** (It's true – please see section 10.3.2)

☐ **FALSE**

FURTHER READING

1. **Flourish** by Martin Seligman

2. **From Strength to Strength** by Arthur C. Brooks

3. **The 7 Habits of Highly Effective People** by Stephen R. Covey

PRACTISING ENTREPRENEURIAL THINKING
MAP YOUR PERSONAL VALUE CREATION

Now, take some time to map what value will mean to you personally. Consider what value you'd like to create in your professional life (e.g., become an expert in something, gain a promotion, change of career, start a business, etc.) as well as your personal life (e.g., take up a new hobby, buy a bigger house, make time for travel, etc.) – and in the intersection of these two worlds.

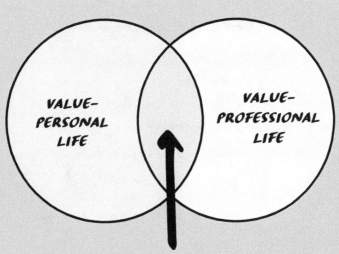

VALUE – INTERSECTION OF PERSONAL AND PROFESSIONAL LIVES

1. Consider what value you wish to create in your **professional life** by following the prompts below:

   • What do you aspire to currently?

   ☐ Promotion (in existing organisation)

   ☐ Move to a new organisation

   ☐ Change of career (new sector)

   ☐ Transition from self-employment to employment

   ☐ Transition from employment to self-employment

   ☐ Reduction of working hours

   ☐ Increase in working hours

   ☐ Increase size of own organisation

   ☐ Decrease size of own organisation

   ☐ Other – please specify ....

   • What value do you expect this to add (perceived value)? Tick all that apply.

   ☐ Financial (more money)

   ☐ Wellbeing (e.g., better work-life balance, more enjoyment, better health/mental health)

☐ Achievement – extrinsic (e.g., more leverage/power/status/recognition)

☐ Achievement – intrinsic (e.g., satisfaction/fulfilment of potential)

☐ Other – please specify ....

- what are you prepared to give up in order to achieve your aspiration (exchange value)? Tick all that apply.

☐ Free time – how many hours per week? ....

☐ Money – how much are you prepared to part with? ...

☐ Effort – more physical/mental exertion?....

2. Consider what value you wish to create in your **personal life** by following the prompts below:

- what do you aspire to currently?

☐ Learn a new skill – please specify ....

☐ Take up a challenge (physical or mental) ....

☐ Move country

☐ Change house

☐ Build a house

☐ Other – please specify ....

- what value do you expect this to add (perceived value)? Tick all that apply.

☐ Financial (more money)

☐ Wellbeing (e.g., better work–life balance, more enjoyment, better health/mental health)

☐ Achievement – extrinsic (e.g., more leverage/power/status/recognition)

☐ Achievement – intrinsic (e.g., satisfaction/fulfilment of potential)

☐ Other – please specify ....

- what are you prepared to give up in order to achieve your aspiration (exchange value)? Tick all that apply.

☐ Free time – how many hours per week? ....

☐ Money – how much are you prepared to part with? ...

☐ Effort – more physical/mental exertion? ....

3. Consider what value might look like at the junction between your professional and personal lives (input into the Figure above).

4. Consider where you are now and where you want to be with regard to the value you have identified.

   - where am I in relation to where I can/want to be?

   - what challenges do I face at this time?

   - what can I do to tackle these challenges?

   - where will I start? what specific actions will I take?

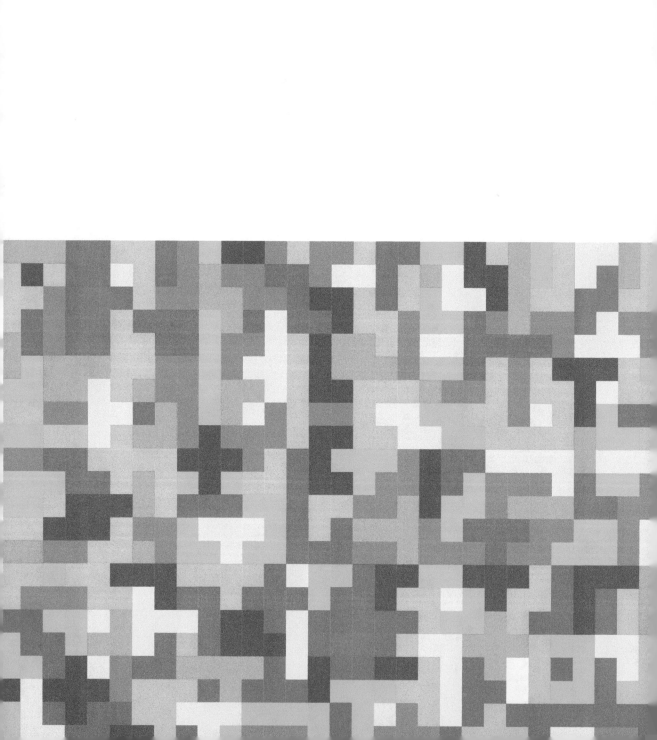

CHAPTER 11

CREATING VALUE FOR OTHERS & TACKLING THE WORLD'S 'WICKED PROBLEMS'

"GREAT THINGS ARE DONE BY A SERIES OF
SMALL THINGS BROUGHT TOGETHER"

– VINCENT VAN GOGH

11.1 INTRODUCTION

Having considered how we can create value for ourselves in Chapter 10, we now turn our attention to how we can extend our creation activities to benefit others. This might mean people in your organisation, your community, or even those further afield. As we've discussed throughout Section 3, creating value is more often than not a collaborative task, where we can draw on different experiences, insights, worldviews, frames of reference and skills in order to create something bigger and better than what we might be able to envision or put into action alone. This is particularly important when we are seeking to tackle complex or 'wicked' problems with no clear boundaries or courses of action.

What skills, interests or experiences do you have that might help tackle the problems that others face? What issues or topics are meaningful for you? Do you feel a 'call to action' to support a particular cause? Who might you collaborate with to take action and initiate change?

This chapter will start by discussing how we can create value for others by identifying, exploring and addressing the problems they face. When we speak about entrepreneurial thinking and action we often jump straight to talk of solving problems, yet taking the time to explore and understand the nature of problems is critical if we are to create meaningful change and thus value. We then consider how value creation for others can take a collaborative form and where bringing people together offers more opportunity for value than individuals working alone. Finally, we consider the manifestation of problems beyond our own families, organisations or even communities. We will discuss how we can approach value creation when tackling those '*wicked problems*' that do not easily lend themselves to being solved but which hold significant potential for creating value.

After working through this chapter, you should be able to:

- differentiate between problem identification, exploration and solving
- articulate the critical role that problem exploration plays in creating meaningful and sustainable value for others
- consider how collaborative entrepreneurial thinking works in practice and the different forms of value that can be created when tackling challenging or 'wicked' problems.

11.2 IDENTIFYING, EXPLORING AND RESPONDING TO PROBLEMS

When we talk about value creation in entrepreneurial contexts, we often think of new products (usually technology based) commercialised by a start-up. Yet as we've discussed throughout this book, value can take a range of forms – *something new, improved, or in a novel space, that an individual or group of individuals considers to have worth*. Within other entrepreneurial contexts, such as in established organisations or even at community level, value may look or feel very different to our mental imagery. Yes, it might take the form of a new product, technology or radical innovation that the world hasn't seen before; equally it might take the form of a series of smaller incremental innovations that, over time, change peoples' lives for the better.

When looking to create value for others, we tend to start from a problem which presents an opportunity for change. This might be eliminating a 'point of pain' (e.g., cutting the time spent waiting on something, or simplifying a process), making life more pleasurable or meaningful for people (think back to Chapter 10) or even tackling wider negative experiences or injustices. While we may be tempted to jump right in to finding solutions to these problems, this is in fact counterproductive to our efforts to create meaningful (and sustainable) value for others! In rushing to develop a solution and making quick judgements (see Chapter 6) we may let our own frames of reference and worldview (see Chapter 3) influence how we see a situation, rather than taking our time to fully explore what is in front of us. We may also not communicate effectively with people experiencing the problem (see Chapter 9), or those who can help us tackle it (see Chapter 7), and thus fail to develop an empathetic understanding of how we can work together to create value (see Chapter 8).

WHERE AM I STARTING FROM?
CHALLENGING THE STATUS QUO

Many would argue that opportunities for value creation are everywhere. As the British entrepreneur Sir Richard Branson famously remarked: 'Business opportunities are like buses, there's always another one coming'. One place to look is in situations where the current way of thinking/acting/doing no longer works — where we need to challenge the status quo. This is particularly so when we're considering creating value for others.

Consider instances where you see that things aren't working as you think they should. Record your thoughts below.

1. What specific problems can you identify? (These could be problems in your workplace, in your community, issues you hear about on the news, etc.)

2. who is being impacted by these problems and in what way?

....

....

3. what do you think might help to address these problems?

....

....

4. what skills/knowledge/experience/perspective could you bring?

....

....

To overcome these challenges, we need to recognise that solving a problem is in fact the last stage in the creation process. Before we are able to develop solutions, we need to first engage in *problem identification and exploration*. This can be challenging as we are likely to be operating in situations of uncertainty (think back to Section 2) or the '*whitespace*', where tried and tested approaches or standardised operating procedures to solve problems are either not available or are unlikely to work and where we may lack resources, knowledge and other structures.[1] As a result, we have a tendency to fixate on what we can easily see (or hear, or understand) linked to our own personal knowledge and experience. In doing so, however, we often confuse the easily identifiable 'symptoms' of the problem with the actual problem itself. We thus need to spend time differentiating the symptoms we see from the *root cause*[2] of the problem in order to ensure that our time and effort is well spent and that we are not missing opportunities to create value.[3]

[1]Maletz, M. C. & Nohria, N. (2001). Managing in the whitespace. *Harvard Business Review, 79*(1), 102–111.

[2]Fischer, A., Greiff, S. &Funke, J. (2012). The process of solving complex problems. *The Journal of Problem Solving, 4*, 1118.

[3]Spradlin, D. (2012). Are you solving the right problem? *Harvard Business Review, 90*, 84.

ENTREPRENEURIAL THINKING AND MINDSET IN PRACTICE

FLORENCE ADU ON CREATING VALUE FOR OTHERS THROUGH INCLUSIVITY

The case study is intended to illustrate the following:

- the impact that small changes can have on the lives and wellbeing of others
- the interrelationship between value for individuals and value for organisations.

This is the case study of Florence Adu, a geologist working in the mining industry. Florence has worked across West Africa and Europe, where she combines her specialist expertise with a passion for assisting the local communities whose lives are impacted by mining operations.

The case is narrated in Florence's own voice.

I'm from originally from Ghana. I work in the gold mining industry and I've worked in different roles, mostly as a geologist, in different countries mostly in French [speaking] West Africa. It's been tough. I was always in an environment where I was probably the only female – or the first female my male colleagues ever had to work with! Anyone who knows me knows that I'm an advocate for diversity, inclusion and equality. Every time I go to a work environment where I was the only female, I made sure I at least double the number. It's not just about the numbers, it's not about just having females. We need them to be there. They have voices to be heard, they have valuable insights. Bring out their creativity, make room for them to be able to speak up and make the workplace safe enough for them to always come to work and to appreciate the work that they're doing.

I was recently nominated as one of the Top 100 Global Inspirational Women in Mining and I saw some of the nominations. One in particular was because I pioneered setting up a lactation room for new mothers in my company.

It's a big deal when you have to return to work, when our self-confidence is even down, and you're thinking about the baby you've left at a creche [nursery] or with someone. It's scientifically proven that breastfeeding, especially in the early months – at least the first six months of the baby's life – is very important. But most women have to return to work in the first three months of the baby's birth, sometimes two months. I always went back after the first three months. I've got two children and I know the challenges that women face when expressing [pumping breastmilk] and have had to use rooms that aren't safe or hygienic places to express [milk] to bring back to the babies.

This was a big deal to me. When I sent this proposal to management this was my first ever business case outside of my geology work and I had to step out of my comfort zone. I had people in HR supporting me as well so I could go to management and say, we need this facility to retain these women at work. Otherwise if a woman decides to have a child we've lost the talent just because they couldn't come back to work safely in the first three or four months after having a baby. With the lactation room they don't have to make excuses to go back home to feed their babies. They get to spend time during the day with their babies. It wasn't easy to push this through, but I was relentless that we were going to push this and make sure that the women felt included, that they enjoy coming to work, and were going to stay with the company.

So yes, it worked out well. The women felt safe and supported at the workplace and they put in everything – I mean 120% – at work. So I don't think the attrition rate in the company is as high as other mining companies.

Identifying and exploring problems has been found time and again to be the most critical part of the creative process – the evidence is quite clear that the more time and effort spent exploring the problem/situation/task at hand, the higher the quality of any output(s).[4] As Albert Einstein famously once remarked, 'If I had an hour to solve a problem I'd spend 55 minutes thinking about the problem and five minutes thinking about solutions'.

Florence's story powerfully illustrates how taking the time and effort to understand a problem can result in opportunities to create unique value. To increase the number of women working at her company, Florence could have adopted common management practices such as instituting affirmative action programmes to encourage the hiring of more women, working to minimise pay gaps between men and women, or offering additional incentives to women such as parental or family leave. Yet, as Florence found, these weren't tackling the root cause of gender inequality in her own specific workplace, which ultimately hinged on the issue of young women not staying in work

---

[4]Getzels, J. W. (1975). Problem-finding and the inventiveness of solutions, *Journal of Creative Behavior*, *9*, 12–18; Getzels, J. W. & Czikszentmihalyi, M. (1976). *The Creative Vision.* New York: Wiley.

after the birth of their babies and thus losing the opportunity to become embedded within the organisation.

To be frank, understanding the nature (or root causes) of problems isn't always straightforward. Sometimes we don't know what to look for, what questions to ask, or even how to make sense of any information we're gathering. To help we can cultivate a number of what are called 'discovery skills',[5] cognitive activities that allow us to engage with problems more meaningfully:

- *associating* – connecting seemingly unrelated questions, problems or ideas, often from different fields or aspects of your life
- *questioning* – asking questions that challenge common wisdom and assumptions, even yours
- *observing* – watching what happens in action and reflecting on the insights you gather
- *experimenting* – tinkering and trying new things whilst embracing the potential for failure
- *networking* – drawing on peer feedback, ideally from different perspectives than your own.

DEEP DIVE
THE POWER OF 'YES, AND ...'

Many of these discovery skills help us to put aside our own biases, assumptions and beliefs, allowing us to have a more open mind when exploring problems and thinking of ideas to address them. A related approach that surged in popularity is the principle of 'yes, and'. Stemming from improvisational comedy, 'yes, and' approaches to problems require us to hear what is being said, to acknowledge it and to **build on it**. This approach prevents us from jumping to conclusions or shutting things down prematurely, encouraging collaborative efforts to come up with new ideas and approaches that may challenge (and perhaps change) our perspectives.

Karen Tilstra, co-founder and director of Florida Hospital's Innovation Lab, talks about how this concept has helped her own work to support creative thinking and innovation in healthcare at **https://youtu.be/ USK_qNLxSU**

---

[5]Dyer, J. H., Gregersen, H. D. & Christensen, C. M. (2009). The innovator's DNA. *Harvard Business Review, 87*(12), 60–67.

11.3 WORKING WITH OTHERS TO SOLVE PROBLEMS AND CREATE VALUE FOR ALL

Networking, the final 'discovery skill', reinforces the fact that exploring and solving problems to create value for others is not something you can do in isolation – it is an inherently collaborative activity. As individuals we have access to limited information and knowledge. Simply put, there is only so much that our brains can collect, and more importantly *retain*, on any given topic!

When we work with others, however, we are able to draw on a much larger body of knowledge and insight.[6] This not only helps us to overcome our own biases of *information asymmetries* (where one side knows more than the other and therefore has more power), but also allows us to tackle problems of greater complexity than we would otherwise be able to deal with alone.[7] This is particularly the case when we work with people from different backgrounds and disciplines[8] and who have different frames of reference and worldview (see Chapter 3) than we do. Not only do these provide us with different ways of identifying and exploring problems, they also allow us to take vague or ill-structured problems and develop a set of structures that will support the development of solutions.

Take, for example, the case of the Italian town of Sciacca that was faced with the daunting choice of either reinventing itself, or losing its residents and cultural history and fading away into history…

ENTREPRENEURIAL THINKING AND MINDSET IN PRACTICE
THE 5 SENSES OPEN-AIR MUSEUM OF SCIACCA

The case study is intended to illustrate the following:

* grassroots collaborative activity to support value creation for individuals and their wider community
* how different forms of value creation can both exist simultaneously and further support one another.

---

[6]Hayek, F. A. (1942). Scientism and the study of society. Part I. *Economica, 9*(35), 267–291.

[7]Wahl, J., Füller, J. & Hutter, K. (2022). What's the problem? How crowdsourcing and text-mining may contribute to the understanding of unprecedented problems such as COVID-19. *R&D Management, 52,* 427–446.

[8]Hong, L. & Page, S.E. (2004) Groups of diverse problem solvers can outperform groups of high-ability problem solvers. *Proceedings of the National Academy of Sciences of the United States of America, 101,* 16385–16389.

This is the case study of Sciacca, a town on the southern coast of Sicily, in the Agrigento province. The area is famous for its historical links to ancient Greece and the Greek temples. The town of Sciacca itself was built by Greeks, who settled there because of the discovery of thermal baths around 400BCE.

The case illustrates the unfolding of a community entrepreneurship initiative that has been recognised through several awards for social innovation and environmental impact, as well as for 'changing minds', an award by the Confederation of Craft Trades and Small- and Medium-Sized Enterprises.

The case has been prepared by representatives of the Sciacca City Council.

THE STRUGGLES

After thriving on tourism linked to the baths over the centuries, the closure of thermal baths in 2015 led to a steady decline in the numbers of visitors virtually overnight. The decline was even more significant during the low season in autumn and winter, leaving the town without one of its main sources of income – tourism.

The economic decline also led to a social, cultural and environmental decline. People felt hopeless and could not envision any route into a prosperous and sustainable future. As a direct consequence, over 6,000 inhabitants migrated, resulting in a steady decline in the population.

Source: Pixabay

THE REINVENTION

In January 2019, a think tank called SOS Centro Storico (SOS Historic Centre) was organised to fight back against the downward spiral that the community had fallen into. It saw representatives of the different economic sectors (both directly and indirectly tied to tourism) and cultural associations come together for the first time. Representatives included coral craftsmen, pottery artisans, carnival associations, theatre associations, B&Bs, restaurant and bar owners, fishing industries associations and other representatives of the community.

The question posed to them all was: 'what would enable us to develop in a fair and sustainable manner?'. Every single person attending the initial meeting had a different answer to the question posed, from sea and beaches to carnival and pottery to coral and fishing, to cooking and traditions. Over subsequent meetings, the discussion evolved into the idea that Sciacca could be seen through the metaphor of an 'open-air museum', where the town squares are exhibition halls, the streets are museum corridors, the craftsmen's shops and the inhabitants' windows are the display cases through which visitors can discover the ultimate treasure of the museum: the PEOPLE who live in it.

From that initial meeting, specialists started crafting the first few visitor experiences and a dedicated website was launched (**www.sciaccaSsensi.it/en/**).

Source: Pixabay

During the summer, the first event took place – the European Night of Museums. Visitors could try different multi-sensorial experiences all over the city and monuments usually closed were reopened, with their past narrated through storytelling. The success of the event sparked more community meetings, increasing awareness of the pool of resources available within the community and of the importance of cooperation rather than competition so that everyone would benefit. **This marked a shift from an ego-system perspective to an eco-system perspective** and Sciacca became a community cooperative and was formally recognised as an Ecomuseum by the Region of Sicily.

Source: Campidoglio in Sciacca

THE TEAM

Sciacca's reinvention was led by Viviana Rizzuto. After working for American multinationals in Switzerland for over 17 years, she decided to return to Sicily as she believed the management techniques she used in her professional role could also be applied to Sciacca as a whole. She refused to accept the negative attitude that some residents felt about the future and was able to bring together sometimes disparate groups by emphasising professionalism, competence, passion and a strong love for her land. A few months in, Emilio Casalini joined as the Chief Vision Officer, bringing with him skills and experience from 20 years working in the world of communication as a professional journalist and correspondent for the Italian national public broadcasting company.

Working closely with Viviana and Emilio is the community of Sciacca, with the project based on three pillars:

- **awareness** of the heritage available but not yet enhanced
- **competence** in transforming resources into social, cultural, environmental, economic, human value
- **connections** in the territories, so essential today, to create synergies for a development that will last over time.

VALUE CREATION FOR THE COMMUNITY AND ITS VISITORS

The initiative has generated a strong value for individuals in the community, for the community as a whole and for tourists visiting the town. Sciacca has started to have a cohesive and healthy community; the way the community interacts and cooperates to co-generate happiness and wellbeing has changed. Diversity has become an additional perspective and a resource for the community. For example, people with disabilities developed experiences to foster perspective and understanding, such as driving a boat blindfolded, through the guidance of Stefano, a visually impaired person.

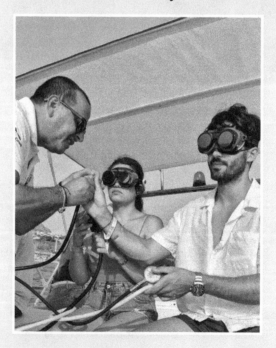

Source: Sciacca City Council

Cultural value has also been created, as tradition and heritage has begun to generate economic value while preserving local history and knowledge. For example, audio guides on Iti.travel have been created by the community to remember and narrate its history.

The community has also reopened the 4,000-year-old Thermal Bath caves, closed for many years, a unique asset in the world. In less than 10 months, with openings managed only by volunteers, only two days a week and for only two hours, more than 6,000 visitors have discovered the caves and their cultural legacy.

Source: Sciacca City Council

Artisans and the cooperative's associates have created more than 50 experiences for visitors to enjoy. The experiences offered to visitors include artisanship and gastronomy, safeguarding and perpetuating intangible heritage. Visitors can try their hand at making pasta, painting ceramics, and sculpting locally sourced material to make jewellery.

Source: Sciacca City Council

Environmental value has been created by making 'local' and 'sustainable' a unique proposition of the community to its visitors. For example, all hospitality structures offer soaps made with organic olive oil and orange blossoms from the territory. The soap is contained in ceramic dispensers, which are unique pieces made by the pottery artisans. In turn, this attention to environmental sustainability is attracting visitors with an appreciation for slow and green tourism, thus creating a virtuous cycle of sustainability both on the side of visitors as well as the community.

All of the above have, in turn, resulted in **economic value creation**. Visitors (or temporary citizens, as they are called) stay longer on average in order to experience the way of life of the local community. They also tend to have higher spending power and are prepared to invest because of the value they perceive they are getting from the experience. The community has also received unsolicited requests for accommodation for digital nomads and employees working remotely. Revenue has increased by 30% for shops located in the regenerated neighbourhoods.

The project is still increasing its influence in the community, contributing to the enhancement of its economic, social and cultural life. It is a way of bringing people together, towards the same goal and through a shared governance that generates value for all.

In this case, Sciacca has been able to draw on a range of skills, interests, experiences and insights – not just from those driving the project, from the whole community. This has supported a range of ideas and resulting initiatives, many of which have only come about due to individuals being empowered to use their specialist knowledge and perspectives. Combined, these different initiatives have helped to bit by bit address the fundamental problem facing Sciacca, to reduce out-migration and support the town to become a place where people want to live, work and stay. These small initiatives have also helped to shape the direction of the project, influencing its aims, objectives and outcomes, as well as providing an impetus to enact further change.

This reflects the concept of ***obliquity***, the process of achieving complex objectives indirectly (as showcased in the Deep dive in Chapter 10). When we are working with problems, we don't always know what action we could (or should) take. Obliquity recognises that,

> ... *complex objectives tend to be imprecisely defined and contain many elements that are not necessarily or obviously compatible with each other, and that we learn about the nature of the objectives and the means of achieving them during a process of experiment and discovery. Oblique approaches often step backwards to move forwards.*[9]

When we're faced with a problem, we often assume we need to do something big to solve it – and then we struggle to persist when we can't figure out what that 'something' big is. Oblique approaches to problem solving are largely built on a number of small innovations and actions which, in combination and over time, culminate to create value. In chaos theory, this is observed as the *butterfly effect principle*, the idea that a small change in a system (e.g., a butterfly flapping its wings in the atmosphere in Brazil) can create turbulence that on a larger scale can disrupt or alter the entire system (e.g., causing a tornado in Texas).[10]

11.4 TACKLING THE WORLD'S 'WICKED' PROBLEMS

This issue of taking small actions that cumulate over time to create meaningful (and more sustainable) value is of particular relevance when looking to create value for our communities, societies or the world at large. In these spaces we are often tackling wider social, political or environmental issues, such as reducing inequalities, fighting poverty, ensuring fair governance and rule of law, or minimising pollution and environmental degradation. These are captured by the UN's 17 Sustainable Development Goals (SDGs) (see https://sdgs.un.org/goals) and are often referred to as 'wicked' problems based on how complex these problems are and how difficult or *wicked* they are to solve.

So what makes a 'wicked' problem? Generally, these are problems that are ill defined, with unclear boundaries, changing requirements, different stakeholders with conflicting

---

[9]Kay, J. (2011). *Obliquity*. London: Profile Books Ltd., pp. 2–3.

[10]Lorenz, E. N. (1963). Deterministic nonperiod flow. *Journal of the Atmospheric Sciences*, *20*(2), 130–141.

needs and values and no clear path to an answer or solution. We can think of them as having a number of distinguishing features:[11]

1. There is no definitive formulation of a wicked problem – they are complex, multifaceted and sometimes contradictory.

2. Wicked problems have no stopping rule – they are so complex that it is impossible to ever say the problem is 'solved'.

3. Solutions to wicked problems are not true or false, but better or worse – this requires us to work in a space of uncertainty (see Section 2) and to make judgement calls (see Chapter 6) on whether we think we are on the right track.

4. There is no immediate and no ultimate test of a solution to a wicked problem – we don't know what outcomes a solution may yield and we need to accept that the solution itself might cause further problems that we need to tackle (think back to how you persist in uncertainty and ambiguity in Chapter 4).

5. Every solution to a wicked problem is a 'one-shot operation' and because there is no opportunity to learn by trial and error every attempt counts – what ever action we take, there will be a lasting effect that we cannot undo, so we need to be able to make judgements and take action we feel confident about (see Chapter 6) while recognising that we may well make a mistake and fail in our goals (see Chapter 5).

6. Wicked problems do not have a describable set of potential solutions or a clear plan of action – we need to work with others (see Chapters 7 and 8) to come up with ideas and to mutually agree a course of action.

7. Every wicked problem is essentially unique – no two are the same.

8. Every wicked problem can be considered to be a symptom of another problem – we struggle to determine cause and effect and so need to carefully consider how to explore and explain the problem at hand.

9. The existence of a wicked problem can be explained in numerous ways – we all make sense of and explain the world in our own way based our own frames of reference and worldview (see Chapters 3 and 7).

10. Those taking action have no right to be wrong – we are liable for the consequences of the actions we generate and how these affect others.

These wicked problems are shaped by – and in turn shape – the uncertain and ambiguous conditions in which entrepreneurial action takes place (see Section 2). As we discussed in Chapter 4, a key capability of entrepreneurial individuals is considered to be their ability

---

[11]Rittel, H. W. J. & Webber, M. M. (1973). Dilemmas in a general theory of planning. *Policy Sciences, 4*(2), 155–169.

to operate – and ultimately thrive – under uncertainty,[12] particularly within what we call VUCA (**V**olatile **U**ncertain **C**omplex **A**mbiguous) conditions:

- Volatility – change is rapid and unpredictable in its nature and extent
- Uncertainty – the present is unclear and the future is uncertain
- Complexity – many different, interconnected factors come into play, with the potential to cause chaos and confusion
- Ambiguity – there is a lack of clarity or awareness about situations.

ENTREPRENEURIAL THINKING AND MINDSET IN PRACTICE
JÉRÉMIE WARNER ON CREATING VALUE FOR DISADVANTAGED COMMUNITIES IN DEVELOPING COUNTRIES

The case study is intended to illustrate the following:

- how small changes can help to address wicked problems such as alleviating poverty and supporting educational attainment
- that economic value creation for organisations is not mutually exclusive with social value creation for other communities and societies.

This is the case study of Jérémie Warner. Jérémie is the co-founder of a 'buy to give' business Power a Life. The company sells portable changers (power banks) to corporate customers for corporate gifting and merchandising. For each charger sold they give a solar light to a child in a developing country. These lights allow children to walk home safely from school and do their homework at night in communities that do not have access to reliable power infrastructure.

The case is narrated in Jérémie's own voice.

BACKGROUND TO POWER A LIFE

I didn't study business, I studied architecture, a creative discipline. I was in Singapore working on what I thought was my dream job. I was working for an architect's practice and we were building luxury houses on private islands. I could see from the projects that what we were building were only making the rich richer and I wanted to use my design skills as an architect to empower the poor, not the rich.

---

[12]Casson, M. (1982). *The Entrepreneur: An Economic Theory*. Washington, DC: Rowman & Littlefield.

So then I came back home, having decided that we need to build a business with social impact. We can make money and do good at the same time, and it was in Singapore that the idea came about. I then did six months in Amsterdam, with lots of free time, asking myself 'How do we build a social enterprise with the challenges in Africa?'. All throughout my final years in the undergraduate degree and my master's degree, everything was geared towards humanitarian design, including a collaborative dissertation focusing on agriculture, health care, energy and education. We had maybe two, three dozen of ideas that we [Jérémie and co-founder Paul] were designing that would be able to alleviate poverty but we knew we needed infrastructure on the ground to get started.

It was at that point that the investment kicked in and we booked flights and went to Senegal. We were very intentional with going to Senegal to begin with. It's considered to be very stable. It's never had a military coup, has always had peaceful transitions of government, their currency is linked to the euro through their French colonial history. So it was a safe place to get your feet wet. Also, it's French speaking and I'm a Belgian national and I speak fluent French, so everything was going through me; I was the only person that could communicate with our friends and partners on the ground.

It's also because that's where a friend of my Dad's was based, Sharif, who does micro finance in West Africa, and who was the CEO of a credit union. At first Sharif was nothing more than a phone number but he became our first employee. We did multiple trips [to Senegal] and we always lived with Sharif and his family in the bush. With no running water, no electricity, we were experiencing the challenges as Sharif and his family did so we could understand the problems.

BALANCING ECONOMIC VALUE AND SOCIAL VALUE

Sales for Power a Life are really trucking. Corporate customers are increasing in size, increasing and scale and the frequency of the orders is also increasing.

We've also delivered about 1,500 solar lights on the ground. I think the first impact report we got back from our charity partner in Zimbabwe was the highest point for us. We were absolutely flabbergasted with the impact we're creating on the ground. In Zimbabwe we set up a monitoring and testing program project where kids in Zimbabwe are tested every couple of weeks in subjects including English and maths and over the space of only two or three months, we could see improvements in every kid's test grades. The biggest improvement was in grade five, with there being almost a tripling of their average class score in only a couple of months. This was phenomenal, we were making a difference and improving kids' grades in schools and we could see it in black and white. The impact was far greater than we thought it could possibly be. That was awesome. That was a really inspiring and certainly very, very motivating for us as a team.

SHARIF'S LEGACY

Sharif wrote an email with something to the effect of 'I'm not well'. At that point, I didn't understand what was going on. I needed to go and make sure he was seen to [by medical professionals] if he's not well. I flew over to Senegal, I took him to hospital and by the end of that week it was me that had to tell him that he had terminal cancer because the doctors were not prepared to tell them. I had to tell Sharif that we needed to start making preparations for him and his family. At that point, I left them all the money I could possibly withdraw [from the bank]. I said 'take care of yourself, please go to hospital, make sure you're comfortable'. It was a month or two after that when there was the phone call from Senegal saying he'd passed away. That is the hardest thing I've ever had to do as a business owner and it comes with the territory of working in developing countries, it comes with the territory of you're working with people who have very little. These communities are off grid and do not have access to healthcare. I think about him all the time and all the lights that we now gift are all gifted in memory of Sharif, and it's a big reason for why we keep doing this after 10 years. I do it out of respect to Sharif.

As Jérémie's story shows, small actions have the potential for big impact, creating value for individuals and communities by making life better. But what might stop us from taking action? As we saw in Chapter 6, we human beings use reasoning shortcuts (heuristics) that generally work well but that do sometimes lead to bias. When it comes to tackling wicked problems, we are likely to be influenced by a number of forms of bias, including *distance bias*, *underestimation bias* and *prisoner's dilemma bias*.

Distance bias means that human beings are not always intuitively able to foresee how the action we take here and now will have implications for events happening at a later point in time or in a different geographical location. This also relates to the *identifiable victim effect*[13] where we tend to be more prepared to help a cause when we can see a specific (identifiable) person (think about Sharif, above). Studies have found that those of us who have a more imaginative brain are better able to overcome distance bias. Why is this the case? The explanation lies in the fact that when we take action we cannot directly observe the outcomes, which occur later in time or in another place. In the absence of our ability to observe outcomes, we need to find a way to 'visualise' them without actually 'seeing' them. Such visualisation requires us to use our imagination and play out such outcomes in our mind. This process will of course require us to have some knowledge and understanding of potential outcomes in the context of the specific global issue under consideration. For example, in order for us to choose to walk a few more steps to put our empty plastic bottle in the recycling bin rather than in the general waste bin closer to us, we will likely to have run a scenario in our mind of what will happen to that bottle if we put it in the general waste (e.g., Will it be incinerated? Will it cause toxic fumes from incineration? Will it end up in a river or ocean?) versus what will happen if we put it in the recycling (e.g., Will it be taken to a remanufacturing centre? Will it be used to make another bottle?). So, if imagination is the engine through which we can visualise outcomes, knowledge is the fuel that allows the imagination engine to function in the specific context of the wicked problem at hand. It follows that it is important to work on our imagination skills, but also to cultivate our learning about issues of global relevance.

Some of us have fundamentally altruistic motives driving our desire to help those in the world who are suffering because of natural disasters, disease, poverty, inequalities, and so on. Others may be driven by a desire to avoid being personally affected by global problems. Fear of pandemics killing us or our loved ones may lead us to take up a vaccine, for example. In such cases, action is more likely to be taken if we perceive a high likelihood of global issues affecting us personally. But how likely are we to visualise bad events happening to us? This is where *underestimation bias* comes in. Researchers have found that we tend to significantly underestimate the likelihood of being personally affected by global issues,[14] unless we have experienced the issue already. This is because the images of those experiences will be vivid and readily available in our minds (think back to the availability heuristic discussed in Chapter 6). It has been suggested that this underestimation is designed to keep us happy and positive. That is because being constantly aware of the likelihood of suffering from the effects of disease, climate change or poverty is associated with depression and low mood.[15] If we find ourselves

[13]Jenni, K. E. & Loewenstein, G. (1997). Explaining the 'identifiable victim effect'. *Journal of Risk and Uncertainty, 14,* 235–257.

[14]Beattie, G. & McGuire, L. (2019). *The Psychology of Climate Change*. Abingdon: Routledge.

[15]Fritze, J. G., Blashki, G. A., Burke, S. & Wiseman, J. (2008). Hope, despair and transformation: Climate change and the promotion of mental health and wellbeing. *International Journal of Mental Health Systems, 2,* 13.

switching off the TV and turning off social media when disasters are being covered, that may be because we are trying to protect our mental health from negativity. Whilst this may be useful to support our own wellbeing (see Chapter 10), it may be less helpful in encouraging us to take action to tackle these problems. What we can do to try to tackle underestimation is to think of different possible scenarios, drawing on our slower and more deliberative System 2 thinking (see Chapter 6).

FOOD FOR THOUGHT
HOW DO DISTANCE AND UNDERESTIMATION BIAS AFFECT YOU?

Most 'wicked problems' are by definition difficult to fully understand. This is particularly true when we consider the impact that human civilisation is having on our natural environment.

If we don't live in an area that is visibly and directly being affected by ecological change or challenges (such as persistent droughts and famine in the Horn of Africa, or constant sea level rises across Pacific Island such as Tonga), we may be affected by both distance and underestimation bias.

Have you ever considered the impact that your own life has on the natural environment?

Are you aware of the impact of your own lifestyle choices?

Would you know how to change them?

To try to combat these biases, an entrepreneurial initiative called the Footprint Calculator (run by the Global Footprint Networks) seeks to help individuals better understand what it means to live on our one planet and the direct impact that each person has in terms of their ecological and carbon footprints

1. Go to **www.footprintcalculator.org/home/en** to calculate your own impact. Record this below.

2. How do you feel about this result? Why? Record this below.

3. Do you feel differently now about the issue of ecological footprint? Why? Record this below.

Finally, another reason why we may not take action is because we are unsure that others will too. This may be accompanied by a sense that other people's inaction or action that impacts negatively may make our own action worthless. This is particularly the case when facing global challenges that require joined up thinking and behaviour in order to succeed. We call this the *prisoner's dilemma* bias, borrowing the term from game theory in economics (think back to Chapter 7). In order for prisoners to escape, they are required to collaborate. However, it would only take some prisoners not to collaborate and the escape plan would not work. This leaves each prisoner with the dilemma of whether to trust that others will follow through with the escape plan. If the prisoner does not trust that this will be the case, he may not collaborate with the rest. If enough prisoners opt not to cooperate, the plan will be ruined for those who attempt the escape. When looking to tackle wicked problems, we look for evidence that others will also take action and that the benefits of this action will be felt widely.

CHALLENGING ASSUMPTIONS
A TEENAGER'S QUEST TO CLEAN UP THE WORLD'S OCEANS

In 2012, an 18-year-old Dutch teenager made headlines for his passionate work to tackle plastic pollution in the world's oceans.

As he asked in his TED Talk [https://youtu.be/ROW9F-cOKIQ], 'why can't we just clean it up?!' Over the years he has talked to – and worked with – others to better understand the scale of plastic pollution in the ocean and to determine a range of approaches to clean it up. Part of this involved working to educate others to better understand the impact that plastic pollution has on oceans, ecosystems and livelihoods. This has led to the creation of the non-profit organisation The Ocean Cleanup [https://theoceancleanup.com/] which focuses on developing and scaling technologies to rid the oceans of plastic. It aims to have removed 90% of floating ocean plastic by 2040 with a longer-term goal of being put out of business – 'once we have completed this project our work is done'.

When people say something is impossible, the sheer absoluteness of that statement should be a motivation to investigate further. (Boyan Slat)

So what can we do then to apply our entrepreneurial thinking and mindset in pursuit of creating value by tackling wicked problems? First, we need to recognise that value creation likely comes in the form of understanding and chipping away at the problem,[16] rather than coming up with a solution.[17] We also want to think about the skills, competences, knowledge and experience that we can bring to our efforts – and how we can draw on others to bring in different abilities as well as perspectives to develop a collaborative approach.[18]

---

[16]Conklin, J. (2006). Wicked problems and social complexity. In J. Conklin (ed.), *Dialogue Mapping: Building Understanding of Wicked Problems* (pp. 3–40). Chichester: Wiley.

[17]Schön, D. A. (1993). Generative metaphor: A perspective on problem-setting in social policy. In A. Ortony (ed.), *Metaphor and Thought* (pp. 137–163). Cambridge: Cambridge University Press.

[18]Roberts, N. (2000). Wicked problems and network approaches to resolution. *International Public Management Review, 1*(1), 1–19.

11.5 SUMMARY AND NEXT STEPS

This chapter has extended our discussion of value from Chapter 10 to consider how we can create value for others by identifying, exploring and addressing the problems they face. We have explored our tendency to jump into 'solving problems' and discussed the importance of problem identification and exploration to differentiate the root cause of problems from any 'symptoms' that we may see. We've also considered how to leverage the skills, competences, insights and perspectives of others to ensure a collaborative approach to working with problems. As we discussed, this is particularly important when we seek to create value for others by tackling wider social, environmental or institutional problems, our so-called 'wicked problems'. Whilst these problems are not easily solved, we can create value for our families, friends, communities and societies through incremental innovations.

WHERE AM I NOW?
VALUE FOR OTHERS

Having worked through this chapter, you've now had a chance to consider how we can approach value creation for others. One way to start is by identifying – and working to – address problems that people face in their lives. This can be at the level of individuals, groups, communities or even society more broadly.

Take a few minutes to reflect on the problems you identified at the start of the chapter (see the 'WHERE AM I STARTING FROM?' box in section 11.2) and how you can work to address these. Record your thoughts below.

1. What problems did you initially identify? (Problems in your workplace, in your community, issues you hear about on the news, etc.)

> ....
>
> ....

2. Of these, which two do you consider to be the most important? Why?

> ....
>
> ....

3. Are these the symptoms of a larger problem? If so, what?

....

....

4. Can these be tackled directly? If so, how? If not, how could they be tackled obliquely?

....

....

5. How do these problems relate to, or draw on, your own foundations for personal flourishing (see section 10.4)?

....

....

11.6 CONTINUE YOUR LEARNING

The following activities are designed to support you on your learning journey, building on ideas introduced in this chapter. These can be completed at any time and in any order, although you may find it helpful to begin with the 'Check your understanding' activity before moving on.

CHECK YOUR UNDERSTANDING

1. Under uncertainty, problem exploration and identification of root causes usually merits less time than problem solving.

   ☐ **TRUE**

   ☐ **FALSE** (It's false – please see section 11.2)

2. Discovery skills are the fastest route to solving problems.

   ☐ **TRUE**

   ☐ **FALSE** (It's false – please see section 11.2)

3. Complex problems benefit from collective input and obliquity.

   ☐ **TRUE** (It's true – please see section 11.3)

   ☐ **FALSE**

4. **VUCA** stands for Valid Uniform Clear Achievable.

   ☐ **TRUE**

   ☐ **FALSE** (It's false – please see section 11.4)

5. The identifiable victim affect can help overcome distance bias in tackling the world's wicked problems.

   ☐ **TRUE** (It's true – please see section 11.4)

   ☐ **FALSE**

FURTHER READING

1. **The Tipping Point: How Little Things Can Make a Big Difference** by Malcolm Gladwell

2. **Eden** by Tim Smith

3. **The Voltage Effect** by John A. List

PRACTISING ENTREPRENEURIAL THINKING
WORKING WITH 'WICKED' PROBLEMS

When we first face a challenging or 'wicked' problem it's often difficult to know where to start. The situation can seem daunting, with no clear parameters or directions to guide our thinking and action. We may get caught up in functional fixedness (think back to Chapter 3) and struggle to see alternative ideas and approaches.

Consider the situation faced by the Apollo 13 crew when, two days into a mission to the Moon, an oxygen tank in the service module failed: **https://youtu.be/YwG4F-16Tno** (10:00)

As the NASA team frantically looked to solve a host of problems, one urgent task was to remove the build-up of carbon dioxide to allow the astronauts to breathe. It was literally a case of trying to fit a square peg in a round hole: **https://youtu.be/ry5S--J4_VQ** (1:15)

One approach to explore alternatives – even under such challenging conditions – is to think about what resources you have available and how you could use these in new ways or in new combinations. To do so, try applying the SCAMPER model[19] to a problem that you find particularly hard to make sense of, using the following prompts to guide you:[20]

Substitute something

Combine it with something else

Adapt something to it

Modify or **M**agnify it

Put it to some other use

Eliminate something

Reverse or **R**earrange it

As the Apollo mission showed, square pegs can be made to fit in round holes: **www.youtube.com/watch?v=Sij7y-EEeiO** (3:22)

---

[19]Serrat, O. (2017). The SCAMPER Technique. In O. Serrat, *Knowledge Solutions*. Singapore: Springer. https://doi.org/10.1007/978-981-10-0983-9_33

[20]Michalko, M. (2006). *Thinkertoys* (2nd edn). New York: Ten Speed Press.

CHAPTER 12

WHAT NEXT FOR YOUR ENTREPRENEURIAL THINKING AND MINDSET?

"Mastering entrepreneurial thinking...
is a journey, not a single act;
It takes practice and no shortcuts
It takes time and dedication
To reach your own value creation"

12.1 WHAT WE HAVE COVERED

Wow! What a journey we've been on together as we've explored your entrepreneurial thinking and mindset!

Over the course of this book, we've covered a range of ideas, concepts and applications of entrepreneurial thinking to support you as a creator of value, for yourself and for others.

In Section 1 (Chapters 1 to 3) we introduced and discussed what we mean by entrepreneurial thinking and mindset. We considered entrepreneurial mindset as the interaction of our *thinking* (cognition) and *emotion* in driving entrepreneurial *behaviour*[1], defining it as 'a set of learnable cognitive and emotional competences conducive to developing and enacting behaviours to support value creation activity'.[2] We also considered your own beliefs, preferences and frames of reference to help you identify where and how you can contribute to entrepreneurial value creation – and equally where you need to shift your thinking to look beyond what is and to consider *what could be*.

In Section 2 (Chapters 4 to 6), we built on our discussions from Section 1, and focused on the uncertainty and ambiguity inherent within value creation activity. After all, value is *something new, improved, or in a novel space, that an individual or group of individuals considers to have worth.* We have explored your own personal responses to uncertain situations in order to determine how you can build your persistence and resilience, developing not only your ability to keep going when situations challenge you but also your ability to learn from these challenges. We've considered the role that our own core beliefs and fears play in influencing our judgements and actions, and discussed how we challenge these when they hold us back from trying new things, making judgements and taking action.

In Section 3 (Chapters 7 to 9) we shifted our focus, considering not just your own entrepreneurial thinking but also how you can encourage and support entrepreneurial thinking and action, among others. As we discussed, value creation is an inherently collaborative activity where we need to draw on different ideas, perspectives, knowledge and skills to create new possibilities. This can happen in a range of entrepreneurial contexts, not just the start-ups that we so often hear about, which requires us to communicate with others who may hold different views. We have discussed how to communicate with others and the role that empathetic communication plays in building trust and psychological safety to support entrepreneurial thinking and action.

---

[1]Kuratko, D. F., Fisher, G. & Audretsch, D. B. (2021). Unravelling the entrepreneurial mindset. *Small Business Economics, 57*, 1681–1691.

[2]Mawson, S., Casulli, L. & Simmons, E. L. (2022). A competence development approach for entrepreneurial mindset in entrepreneurship education. *Entrepreneurship Education and Pedagogy, 6*(3), 481–501. https://doi.org/10.1177/25151274221143146

Finally, in Section 4 (Chapters 10 to 12) we built on ideas and concepts introduced throughout the book to consider what entrepreneurial thinking and action means for your own value creation activity. We considered value for yourself, thinking about a range of ways that value links to achievement, wellbeing and personal flourishing. We also considered how you may be creating value for others by addressing the problems people face, even if only in a small way that builds momentum.

As you have worked your way through the sections and chapters, you've been challenged to develop your own entrepreneurial competences. These competences have included the development of an **action orientation**, where you actively gather information and feedback from the environment, evaluate it and engage in **judgement** and *decision making* that determines your plans and actions.[3] You have also developed your *cognitive flexibility* linked to *open-mindedness* and a *growth **mindset*** in order to support your sense of **self-efficacy** and **creative thinking** to look beyond the status quo and think about what could be. The different exercises and activities you have completed have supported you to shift from unconscious incompetence towards unconscious competence, where you develop *mastery*.

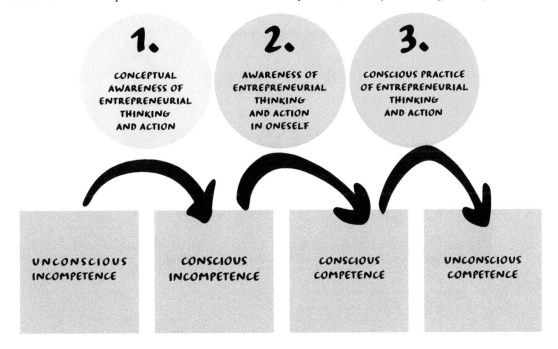

So, having done all that, where are you now? Just as when you started with this book, you may be feeing a range of emotions now that it is coming to an end and you approach another 'new beginning'.[4]

---

[3]Dimov, D. (2010). Nascent entrepreneurs and venture emergence: Opportunity confidence, human capital, and early planning. *Journal of Management Studies, 47*(6), 1123–1153.

[4]Bridges, W. (2004). *Transitions: Making Sense of Life's Changes.* Cambridge, MA: Da Capo Press.

WHERE AM I NOW?
SEEING HOW FAR YOU HAVE COME

When you started this book, we asked you to record your thoughts on how you were thinking and feeling as you embarked on your personal learning journey to develop your entrepreneurial thinking. Having worked through this book – and having started putting your learning into practice – where are you now? Spend a few minutes reflecting on how you are thinking and feeling now. Record these below.

1. How are you feeling having worked through this book?

2. What worries or concerns do you have?

3. What do you feel excited or optimistic about?

4. What have you got out of this learning journey?

5. What else do you need to learn more about or practise further?

12.2 WHAT NEXT FOR YOUR ENTREPRENEURIAL THINKING AND MINDSET IN ACTION?

When we're starting something new it can be hard to see that we are making progress. Yet little by little our abilities (and confidence) grow and we start to see the outcomes of the hard work we are putting in. Eventually, we start to demonstrate *mastery*. While we often assume that *mastery* means complete 100% knowledge, or skill, or behaviour, it is in fact a journey, rather than an end state. Usually, the more we know about something (or the better we get) the more we realise we have room for improvement.[5]

So how will you be able to tell you're on the right path to creating value? Think back to when we talked about creating value for yourself in Chapter 10 and for others in Chapter 11. What was it you identified as being important? Were you focused on achievement? Wellbeing? A sense of purpose? Tackling a social or environmental problem? Helping a person, a team or society at large? To determine where to start, you may want to take those ideas of value and translate them into a more specific set of ***goals*** – our aims or desired results.[6] Goal-setting is recognised to work best when:[7]

- goals are detailed rather than general (i.e., avoiding general statements like 'I'll do my best' in favour or something more specific)
- goals are ambitious and push you to your limits (think back to our discussion of *flow states* in Chapter 10)
- goals are aligned to specific rather than loose deadlines (tighter deadlines encourage action, which is particularly useful for System 2 thinkers – see Chapter 6)
- goals are shared with others (we feel more accountable and thus personally committed, particularly when operating in a place of psychological safety – see Chapter 8).

These principles underpin the commonly used SMART framework[8] for goal-setting:

Specific	Make goals detailed, rather than general. Think which action words you will be using.
Measurable	Identify how you will measure the progress (or outcome) of the goal. Use metrics or data where possible.
Achievable	Aim high, but within the realm of your skills and abilities given the time you have available and your ability to take action.

---

[5]https://en.wikipedia.org/wiki/Dunning%E2%80%93Kruger_effect

[6]*Oxford English Dictionary* (2023). www.oed.com/

[7]Locke, E. A. & Latham, G. P. (2002). Building a practically useful theory of goal setting and task motivation. *American Psychologist, 57*(9), 705–717.

[8]Doran, G. T. (1981). There's a S.M.A.R.T. way to write management's goals and objectives. *Management Review, 70*(11), 35–36.

| Relevant | Make sure specific goals link clearly to, and support, your overall goal/vision/strategy. |
| Time-bound | Set specific deadlines but be reasonable about how long things will take. |

For example, we may seek to create value in our lives by 'having a healthier lifestyle'. As it stands, it's hard to know what to do first. We can start breaking it down by developing specific goals, perhaps based on key areas for improvement we've already identified. Perhaps this is not doing enough exercise, eating too much sugar, or not getting enough rest. A SMART goal could thus look like:

Specific	I will get at least 7hrs of good quality sleep each night during the work week, Monday through Friday.
Measurable	I will use my Fitbit to see how many hours I slept each night and the quality of that sleep.
Achievable	I need to be up at 6am. I often work until 11pm and then spend time scrolling social media for at least another hour. If I don't open social media I have a 7-hour window for sleep to achieve this goal. I can also create more time by stopping work an hour or more earlier as my work day officially finishes at 6pm.
Relevant	When I am tired, I drink too much coffee, make bad food choices and don't have enough energy to exercise. In getting more sleep I should be able to address my overall goal of having a healthier lifestyle.
Time-bound	I will do this for the next two calendar weeks (14 days) and then assess the data I have collected.

PRACTISING ENTREPRENEURIAL THINKING
DEVELOPING YOUR OWN SMART GOALS

Thinking about how you can use your entrepreneurial thinking and mindset to create value, where might you start? See if you can develop at least two SMART goals to help you on your way.

Step 1. Consider what 'value' means for you and what kind of value will you seek to create.

....

....

....

....

Step 2. From step 1, identify two SMART goals.

GOAL 1	
Specific	
Measurable	
Achievable	
Relevant	
Time-bound	

GOAL 2	
Specific	
Measurable	
Achievable	
Relevant	
Time-bound	

Now that you have some goals to start with, what next? While goal-setting can be helpful in determining priorities and time-bound courses of action, we want to think about how we can sustain our actions over time. Specifically, we want to build *unconscious competence*, where our (small) daily behaviours and actions build into big results over time.

Habits are the small decisions you make – and resulting actions that you take – every day. These are usually small and, once they are established, you may not even think about them! For example, every morning you may get out of bed, go into your kitchen, and put on your coffee machine – all before you're fully awake and perhaps even aware of what you're doing! Every habit starts out as a conscious action; it's only because we have done the action so many times that we no longer actively think about it. The same holds true for our entrepreneurial thinking and competences as we engage in value creation. By embedding actions into our daily routine in the form of habits, we can take our broad aims and goals for value creation and transition them into sustained activity to support unconscious competence.

To develop new habits, we can draw on four guiding principles or 'laws':[9]

1. *Make it obvious.* Become aware of what you are doing by actively tracking your habits. Be clear and specific WHAT you will do, WHERE and WHEN. Leave visible cues to remind you of what you should be doing.
2. *Make it attractive.* Do something you want to do in combination with what you need to do to feel motivated. Find a place where your desired behaviour or actions are the norm, rather than the exception.
3. *Make it easy.* Keep your habit simple and minimise the number of steps/actions to be taken. Leave cues and reminders (see #1) and be realistic about the time you spend (try to get it done in two minutes or less).
4. *Make it satisfying.* Keep a record of what you're doing (see #1) and try not to break your 'streak' (using #2 and #3). Reward yourself often for staying on track.

PRACTISING ENTREPRENEURIAL THINKING
TRACKING HABITS

Take some time to consider the two SMART goals you identified above and develop relevant habits that you can implement and track to determine your progress.

Continuing with our example of creating personal value through 'having a healthier lifestyle', we've identified that a SMART goal would be to 'get at least 7hrs of good quality sleep each night during the work week, Monday through Friday'. To turn this into a set of habits, we can draw on the four laws above. For example, you could set an alarm on your phone to stop work by 9pm, shutting down the computer and putting your phone on 'sleep mode'. You could then engage in an activity you enjoy to transition from 'work mode' to 'sleep mode', such as having a bubble bath while listening to music before putting on your pyjamas and getting into bed by 10:30pm.

---

[9]Clear, J. (2018). *Atomic Habits.* London: Random House Business Books.

EXAMPLE HABIT	MON	TUE	WED	TH	FRI	SAT	SUN
Alarm goes off at 9pm to stop work	X	X	X	X	X	X	X
Shut down computer and turn phone on sleep mode	X	X		X	X	X	X
Take a 20-minute bubble bath with favourite playlist	X			X	X	X	X
Put on pyjamas (positioned next to bath)	X	X	X	X	X	X	X
Into bed by 10pm			X	X	X	X	X

Step 1. For each of your smart goals, identify a number of habits based on the four laws above. Track these for at least one week.

GOAL 1 HABITS	MON	TUE	WED	TH	FRI	SAT	SUN

GOAL 2 HABITS	MON	TUE	WED	TH	FRI	SAT	SUN

Step 2. Once you've tracked your habits for at least one week, make a note of any variation and why this occurred. How well are you persevering? Why? Do any of your habits need to be tweaked as a result of your tracking?

When we start taking action and building new habits it can feel like we're just adding more to our day and our 'to-do' list. In this age of 'time famine',[10] we may feel as though we don't have enough hours in the day to accomplish all the tasks we need to do, let alone those we want to do. Yet research has shown that we often have more time than we think – we just aren't using it in the most effective way to achieve our goals and build our competences.[11] If we think of Law #3 of habits, we can start small, spending two minutes or less on specific actions.[12] If we add a little at a time, we can take action and build momentum. After all, 'if you want to do something or become something – and you want to do it well – it takes time'.[13] And we have the power to choose how we use our time. Sometimes this will mean choosing to use our time for things that we know are important to our overall goals, even if it doesn't result in direct satisfaction or outcomes right now. This is particularly important and you continue to use your entrepreneurial thinking and mindset to create value. As we've spoken of at length, creation is an act that requires us to see beyond what exists. To do so, we need to make time to watch, listen and reflect – on ourselves as well as on the world around us.

ENTREPRENEURIAL THINKING AND MINDSET IN PRACTICE
CECILIA LIVINGSTON ON CREATIVITY AS A HABIT

Cecilia Livingston is an internationally celebrated composer, specialising in music for voice as well as modern opera. She composes for a range of audiences in the UK, Canada and the US.

The case is narrated in Cecilia's own voice.

---

[10]Perlow, L. A. (1999). The time famine: Toward a sociology of work time. *Administrative Science Quarterly, 44*(1), 57–81.

[11]Vanderkam, L. (2010). *168 Hours: You Have More Time Than You Think.* New York: Penguin Group.

[12]Clear, *Atomic Habits.*

[13]Vanderkam, *168 Hours.*

Photo by Daniel Alexander Denino

I think it can be easy in a creative career to be intimidated by the idea of the blank page. And in my line of work I have to get up and face the blank page every single day. So I try to be quite conscious about what my routines are and what my habits are for overcoming that daunting moment.

I've come to believe that professional creativity requires creativity that's like a habit. Creativity is like a muscle: if you don't go to the gym, you're not going to have the strength. So for me, it's really important that I've routinised my creative time so that my brain knows this is the time to focus. I'll set an achievable goal for that period of time and then it'll be possible to do something else to rest afterwards. Building in routine and breaking things down means that projects don't feel so enormous. This is particularly true in composing opera. I may think 'I have to write an hour and a half of music', which sometimes feels impossible! But thinking 'I actually just have to write another minute to get to the end of the section' makes the project seem much more doable.

The really important part, for me, is recognising that I do a lot of my creative thinking in my 'time off', when I'm going for a run or doing something with my hands like tasks around the house. That seems to allow my brain to process the creative work I've done earlier in the day and I've learned that this 'background simmering' is a valuable part of my creative routine.

When we are able to sustain our habits over time, we are able to develop unconscious competence. Yet it is hard to keep track of where and how our competence is shifting. Where does conscious competence end and unconscious competence or mastery begin, for example?

Whilst it's hard to pinpoint these changes precisely, we can collect data to confirm if we're on the right track!

PRACTISING ENTREPRENEURIAL THINKING
THE 'JAR OF AWESOME'

How can we tell we're achieving and sustaining mastery?

Linked to the fourth law of habits, one approach you might want to consider is what Tim Ferris describes as the 'Jar of Awesome'. This is a collection of words or objects that help you to keep track of – and celebrate – your wins, no matter how small. It also help you to see how far you have come. See:
https://youtu.be/LWCvOzAnqWO

1. what will your 'Jar of Awesome' look like?

2. How will you keep track of your successes?

3. How will you celebrate your successes, no matter how small?

....

....

....

....

Throughout this book we have explored how you can develop your entrepreneurial thinking and mindset, building and sustaining entrepreneurial competences regardless of where you are starting from. As you'll now know yourself, this journey is far from an easy one, but it is one filled with possibility. Entrepreneurial thinking and action through value creation can be a force to support your own personal growth and fulfilment; equally, it can be a force for change and empowerment in the world.

We hope this book has helped you to identify how you will take entrepreneurial action to achieve your goals, creating value for yourself and for others. The road to success is long and full of unexpected detours, but if you can take the first step and persist in moving forward, the journey will be well worth the effort.

"IF YOU CAN'T FLY THEN RUN, IF YOU CAN'T RUN THEN WALK, IF YOU CAN'T WALK THEN CRAWL, BUT WHATEVER YOU DO YOU HAVE TO KEEP MOVING FORWARD."

Martin Luther King Jr.

FURTHER READING

1. **Atomic Habits** by James Clear
2. **168 Hours: You Have More Time Than You Think** by Laura Vanderkam
3. **Tools of Titans** by Tim Ferriss

GLOSSARY

achievement – goal striving and ambition, usually aligned to our own personal interests, inclinations and potential

action orientation – when we actively gather information and feedback from the environment, evaluate it and then determine our plans and actions

cognition – how humans make sense of and process information including perception, memory, learning, judgement and decision making

cognitive flexibility – one's ability to think about multiple concepts at the same time, or switch between different concepts and ideas in response to changing situations

cognitive schemas – your knowledge, beliefs, experiences, etc. that are the 'files' within your memory

communication – how we craft, send and decode messages with others, both including both verbal and non-verbal elements

core beliefs – the deep-seated beliefs we hold about ourselves, the world and our future

creativity – the ability that human beings have to think beyond 'what is' in order to develop novel objects, ideas, processes or behaviours

effect uncertainty – when we cannot predict what impact a future (or potential future) change will have on us

einstellung effect – the tendency for people to behave or respond in a way that they have done before, even if it is no longer the most appropriate (or effective) way given the current circumstances

empathy – the cognitive and affective process fostering the capability of understanding and appreciating the feelings, thoughts and experiences of others

entrepreneurial cognition – how our thinking leads to the identification and enactment of opportunities through creative ideas

entrepreneurial competences – a way to think, feel and act that leads to value creation

entrepreneurial context – how spatial, temporal, institutional, social and societal elements combine to influence 'where' and 'when' entrepreneurial thinking and action take place

entrepreneurial leadership – a set of leadership behaviours emphasising trying, learning from mistakes and removing obstacles to creativity and innovation amongst employees

entrepreneurial mindset – a set of learnable cognitive and emotional competences conducive to developing and enacting behaviours to support value creation activity

entrepreneurial team – a group of individuals that share a common goal and that achieve the goal by combining individual entrepreneurial actions

entrepreneurial traits – stable elements in our neuropsychic system or, more simply, the way in which we are 'wired'

environmental uncertainty – shaped by state and effect uncertainty, where we have a limited set of courses of action but a wide range of possible outcomes from that action

flourishing – a personal state where both wellbeing and achievement are high

frames of reference – the mental structures that allow us to understand our own reality and to create a sense of (personal) meaning

goals – our aims or desired results

habits – the small decisions you make, and resulting actions that you take, every day

imposter phenomenon – the belief that we are not intelligent or capable enough to do what we're supposed to be doing linked to worry about being exposed as a fraud

judgement – a form of thinking and the precursor to decision making which involves weighing up options based on the information available and deciding the likelihood of a certain outcome based on certain actions

metacognition – how we think about (and make sense of) our own thinking

metaphor – a figurative rather than literal comparison with something that already exists

mindset – how we become aware of (and make sense of) what we think, how we think and how we leverage that thinking (or not) to pursue our ambitions and goals through our behaviours

neuroplasticity – the ability of one's brain to change and form new neural connections and networks in response to learning, experience or injury

obliquity – the process of achieving complex objectives indirectly

organisational entrepreneurship – the embodiment of entrepreneurial efforts that require organisational sanctions and resource commitments for the purpose of carrying out innovative activities in the form of product, process and organisational innovations

persistence – the combination of our own internal motivation and the skill to mobilise our energies and keep going, regardless of setbacks

psychological safety – a shared belief that the team is safe for interpersonal risk taking and that the team will not embarrass, reject, or punish someone for speaking up

resilience – our ability to grow in the face of adversity

response uncertainty – when we don't know what we can do/how we can respond, linked to the inability to predict the consequents of our responses/actions

self-awareness – one's ability to know and understand one's thinking and feelings and appreciate how they impact – and are impacted by – behaviour

self-determination – a person's ability and freedom to manage themselves, to make choices and to think for themselves

self-efficacy – the belief we hold in our own ability to cope with specific tasks or situations

self-esteem – how we judge our own worth

state uncertainty – when we observe or perceive an environment to be unpredictable

trust – a person's willingness to be vulnerable toward another person and, as a consequence, to take the risk that they may get hurt

uncertainty – see effect uncertainty, environmental uncertainty, response uncertainty or state uncertainty

value – the creation of something new, improved, or in a novel space, that an individual or group of individuals considers to have worth

value creation – taking action to change the status quo and thus trading the 'known' for the 'unknown'

wellbeing – being both physically and psychologically healthy and therefore experiencing life positively

wicked problems – problems that are ill defined, with unclear boundaries, changing requirements, different stakeholders with conflicting needs and values and no clear path to an answer or solution

worldview – the information through which we understand the world (and which shapes our frames of reference)

INDEX

Page numbers for entries in the glossary are followed by (g)

Printed in the USA
CPSIA information can be obtained
at www.ICGtesting.com
CBHW082058150524
8518CB00005B/46